THE TAYLOR MAC BOOK

TRIANGULATIONS
Lesbian/Gay/Queer ▲ Theater/Drama/Performance

Series Editors
Ramón H. Rivera-Servera, University of Texas Austin
Sara Warner, Cornell University

Founding Editors
Jill Dolan, Princeton University
David Román, University of Southern California

THE TAYLOR MAC BOOK

Ritual, Realness and Radical Performance

David Román & Sean F. Edgecomb

UNIVERSITY OF MICHIGAN PRESS

Ann Arbor

For questions or permissions, please contact um.press.perms@umich.edu

Published in the United States of America by the
University of Michigan Press
Manufactured in the United States of America
Printed on acid-free paper
First published February 2023

A CIP catalog record for this book is available from the British Library.

Library of Congress Cataloging-in-Publication data has been applied for.

ISBN 978-0-472-07527-0 (hardcover : alk. paper)
ISBN 978-0-472-05527-2 (paper : alk. paper)
ISBN 978-0-472-22002-1 (e-book)

To artists who persevere in times of crisis,
and in memory of Barbara Maier Gustern.

Fig. 1. Taylor Mac resplendent in a costume by Machine Dazzle and makeup by Anastasia Durasova (2020). Photo: Machine Dazzle.

Contents

Digital materials related to this title can be found on the Fulcrum platform via the following citable URL: https://doi.org/10.3998/mpub.12004355

Acknowledgments

We are grateful for the many individuals and organizations who helped to make this collection happen, nurturing the conversations and collaboration essential to the project.

First and foremost, we must thank Taylor Mac, whose vision, work, and ongoing commitment to artistic collaboration toward social justice, representation, and inclusion inspired the collection.

Second, it has been a joy collaborating with the contributors to this volume, a diverse group of scholars and artists whose engagement, critical analyses, and thoughtful reflections have been a delight.

The seeds for *The Taylor Mac Book* were planted during the marathon concert of *A 24-Decade History of Popular Music* in October 2016, which provided not only a once-in-a-lifetime experience, but an opportunity for many of the collaborators to connect. Linda Brumbach and Pomegranate Arts have been supportive of our work, and we greatly appreciate their vision of encouraging and disseminating Taylor's ongoing performances.

A conference panel arranged by Jen Parker-Starbuck at the American Society of Theatre and Performance Research in Atlanta (2017) allowed some contributors to come together to reflect on Taylor, inspiring ideas that found their way into some of the essays in this volume. In September 2019 Brown University sponsored a morning symposium following a touring abbreviated performance of *A 24-Decade History of Popular Music*, and we are grateful to Patty Ybarra for organizing a panel that gave us a chance to engage directly with Taylor and an insightful, gathered audience.

We are grateful to our two outside readers for useful reports that helped to shape the book as you see it now. We also want to express our thanks to LeAnn Fields, Flannery Wise, Marcia LaBrenz, and the entire hardworking team at University of Michigan Press.

Funding from the University of Southern California's Dornsife College of Letters, Arts and Sciences helped support the inclusion of photographs in the volume. Our thanks to the Department of English and the administrative staff at USC.

Sean would like to thank the Research Foundation of CUNY for a generous award that helped to support the costs of this manuscript. He also would like to thank Fiona Coffey, Natasha Korda, and the staffs of the Department of Performing Arts and the Wesleyan Humanities Center, who organized and facilitated a weekend of events and performance that not only celebrated Taylor Mac but led to some important questions and inquiries around the work. Sean also thanks his supportive colleagues in the PhD program in Theatre and Performance at the CUNY Graduate Center, particularly Peter Eckersall, David Savran, Jean Graham-Jones, Erika T. Lin, James Wilson, and Edward Miller, and the students who helped organize the Edwin Booth Award in 2017, particularly Janet Werther, Dan Venning, and Elyse Singer. He would like to also thank Sean Metzger, Claire Conceison, Benjamin Gillespie, Helen Lewis, Penelope Farfan, Angela Fan, the Drama Book Shop, and Cullan Riley. Finally, a multitude of thanks to David Román, whose work continues to be essential to my own scholarly journey.

David also thanks the University of London's Royal Central School of Speech and Drama, where he was in residency during the spring of 2019, for their engagement with his work on Taylor Mac. David also thanks Richard Meyer, Kevin Sessums, Lisa Freeman, Peggy Gillespie, Barbara Maier Gustern, Marisa Maneri, Peter Staley, Kareem Khubchandani, Jordan Shildcrout, Scott Poulson-Bryant, Zak Wolf, Josh Abrams, Alex Luu, Isaiah Wooden, and especially Sean F. Edgecomb for engaging his ideas about Taylor Mac's work. David would also like to thank Linda Brumbach and everyone at Pomegranate Arts for their ongoing support of my work on Taylor Mac.

On Queer Pronouns and Gender as Performance

Taylor Mac's positionality is clearly queer, but at the same time Mac is a civically engaged artist activist, not a politician. There has been a tendency over the past decade to attempt to police Mac's gender pronouns out of a fear of getting it wrong or offending someone. Mac, along with queer performer Mx. Justin Vivian Bond and others, is responsible for our growing awareness of gender as fluid, constructed, and performed, but does not shame those who misgender or mislabel, preferring a sensitive reminder or conversation.

Mac relates: "I kind of identify as a gay male; I kind of identify as genderqueer. Really, my gender is *performer* because I feel like I'm always performing gender."[1] While Taylor Mac the performer/playwright now uses "judy" as their gender pronoun, Taylor Mac Bowyer the citizen often uses male pronouns, or "they," or a mix of the two, and in fact, more consistently used male pronouns before "judy" was introduced.

For this very reason, as the editors of this volume, we have not overly policed the pronouns used in the following essays and reflections. Most contributors employ the neutral "they" or refer to Mac by name, as we have primarily done. It is also important to state that while Mac often deconstructs gender in performance, unlike Justin Vivian Bond, they are not transgender in daily life. More often than not, when we meet Mac for a social outing, they are sporting what Mac refers to as "boy drag"— whether a baseball cap and jeans or a beautiful custom suit—and Mac is open to other or "any" pronouns, including he/him/his, she/her/hers, or they/them/theirs in their life offstage.

---

1. Michelle Ruiz, "Tony-Nominated Taylor Mac on 'Camping with Radical Faeries,' Penis Jokes and His Gender Pronoun," *Vogue* (June 7, 2019), last accessed February 9, 2022. https://www.vogue.com/article/taylor-mac-gary-tonys-interview

Introduction

Sean F. Edgecomb

I'm a storyteller . . .
   —Taylor Mac

The Taylor Mac Book is a volume of essays, reflections, and interviews intended to describe, analyze, and celebrate the work of contemporary actor, performance artist, songwriter, self-professed storyteller, and playwright Taylor Mac. Mac's numerous honors include two Obies, a MacArthur "genius" award, and recognition from the Guggenheim Foundation and the Drama League. Among many other performances and accolades, their critically celebrated *A 24-Decade History of Popular Music*, which culminated in a twenty-four-hour marathon at St. Ann's Warehouse, Brooklyn, in 2016, was a finalist for the Pulitzer Prize in Drama. Mac has developed their unique career over the past two decades by performing (and having their plays produced) across diverse venues, from clubs and downtown New York bars to off-off-Broadway, off-Broadway, and on Broadway, to college campuses, lesser-known regional theaters, and famous playhouses across the globe.

Queer Collaboration

My interest in Taylor Mac began early in my scholarly career, with a dissertation and then a book about Mac as a legatee of queer playwright and performer Charles Ludlam. My co-editor David Román's work has been foundational to the development of queer theater scholarship since the

1990s. David and I chose to collaborate on this particular project because we are both passionate about Mac's work, but our collaboration has also been an attempt to create a process and product that serves as an example of intergenerational and cross-cultural queer scholarship, kinship, perspective, and creative cultural production. In a sense, this is a book about how Mac acts as a conduit to link together a variety of people in the United States and beyond who are passionate about a theater that makes space for inclusion and representation while it attempts to enact social change through art. As Mac relates, "my job as a theater artist is to remind people of the things they've forgotten, dismissed or buried, or that other people have buried for them."[1] We hope that this book is an informative, thoughtful, and even fun extension of Mac's call for representation, reparation, celebration, and queering as a form of both art and activism.

The book's contributors—theater and performance scholars, working artists and performers who have collaborated with Mac, as well as a voice teacher, a producer, and a journalist—provide a rich variety of perspectives and accounts of Mac's work. All of the authors admire Mac and their work. While the essays, interviews, and reflections that make up this volume include some rigorous criticism and questions about the work, they are for the most part celebratory, laudatory, and even joyful—entirely in keeping with a performer whose work encourages queer kinship through togetherness and community organization as a form of performance. In this sense, while the essays (if not the reflections from collaborators) retain a critical, scholarly lens, we also invited contributors to consider a methodology of queer subjectivity and even affectiveness. This is not only because of the queer nature of Mac's work, but because the essays were composed in response to experiencing the live performance(s) of a living artist. Thus, at its core, this is a queer book—queer in its focus on artists who are members of the LGBTQ+ community (and more specifically focused on Mac as the brightest star in the constellation); queer because it was conceived and edited by two gay men committed to queer performance studies, queer historiography, and/or queer theory; queer in its approach to thinking about theater scholarship outside of a more traditional and thus normative, patriarchal box; and finally, queer in its vision, process, and attempt (never aiming for a truly comprehensive approach or total coverage of Mac's dazzling career).

The book's thirteen sections roughly follow the chronology of Mac's career to date, but readers are encouraged to forge their own queer path of engagement with the work, reading and reordering in a personal way

Fig. 2. Taylor Mac plays the banjo, awash in their signature glitter and sequins at St. Ann's Warehouse, October 2016. Photo: Teddy Wolff.

that best suits their own interest. The collection embraces a kind of queer teleology (offering a variety of ways to enter the essays and reflections while devising various origin points for personal engagement) and queer temporality (which can be manipulated by reordering chapters from the roughly chronological table of contents), which allows a reader to explore, collage, skip over, pause, and even deviate to pursue new ideas about Mac and their work. Ideally readers unfamiliar with Mac will be inspired to seek out the work, while readers who are more familiar will be moved to reflect on their own experiences with Mac in order to relay or set down their own queer anecdotes or stories.

While we hope that this collection lives on and finds readers who engage for pleasure, scholarly research, or artistic inspiration, it is essential to note that it was largely conceived and created during the Covid-19 pandemic between 2020 and 2022. While chapter 13 discusses this more explicitly, all of the writing inherently reflects a tone of what it meant to be writing about live theater during an uncertain time when performances were indefinitely on hold, across the world.

Taylor Mac in Performance: A Brief History

In 2000, performance artist Taylor Mac (né Taylor Mac Bowyer) summered in Provincetown, Massachusetts. Located on the tip of Cape Cod, "Ptown," a historic and storied gay resort, was a place where Mac could escape from the hustle and bustle of New York City.[2] Following their graduation from the American Academy of Dramatic Arts in 1996 at age twenty-three, Mac had begun a career as an actor in touring productions while also writing original one-act plays (including the *Dilating Cycle*: *Okay, Maurizio Pollini, The Levee,* and *A Crevice*), but frustration with the casting system inspired their escape to this queer enclave. It was in Ptown that Mac began experimenting with cabaret-style solo performances, featuring original songs (self-accompanied by the self-taught ukulele) and monologues. Aesthetically, Mac used what they could access to create a character—a "stage-worthy version of [Taylor Mac]"—relying on a creative assemblage of trash and thrifted materials for original "metaphoric" costumes and clownish white face paint, highlighted with drugstore makeup and glitter.[3]

These early drag performances would establish Mac's signature messy aesthetic, but also began garnering comparisons to queer downtown New

York performers of an older generation, including Jack Smith, Charles Ludlam, and Ethyl Eichelberger. On returning to New York that autumn, Mac began immersing themself in the plays and archived performances of these three key figures in the development of American LGBTQ+ theater as a genre with distinct individual styles. In performances that featured drag, camp, improvisation, clowning, and curated amateurism, Smith, Ludlam, and Eichelberger contributed to the creation of Theatre of the Ridiculous, which parodied heteronormative culture through performances "used as vehicles for social commentary and/or humor."[4] Mac would take this style and develop their own fool persona, a stage version of themself who could act as a queer medium to comment on contemporary culture and queer positionality through performance art.

Mac's early research on queer Ridiculous forebears inspired new solo performances that spoke to queer life in the contemporary United States—including criticism of the George W. Bush administration and its response to the 9/11 terrorist attacks—while also continuing the queer legacy of Smith, Ludlam, and Eichelberger, all artists who had tragically died of AIDS-related complications. Mac's foundational performances took place in various sites in lower Manhattan, including the Slide Bar and HERE Arts Center, helping to establish them as an up-and-coming queer voice in postmillennial New York. It was also during this period that Mac became acquainted with boylesque performer James Tigger! Ferguson, who would become a long-time collaborator.

In 2002 Mac presented their first official performance art cabaret, *The Face of Liberalism*, which led to an invitation to collaborate on *Live Patriot Acts: Patriots Gone Wiiiiildd!*, a response to the Republican National Convention, which was to take place at Madison Square Garden the following year. Simultaneously, several of Mac's one-act plays found productions in small theaters across Manhattan. Additionally, Mac premiered their solo show, *Cardiac Arrest or Venus on a Half Clam* (2004) at the Fez performance space before it moved to become a headline event at the Queer at HERE Festival. Mac's ceaseless work ethic and growing fame resulted in their selection as the winner of PS 122's inaugural Ethyl Eichelberger Award. The associated funding was used to write and produce *Red Tide Blooming* (2006), which was written in the style of Ludlam's Ridiculous and tackled themes such as transphobia, capitalism, and the threat of climate change, set in a gay fantasia of Coney Island's annual Mermaid Parade.

Following a much-lauded run of a new, pastiched, one-person show, *The Be(A)st of Taylor Mac* (2006), at the Edinburgh Fringe Festival, Mac began to tour regularly while completing their autobiographical play, *The Young Ladies of . . .* (2007), which also premiered at HERE Arts Center. Following the foundational first phase of their career, Mac continued to adapt their fool persona into critically celebrated shows that would lead to a new era of critical praise and international fame. After the success of *The Young Ladies of . . .* at HERE Arts Center, Mac was invited to create their first durational performance, the five-hour *The Lily's Revenge* (2009), which tackled the topic of marriage equality in the United States through a critique of nostalgia as violence. This production was a harbinger of the 2015 Supreme Court ruling that made same-sex marriages legal in all fifty states. In addition to winning an Obie, *Lily's Revenge* set in motion relationships with composer/arranger Matt Ray, director Niegel Smith, costume wunderkind Machine Dazzle, and guitarist Viva DeConcini, who would soon become Mac's permanent collaborators.

It was during the period of *Walk Across America* that Mac was cast in a variety of productions, including the roles of Puck/Egeus in the Classic Stage Company's production of *A Midsummer Night's Dream* (2012); as the Emcee in PlayMaker's Repertory Company's production of *Cabaret* (2013); as Shin Te/Shui Ta in the Foundry Theatre's production of *The Good Person of Szechuan* (2014); and in collaboration with Mandy Patinkin in *The Last Two People on Earth: An Apocalyptic Vaudeville* (2015) at the American Repertory Theatre in Cambridge, Massachusetts. It was also during this period that Mac introduced "judy" as their preferred gender pronoun in performance. (As explained elsewhere, contributors to this volume have employed the gender pronoun that they typically use with Mac, since "judy" is used primarily in performance. Mac is open to other pronouns, including he/him/his, in their life offstage.)

As Mac garnered critical acclaim, including being called a "future theatre legend" by *TimeOut New York* magazine, and earning the Peter Zeisler Memorial Award for "ingenuity, artistic integrity [. . .] and exemplifying pioneering practices in theatre," they also continued playwriting scripts in which they would not appear.[5] Inspired by the Dionysia Festival and more specifically the spirit of Greek mimes (proto-fools) in ancient Athens, Mac began a cycle of four plays. Part 1, *The Fre*, originally commissioned for Children's Theatre Company, premiered at the Flea Theater (2020). Part II, *Hir*, premiered at San Francisco's Magic Theatre (2014) before transferring off-Broadway to Playwrights Horizons the following year, directed by Niegel Smith and starring Kristine Nielsen. Thereafter, Smith would become Mac's director of choice. Part III, *The Bourgeois Oli-*

garch, which has yet to be produced, and Part IV, *Gary: A Sequel to "Titus Andronicus,"* which opened to mixed reviews on Broadway (2019) starring Nathan Lane, directed by George C. Wolfe, received seven Tony nominations, including the category of Best Play.

Perhaps Mac's most celebrated project to date is *A 24-Decade History of Popular Music*, which after years of marathon-style training (with ever-lengthening performances), culminated in a twenty-four-hour performance at St. Ann's Warehouse in Brooklyn, New York, October 8–9, 2016. It was produced by Linda Brumbach and Pomegranate Arts. The immersive performance was inspired by an early AIDS walk that Mac had participated in as a teenager in San Francisco. Mac reminisces that the event embodied "a community coming together [as] it was being torn apart."[6] The concert reframed this memory within the format of a "radical faerie realness ritual sacrifice" intending to symbolically purge the violence and intolerance of America's difficult past through performance, in order to communally envision a more inclusive future for its marginalized people.[7] Over a period of twenty-four hours (noon on Saturday to noon on the following day), Mac dedicated each hour to a particular decade since the country's founding, starting with 1776–1785. Each hour thereafter Mac changed into a new outré costume (by Machine Dazzle), symbolic of each era, without a pause in the performance. Throughout the event, the performance space was continuously changed as a form of creative disruption. Both the stage and the auditorium were carefully shifted and reset—moving not only performers and set pieces, but also audience members and chairs through a consciously designed choreography that changed the physical layout of the audience at least once every few hours. Not only did this keep the audience engaged, it reflected the theme of each decade. For example, dinner tables were brought into the space to serve food, but also to symbolize the idea of homecoming following the Civil War. Mac invited people of color in the audience to sit front, center stage, while white attendees were asked to retreat to the margins of the space as a reenactment of 1950s suburban white flight.

Throughout the concert, a group of artists known as "Dandy Minions" (a carefully curated group of queer, downtown New York artists curated by Indigenous performer Timothy White Eagle) helped Mac facilitate the changes, ensuring that everything ran smoothly and on schedule. The performance featured Mac as a shape-shifting fool, who adapted to comment on various periods in American history, expansively queering the notion of linear time to reflect positions from both the past and the present.

Embodying the now-ubiquitous notion (at least within theory-driven scholarship) that queer time exists outside of the controlling power structure of heteronormativity, *A 24-Decade History* allowed all audience members to form bonds of queer solidarity through curated time travel, alternative family modeling, and the resultant kinship. Moreover, the concert, which began at hour one with a full, twenty-four-piece orchestra and supporting cast members, engaged the convention of removing someone from the stage with each hour and decade that passed. Thus, at the end of the performance, Mac was left alone on the stage, nearly naked, strumming their ukulele and singing original songs. This final hour harkened back to Mac's very first performances in New York, such as *The Face of Liberalism*, highlighting the Ridiculous fool persona that continues as the creative center of their work. In addition to critical and scholarly praise for *A 24-Decade History of Popular Music*, Mac was awarded the Edward M. Kennedy Prize, a Guggenheim Award, the Doris Duke Award (2016), a MacArthur "genius" grant, a Special Citation Obie, and a selection as finalist for the Pulitzer Prize (2017).

A 24-Decade History then toured around the globe while Mac and composer/arranger Matt Ray conceived an annual seasonal show, *Holiday Sauce* (2017), which premiered at Manhattan's storied venue, Town Hall. *Holiday Sauce* extended the legacy of the marathon concert and was dedicated to Mac's late drag mother, Flawless Sabrina, who gained cult fame in the documentary *The Queen* (1968). Mac continued through the Covid-19 pandemic to produce new virtual work, including a prerecorded *Holiday Sauce* (in 2020 and 2021), and a series of short films that queer Walt Whitman (supported by a residency at ALL ARTS in 2021), which received the prestigious Ibsen Award. In June 2021 Mac made their post-Covid debut as part of Lincoln Center's Restart Stages (outside on the plaza) in celebration of LGBTQ+ Pride, with a performance entitled *Egg Yolk*. The concert included new songs that will become part of Mac's ongoing project that celebrates queer icons of the twentieth century.

In fall 2021, the Magic Theater in San Francisco was set to premiere Mac's new play, *Joy and Pandemic*, set during the 1918 influenza pandemic, but it was postponed indefinitely with the onset of the Covid-19 Delta variant and its spread. The play, an ode to Mac's late mother Joy Aldrich (much like *The Young Ladies of . . .* focuses on their deceased father), takes place in a children's art school, like the one their mother ran in Stockton, California. According to press releases, one of the themes of *Joy and Pan-*

demic is the Christian Science faith that their mother practiced devoutly, which largely rejects modern medicine.

In January and February 2022, again in collaboration with Matt Ray and Machine Dazzle, Mac performed in the premiere of a new self-penned opera, *The Hang*, at HERE Arts Center in Manhattan. Reframing the final hours of Socrates, this production served as a dynamic opportunity for queer communion through a return to live performance following the theater lockdowns required by Covid-19 mandates. These new works from this remarkably creative and productive artist reflect Mac's return to their own roots, by returning to the places and even venues where they started their career over two decades ago. Mac continues to make new work.

The Collection: Chapter Overview

In chapter 1, "The Early Performance of Taylor Mac," I describe and ana-lyze the early performances from 2000 to 2007, employing theater his-tory and queer theory to link Mac's particular style and legacy to queer predecessors. Covering these earliest works reveals the influences, prac-tices, and philosophies that populate Mac's later, better-known works. The chapter also traces the development of Mac's persona as a postmodern fool, grounded in part in the clown work of queer pioneer and Ridiculous Theatre champion Charles Ludlam.

In chapter 2 Carrie J. Preston reflects on *The Lily's Revenge* in her essay "Participation, Endurance, and the Pucker in Taylor Mac's *The Lily's Revenge*," describing divergent reactions to Mac's work and how different, vulnerable audiences (for example, survivors of trauma or persons who are immunocompromised) can experience audience participation in very different ways. In chapter 3, "Between *Hir* and There: Considering Taylor Mac's Work as Bridging Genres," Kelly I. Aliano highlights the concept of "Absurd realism" as a lens to analyze *Hir* and focuses on gender roles and alternative queered family structure, particularly as read through the experiences of the trans male character Max.

Because of the magnitude of the ongoing *A 24-Decade History of Popu-lar Music*, three chapters are devoted to it, each providing a distinct lens to analyze and assess the cultural importance of the Brooklyn marathon performance. In chapter 4, "Queer Pussy Time: Taylor Mac's Lesbian Decade," Kim Marra focuses on the second-to-last hour (the Lesbian

Decade) of *A 24-Decade History*, which honors the lesbians who acted as caretakers for persons with AIDS, features music popular among radical lesbians from roughly 1996 to 2006, and signals the notion of "queer pussy time" as a timely feminist queer intervention. Lisa A. Freeman dedicates chapter 5, "Too Slow: Taylor Mac and the Rubs of Time," to the fifteenth decade (1916–1926) of *A 24-Decade History*, highlighting Mac's "queering" of American history, the collaborative nature of the work, audience participation, and the trauma of war. Rounding out a trio of essays that analyze the marathon concert, Jen Buckley's chapter 6 essay, "Taylor Mac, Walt Whitman, and Adhesive America: Cruising Utopia with the Good Gay Poet," proposes the centrality of the American poet Walt Whitman's "aesthetic and political place in the *24-Decade History of Popular Music*," as reflected especially in the 1846–56 hour and unpacks Whitman's racial politics, Mac's noted elision of this controversy, and the particularities of queer durational performance.

Erika T. Lin's essay, "Circles and Lines: Community and Legacy in Taylor Mac's *Gary: A Sequel to 'Titus Andronicus,'*" in chapter 7, focuses on Mac's script for *Gary*, offering a reading of early modern theatrical conventions and Mac's engagement with and subversion of these, focusing on narrative content and presentational experience.

The next two essays, by Sissi Liu and David Román, extend the theme of *A 24-Decade History* beyond the performance space to consider its aesthetic and cultural legacies in an American context. Liu's chapter 8 essay, "Designturgy, Being Queer: Taylor Mac Wears Machine Dazzle in 24 Decades," focuses on Dazzle's remarkable costumes at the 2017 San Francisco performance of the concert, the year after the Brooklyn marathon, arguing for their centrality to the dramaturgical framework of the show as it continues to shift. Finally, in chapter 9, "Sing the Revolution: Lin-Manuel Miranda, Taylor Mac, and the Great American Songbook," Román, who has followed *A 24-Decade Concert* through its long development, reflects as an audience member on Mac's use of the American Songbook, tracing the cross-temporal connections the work makes with other performers, including Lin-Manuel Miranda, Linda Ronstadt, Aretha Franklin, Barbra Streisand, and Ella Fitzgerald.

Following these critical essays, the volume moves from the perspectives of scholars and critics to commentary by Mac's collaborators—and by Mac himself. In chapter 10, "*The Walk Across America for Mother Earth*," Paul Zimet focuses on the process of collaboratively composing *Walk*, conceived as a rewriting of Chekhov's *The Three Sisters* that also borrows elements from *Waiting for Godot*, commedia, burlesque, and cabaret—highlighting the use of pastiche that remains a hallmark of Ridiculous-style performance in its contemporary form. In chapter 11 we hear from the artist himself, in an interview with Mac by Kevin Sessums that reveals not only Mac's personal ideas about the work, but also gestures to the future. Chapter 12 provides a series of original reflections on collaboration with a variety of artists, including Matt Ray, Machine Dazzle, Niegel Smith, Viva DeConcini, Tigger! Ferguson, producer Linda Brumbach, and Mac's longtime voice teacher the late Barbara Maier Gustern.

Finally, chapter 13 takes the form of a conversation between David Román and myself. In it we trace the origins of this project, casually reflect on what Mac has meant in the formation of our professional relationship and friendship, on the importance of queer mentorship, and on Mac's role as a community organizer and the quest for empathy that we believe ties together Mac's work and this edited collection. Additionally, the conversation acts as a reflection on the role of theater and live performance during the Covid-19 pandemic, when playhouses and performance venues were forced to lock their doors and turn out their lights for over a year.

Because this collection is an analytical celebration of Mac's work to date (and because Mac is so amazingly productive), the deadlines of writing and publishing make it impossible to ensure that the collection will be up-to-date at the time of its release. The book is not intended as an analysis of culmination, but rather as an invitation for others to observe, analyze, discuss, and celebrate Mac's ongoing work as a queer performance artist and activist performer.

Notes

1. Garth Greenwell, "Hero's Journey: An Interview with Taylor Mac," *Paris Review* (June 25, 2018). https://www.theparisreview.org/blog/2018/06/25/heros-journey-an-int erview-with-taylor-mac/

2. For more on Taylor Mac's childhood and early life, see chapter 1, "The Early Performances of Taylor Mac."

3. Sean F. Edgecomb, "The Ridiculous Performance of Taylor Mac," *Theatre Journal* 64, no. 4 (2012): 553.

4. Stephen J. Bottoms. *Playing Underground: A Critical History of the 1960s Off-Broadway* (Ann Arbor: University of Michigan Press, 2006), 215.

5. "The Latinx Theatre Commons' Peter Zeisler Memorial Award Acceptance Speech," *howlround.com* (June 14, 2017). https://howlround.com/latinx-theatre-commo ns-peter-zeisler-memorial-award-acceptance-speech

6. WFMT Blog, "12 April 2016.blogs.wfmt.com." http://blogs.wfmt.com/offmic/20 16/04/12/how-1-artist-is-condensing-24-decades-of-american-popular-song-into-a-si ngle-24-hour-performance/

7. Maddie Hopfield,. "Taylor Mac: Distilling the Past to Imagine a Future," *theatre. philadelphia.org* (June 25, 2018). https://www.theatrephiladelphia.org/theatre-news/tay lor-mac-distilling-the-past-to-imagine-a-future

ONE

The Early Performances of Taylor Mac[1]

Sean F. Edgecomb

Taylor Mac's remarkable oeuvre carries on the tradition of Charles Ludlam, who is identified as the auteur of the Theatre of the Ridiculous genre through his writing, directing, and appearing in twenty-nine original plays for his Ridiculous Theatrical Company (RTC) between its founding in 1967 and his untimely death in 1987. Ludlam's Ridiculous aesthetic juxtaposed the modernist tradition of the avant-garde (even though Ludlam rejected the term) with camp, clowning, and drag. Forming within the gay community at the watershed of gay liberation, it was one of the first fully realized queer theater forms in the United States. More specifically, it mixed high literary culture with low pop culture, generating a pastiche that reflected and satirized contemporary society. Farcical in nature, the Ridiculous contributed to the emergence of the postmodern clown, a comic figure who appropriates traditional clowning skills and "fragments, subverts and inverts" them to create a self-reflexive and deconstructive performance. After solidifying their reputation as an actor the 1990s, Mac embraced this aesthetic, provocatively adopting and extending Ludlam's Ridiculous, employing it as a fool for political satire and radical social commentary, by layering Ludlam's clown (an entertainer combining traditional comic skills with camp) with the alternative persona of the fool (a figure whose comic identity is a reflection of their status as a born outsider).

While other contributors to this collection take up aspects of Mac's broad oeuvre, this chapter focuses on the period before 2009, the foundational period in Mac's development as a neo-Ridiculous artist. It treats four

Fig. 3. Taylor Mac in *The Be(A)st of Taylor Mac*, in trademark Pierrot-inspired makeup, c. 2006. Photo: Lucien Samaha.

works that followed the terrorist attacks of September 11, 2001: *The Face of Liberalism* (2002), *Red Tide Blooming* (2006), *The Be(A)st of Taylor Mac* (2006), and *The Young Ladies of . . .* (2007). It was through these shows that Mac laid the groundwork for their signature fool persona through a personal interpretation of their distinct neo-Ridiculous aesthetic, which evolved from an amateur, queer one-person show in a Manhattan bar to Mac's more fully developed plays.

In their performances, Mac is consciously haunted by the ghost of the original Ridiculous, but rather than acting as someone possessed, they act as a medium to the spirit, which, in the words of Joseph Roach, allows them to "bring forth, to make manifest, and to transmit."[2] Roach suggests that the making of culture through the practice of performance is inherently re-inventionist, allowing for a process that is generative and nonbiologically productive. In their contemporary Ridiculous performance, Mac seeks both to resurrect and to transform predecessors such as Ludlam. In this way, their Ridiculous aesthetic exemplifies the operations of queer legacy in David Román's sense of "provisional collectives," where "certain artists mark themselves as historical subjects whose genealogies might be found outside of traditional systems of identification and belonging."[3] Román elucidates his concept through the notion of "archival drag," which refers to "the nature of contemporary performances that draw on historical reembodiment and expertise."[4] When brought into conversation with Elizabeth Freeman's "temporal drag," which she defines as "a kind of historical *jouissance*, a friction of dead bodies upon live ones, [and] obsolete constructions upon emergent ones," drag is extended beyond early utopian notions introduced by Judith Butler and favors particular acts of drag drawn from social histories.[5] If the Ludlamesque legacy is what Mac figuratively drags behind themself as a connection to the past, the acknowledgment of this trailing history allows Mac to cut the ties, creating a momentum that propels them forward into new performative manifestations of the Ridiculous that provide queer commentary on the contemporary United States.

Formative Years

Taylor Mac (Bowyer) (1973–) was born in Laguna Beach, California, and grew up on the West Coast with no access to downtown New York theater until they were an adult.[6] Because of this distance in both location and culture, their approach to performance developed independently until they eventually became part of New York City's queer performance tradition. After graduating from high school in Stockton, California, in 1991, Mac moved to San Francisco, "because it was the closet city, and the gayest city," and the ideal place for them to come out of the closet.[7] San Francisco offered Mac a hodgepodge education that included professional acting training and practical experience as a working actor.[8]

Mac moved to New York City in 1994 to attend the American Academy of Dramatic Arts (AADA), where they continued their acting training, studied theater history, and also learned that the AADA had been the training ground for Ethyl Eichelberger (né James Roy Eichelberger, 1945–90), who would influence their emerging interest in the Ridiculous aesthetic.[9] A classically trained actor like Ludlam, Eichelberger developed their unique Ridiculous sensibility while working with Ludlam and the RTC. After leaving the company to pursue a career as a solo performer, they migrated from the West Village to the bohemian world of the Lower East Side in the early 1980s (a period now deemed the East Village Renaissance) and became known for their solo drag shows featuring iconic women from history and mythology, including *Nefert-iti* (1978), *Jocasta* (1982), and *Medusa* (1985). Eichelberger was a seminal figure in the post-Stonewall queer theater movement before dying by suicide in 1990, unable to tolerate the harsh side effects of their prescribed AIDS medication.[10]

On graduating from the AADA, Mac performed in regional theaters across the United States and began developing their own ideas as a playwright. Seeking an outlet to express their frustration with the state of US theater, Mac began writing what they call "kooky" plays with traditional dramatic structures, such as *The Hot Month* (written in 1999), in which the beat of a heart monitor sets the pace and tone of the play as a sister, a brother, and his male lover struggle to find their identities and come to grips with one another in the face of death, and *The Levee* (written in 2000), a kitchen-sink drama about a heterosexual couple attempting to deal with the pain and pressure of repeated miscarriages. In the summer of 2000, Mac headed to the gay resort of Provincetown, Massachusetts, to focus on their newfound vocation as playwright and to experiment with thrift-store drag performances. Because "PTown" constitutes a living archive of intergenerational activity, particularly among gay men, Mac's drag appearance on the scene inspired comparisons to Ridiculous founders, including Smith, Tavel, Eichelberger, and Ludlam. Such comparisons motivated Mac to immerse themselves in the Ridiculous canon and to learn its history. They discovered that the first manifestation of the Ridiculous took place in 1965 at the Play-House of the Ridiculous (PHR), founded by Tavel as resident troupe playwright and John Vacarro as director. Tavel and Vaccaro formulated the pastiche style of the Ridiculous in early plays such as *Shower* (1965) and *The Life of Juanita Castro* (1965), both of which were intended for but rejected by Andy Warhol's Factory. In 1966, Ludlam, fresh from the drama program at Hofstra University, joined the Play-House of the Ridiculous as an actor and playwright, and his Ridiculous fate was sealed. A year later, he mutinied from Tavel and Vaccaro with a majority of the company members in tow, formed the RTC, and became the key figure in the movement for the next twenty years. Many of the summer residents in Provincetown had firsthand recollections of Ludlam both personally and in performance, providing Mac with an education drawn from memory and experience.

During this summer, Mac also discovered the Ludlamesque interpretation of the clown. Ludlam was notorious for channeling his comic stage personae through a distinctive clown character pastiched from a grand tradition of clown types, including Greek mimes, the auguste, Arlecchino, the scapegoat, and the medieval court jester, and he exemplified in his characters Saint Obnoxious (*Turds in Hell*, 1968), the Fool (*The Grand Tarot*, 1969), and Mr. Foufas the farceur (*Le Bourgeois Avant-Garde*, 1983). Ludlam relied on camp to construct his clown characters, becoming a covert spokesperson for the gay community that was gaining visibility in New York in the 1970s. His distinct sense of camp as "an outsider's view of things"[11] was employed as a method by which marginalized outsiders (queers) could communicate with like-minded individuals through a series of codes—a secret language.[12] For Ludlam, the concept of camp was thus a combination of the ideas inherent in his plays and the larger-than-life aesthetic choices in his productions.

Ludlam further fashioned his clown through the practice of "gender-fuck" drag, which hyperbolizes expressions of artificiality (both aesthetic and gestural) to "fuck" with gender perceptions. A signature feature of Ludlam's stage clowns, this gender-fuck camp aesthetic distinguished his groundbreaking interpretations of Norma Desmond (*Big Hotel*, 1967), Maria Magdalena Galas (his homage to Maria Callas; *Galas*, 1983), and Lady Enid (*The Mystery of Irma Vep*, 1984), as well as his performance in his 1973 adaptation of *La Dame aux Camélias* by Alexandre Dumas fils. In Ludlam's *Camille*, the doomed romantic relationship between the courtesan Marguerite Gautier (Ludlam) and her lover Armand Duval, played by RTC member Bill Vehr, respectively, demonstrates how Ludlam strategically mimicked a heteronormative relationship to openly depict a gay romance onstage. Although portrayed by two openly gay men, Marguerite and Armand's relationship was approached with complete sincerity and dedication in an effort to facilitate what Ludlam referred to as "believ[ing] in the character beyond the gender of the actor."[13] Even though Ludlam proudly displayed his hairy chest and arms in his low-cut, nineteenth-century-style gown, he drew the audience into the story enough to forget the intentional artificiality, camp, and anarchic disregard for verisimilitude in the production.

Drawing on Ludlam's distinct drag aesthetic and understanding of camp, Mac filters the practice of gender-fuck through the figure of the fool, drawing on the color, tone, and infrastructure of the time and place in which they live. Scholar Enid Welsford defines the fool as one who is "the mouthpiece of a spirit, or power external to himself, and so has access to hidden knowledge—especially to knowledge of the future."[14] The fool possesses a seemingly clairvoyant ability to see beyond the imposed boundaries of a society, making him a gauge of the moral underpinnings of a civilized culture. Mac's version of the fool lies closest to what Louis Pétit de Julleville refers to as *"la jeunesse abondonée à la nature*,"[15] the fool who is cast out by the civilized into the wilds, where they adapt to and eventually rule their surroundings. In the first phase of Mac's career (analyzed herein), they originally represented the gay youth rejected by a normative culture and given up to the wilds of New York City, where they find respite from homophobia through opportunities to form community. In this context, Max as fool found the opportunity to establish their own fool society, inviting audiences into their own queer space rather than entertaining the mainstream. As Mac's career and notoriety have grown, however, their current works expand the notion of community, working toward inclusion and representation of anyone willing to work for social justice in the United States. This is particularly evident in the ongoing *A 24-Decade History of Popular Music*, which attempts to resurrect lost narratives of all marginalized or oppressed Americans over the past 240 years.

After fashioning an early version of their gender-fuck fool character ("a Pierrot figure for the modern age,"[16] and a "stage-worthy representation of [them]self"[17]) following Mac's Provincetown sojourn, Mac began doing short performances at NYC gay bars, including the Marquis and the Slide. Performing brief comic vignettes, they began to gain some celebrity among the subcultural coteries of downtown Manhattan. This early-career approach to performance in a variety of found spaces reflected Ludlam's origins, when he and the Play-House of the Ridiculous performed *Turds in Hell* in a porno cinema on 42nd Street and the RTC presented *Bluebeard* (1970) on reclaimed boards laid precariously across the bar at the West Village watering-hole Christopher's End.[18]

Describing their stylistic approach as "Hey, let's put on a show!,"[19] Mac took up the tradition of the "moldy aesthetic" introduced by Jack Smith, an approach that creates art from the discarded refuse of others, often coating it in glitter. In his 1962 essay, "The Perfect Filmic Appositeness of Maria Montez," Smith states that "trash is the material of creators."[20] The communal freedom and opportunity for improvisatory creation or destruction implied by Smith's eccentric vision was communicated directly through his underground films *Flaming Creatures* (1962–63) and *Normal Love* (1963) and his play *Rehearsal for the Destruction of Atlantis* (1965). Smith's work was irrefutably political in its attack on American capitalism, which was couched in metaphors such as his use of a Lobster to represent the "epitome of the avaricious landlord [. . .] who increasingly held the world in his grip."[21] The theme of material and social refuse became emblematic of the era, with queer works such as John Waters's *Mondo Trasho* (1969) and Andy Warhol's *Trash* (1970). Ludlam continued this adoration of the disposed-of by rifling through trash to compose his distinct plays and performances.[22]

Following in this tradition, Mac began to create new art thematically born from the destruction and refuse of the 9/11 terrorist attack in the same way that their predecessors had created work from their own beloved trash heaps. Mac's early drag aesthetic was "glamorously beaten" in style, with smeared makeup and layers of violently ripped garments.[23] A mélange of enlightened precision and premeditated disarray, Mac's drag became the omnipresent metaphor steering their artistic practice, their at-odds aesthetic serving as a visual allegory for the political themes on which their work is based. For example, in early performances a homemade dress of dirty latex gloves was a metaphor for "the War on Terror," the filthy, cheap, and intentionally haphazard garment physically representing what Mac calls the "mess" in the Middle East.[24] Mac's image thus reflected their frustration with the state of the war-driven, jingoistic American political climate post-9/11.

Although Mac had lived in the East Village for several years, the period directly following 9/11 was their first opportunity to perform in the unconventionally laissez-faire climate of downtown Manhattan, where the theater scene provided room for experimentation and failure that enabled them to thrive, As Mac has explained, "Uptown, failure is unacceptable, but suddenly downtown I found this access to a world that was just embracing of performance, and of difference, and of being in the moment, and kookiness and failure. [Downtown] they'll clap for you if you fail."[25] These foundational ideas would lead to Mac's ongoing, often-repeated mantra: "perfection is for assholes." Mac's reflections on the power of failure resonate with J. Jack Halberstam's view that in a queer context, failure may "offer more creative, more cooperative, more surprising ways of being in the world."[26]

Fig. 4. Mac in their bespoke garment composed of latex gloves as a metaphor for "The War on Terror." Photo: Lucien Samaha.

The Face of Liberalism *(2002)*

Following out of these formative years, Mac turned to political performance, motivated by the goal of revealing what they consider to be "the end of the American empire."[27] Their solo show *The Face of Liberalism* was prompted by the White House's response to the terrorist attack on the World Trade Center. In developing the show, Mac began to evolve their signature fool persona as an extension of themself, a social commentator who reveals truth, bravely speaking against dominant sociopolitical beliefs, in this case the United States in the aftermath of 9/11. Mac's fool is a hybrid of traditional fool archetypes; as an artist, they are an artificial fool who uses slick wit to comment and entertain the audience, but Mac also takes on the role of the natural fool, a figure shunned as an outsider and ostracized as a self-identifying queer. When in this fool mode, Mac refers to themself as "a bedazzled creature [who] builds community."[28] Mac's ideal vision of this community is as a magnanimous collective composed of self-identifying queer activists and their allies. Mac extends this even further in more contemporary, participatory works, including *The Lily's Revenge, A 24-Decade History*, and *Holiday Sauce.*

Premiering in 2002 (though a longer run would follow in 2003) in the basement of the Slide Bar on the Bowery in New York's East Village, *The Face of Liberalism* was among the very first theater pieces to interrogate and satirize the climate of fear and resultant xenophobia that Mac suggests came from the Bush White House following 9/11. Reinventing the Ridiculous genre as "in-yer-face" Americana, Mac succeeded in this work in morphing Ludlam's midcentury gay theater into a more socially conscious version, while preserving the extremist and histrionic nature of the original. Just as Ludlam's Ridiculous had thrived on the creation of exclusive safe space as a site for politically unrestrained expression, *The Face of Liberalism* invited participants into an alternate world, where Mac played the role of a postmodern Lord of Misrule. Describing the show as "a subversive jukebox musical," Mac relied on the preferred Ridiculous practice of pastiche to formulate the highly politicized work.[29] Advertised as "a mishmash of original songs, parodies, stories and mental illness,"[30] the show was based around a set list that included "War Criminal Romp," a New Orleans–style jazz tune in which the lyrics are a recitation of the names of supporters of the Bush administration, and "Fear Itself," a thoughtful ballad that Mac sang without accompaniment, pointedly closing the show with the lyrics: "I'm afraid of patriotism, and nationalism and jingoism /

We've nothing to fear but fear itself, fear itself, fear itself."[31] Although the songs remained mostly the same for each performance (with room for Mac's now-trademark improvisational commentary), they added transitional topical and anecdotal monologues about the state of US society in the period following 9/11. In one such monologue, Mac explored tackiness through the persona of a disenfranchised teenage Goth: "People are selling baby American flags on the street for two dollars when you know they only cost like two cents and were made by some Taiwanese premi-baby in their makeshift bamboo incubator."[32]

In addition to such criticism, Mac improvised dialogue rooted in the news of the day, and each night, in a postmodern riff on the Federal Theater Project's Depression-era "living newspapers," they pasted headlines on their mostly nude body. For the first performance, for example, Mac's body featured the headline "Liza Beat Me" in boldface type, referring to the accusations of David Gest against his ex-wife Liza Minnelli. This absurd recipe of pointed references to current events and gay diva worship exemplifies Mac's particular Ridiculous sensibility.

Inspired by the themes and aesthetic of *The Face of Liberalism*, Mac developed a distinctive makeup scheme in collaboration with makeup artist and designer Derrick Little, though it wouldn't appear until a year later in the political cabaret *Live Patriot Acts: Patriots Gone Wiiiiildd!* (2004). It entailed messily painting their face with the stars and stripes of the American flag, applying thumbtacks to their jaw with spirit gum—points facing outward, and wearing a curling-ribbon red-white-and-blue wig. The deconstructed flag motif, created with drugstore cosmetics and stationery-aisle craft supplies, was a visceral expression of Mac's agenda as a citizen/artist to "reveal the truth," their face a billboard for self-created graffiti, articulating their identity through metaphor and its hyperbolized freakish interpretation of the queer fool.[33] Mac's practice of employing their body as a canvas marks them as a queer subject, their changing physical appearance a metaphor for performative gender. In a state of constant transformation, Mac creates a sense of agency that, in Victoria Pitt's words, "underscores the body's symbolic significance as a site of public identity and a resource for opposing (hetero) dominant culture."[34] In this vein, Mac offers his physical body as a corporeal representative of the liberal body politic, embodying the Foucauldian notion of the body as a text on which social reality is inscribed.[35]

The Face of Liberalism provided a potential refuge for like-minded audience members who openly criticized the conservative political majority during a time of jingoistic fervor—the period directly following 9/11. Although audiences for the run of the show were admittedly limited, the performance space successfully doubled as a site of refuge and communion for urban Americans who harbored similar feelings of frustration with prevailing hegemonic ideologies that promoted xenophobia and absolutism. Mac embodied, hyperbolized, and performed the minority position through their carefully constructed image: a voluntary scapegoat, the traditional fool archetype reclaimed as a figurehead with a political agenda. In offering up their cosmeticized visage for consumption, Mac willingly became the unlikely "face" of liberalism. Mac's continuing political stance as a self-proclaimed liberal (though more contemporarily, they might prefer "progressive") is driven by their belief in a democratic society that supports the expression of individual freedoms across "a range of humanity."[36] When read in combination, themes discussed in *The Face of Liberalism*, including blind patriotism and subsequent threats to individualism and representation, offer a subtle critique of neoliberalism and the social detachment that Mac sees as a destructive consequence of its global proliferation.

The Face of Liberalism stands apart from Mac's later works because of its underground origin and nature. Positioned as a piece of provocative antipatriotic art and located surreptitiously in an East Village basement with limited advertising or press, this foundational performance marked the materialization of Mac's fresh take on the Ludlamesque Ridiculous tradition in a postmillennial context.

Red Tide Blooming *(2006)*

In 2005, Mac was the inaugural winner of the Ethyl Eichelberger Award, a commissioning prize given in recognition of an artist who embodies Eichelberger's uninhibited aesthetic and spirit. As such, Mac was invited to compose, and funded to produce, an original work. In homage to Mac's Ridiculous predecessors, Mac elected to create *Red Tide Blooming*, a play about disenfranchisement and a search for belonging inspired by the early epic plays of Tavel and Ludlam in the genre of Ridiculous pastiche.

The plot of *Red Tide Blooming* is based on the gentrification of the Coney Island Mermaid Parade, where bohemians dress up in outré costumes as marine creatures, both real and mythological, in a contemporary Feast of Fools. The capital-driven metamorphoses of the former bohemian enclaves of lower Manhattan into now one of the city's most unaffordable neighborhoods has forced artists to seek new haunts beyond the city proper, among them Coney Island. This migration of New York City's artists and creatives to the far edge of Brooklyn, along with Coney Island's colorful past as a nonstop carnival that provided escapist amusement away from the city, inspired the creation of the Mermaid in 1983. As a celebration for and of self-declared "freaks," the parade took a cue from the practice of Gay Pride parades (and specifically NYC Pride), the popularity and carnival atmosphere of which led in the 1980s to large marketing campaigns and opportunities for the business-minded to capitalize on and profit from the crowds that gathered. Similarly, as the Mermaid Parade grew in size and popularity, the celebration that had been created as an alternative by and for disenfranchised members of society (both gay and straight) became a magnet for a wider audience.

Red Tide Blooming is a metatheatrical pageant with characters and parade participants presenting a play that seeks to answer the question, What happened to all of the freaks? Mac carefully curated a cast of "outsiders" that included burlesque performers, performance artists, trans activists, drag queens, radical Faeries, a self-proclaimed slut, naked bodies of all shapes and sizes, four generations of performers, all different kinds of celebrated sexual perversions, and even former Play-House of the Ridiculous veteran superstar Ruby Lynn Reyner. In bringing together a variety of well-known performers from across generations, the cast embodies the legacy of the Ridiculous tradition in a histrionic family reunion. The decision to construct the play around contemporary stock characters is directly borrowed from Ludlam, who, as a trained expert in commedia dell'arte, frequently built texts around archetypes and situations from the early modern Italian drama.[37] The play would also provide foundational understanding of commedia, which Mac expanded on in their production of *A Walk Across America for Mother Earth*, which premiered at LaMaMa in collaboration with Talking Band in 2011.

Red Tide Blooming centers around Mac-as-Olokun, a hermaphrodite sea creature who has secured their phallus to their posterior with duct tape—what drag queens refers to as "tucking." Mac borrowed the name Olokun, an Orisha spirit of the ocean who embodies equally male and female characteristics, from the religion of the Yoruba of West Africa. Appearing onstage on a desert island of discarded toys reminiscent of Smith's vision of a trash-heap metropolis, Mac-as-Olokun elucidates their desire to find and commune with other freaks like themself: "All freaks?

Disappeared? They can't have disappeared. Maybe they've gotten sad and have hidden away for a time."[38] Mac's interpretation of the freak resonated with Michel Foucault's views on insanity and how, as Chris Baldrick has summarized, "the freak must have a purpose: to reveal the results of vice, folly and unreason as a warning to an erring humanity."[39] Rather than moralizing or condemning sexual liberation, the "erring humanity" that Mac attempts to combat in *Red Tide Blooming* is the conservative American right wing. On a Candide-like journey, Mac-as-Olokun encounters a cast of "citizens" who declare their distaste for diversity, led by the Collective Conscious, a sweater puppet who condemns social subversion with Wizard of Oz–like brainwashing. The play-within-the-play warns of an impending Armageddon brought on by the conformist agenda of the first decade of the twenty-first century.

Among the characters reveling in this satirical end of days are US vice-presidential spouse and former National Endowment for the Humanities chair Lynne Cheney and Iraqi dictator Saddam Hussein. Cheney, who took part in the construction of the Collective Conscious, has been thrown out of the upper echelons of political power because her penchant for writing lesbian romance novels and having a secret love affair with Hussein. The character of Hussein is portrayed in Arabian Nights drag, a distinct reference to Jack Smith's affinity for Middle Eastern glamour.[40] While the caricatures of Cheney and Hussein are extreme, Mac presents them with empathy as two more uncomfortable freaks attempting to masquerade as normal.

Red Tide Blooming's concern with the disenfranchised Other is reiterated at the play's conclusion when the character of Constance Faubourg, an anxiety-ridden, germ-obsessed housewife who helps to manipulate the Collective Conscious (with Beep, a bearded lady as a male corporate cliché), exposes Olokun not as a hermaphrodite, but as a transgender nudist. Olokun responds by ripping the duct tape from their genitals, refigured through the act of fetishistic body modification as a symbolic expression of trans identity for the stage. This practice not only suggests an agency of choice and queer authority, but embodies a sort of physical deviance, what Michael Atkinson refers to as a "flesh journey: [the] process of intentionally constructing the corporeal in order to symbolically represent and physically chronicle changes in one's identity, thought, relationships and emotions."[41] After manifesting such a change in revealing their nude body (painted an electric shade of green), a less-than-discreet metaphor for the baring of their soul, Olokun exposes the cast (as representative of the whole of society) for their own freakishness and for masking their individuality in an attempt to pass as normal.[42] Olokun specifically points to Colin Clement, a television weatherman-cum-celebrity whose overdeveloped muscular body suggest the gay subcultural aesthetic that developed in the late 1970s and early '80s.

The exposure of Mac-as-Olokun's genitals is drawn from Ludlam's play *Bluebeard*, in which the tortured title character struggles to create a third "gentler genital" representative of homosexuality: "Love must be reinvented / Sex to me is no longer mysterious / And so I swear that while my beard is blue / I'll twist some human flesh into a genital new."[43] In the original 1970 Ludlam production, the third genital was revealed at the end of the play—a chicken foot attached to an eggplant that protruded from the crotch of the ingénue Sybil (as played by original RTC troupe member Black-Eyed Susan). In a *New York Times* interview, Ludlam explained that the third genital "means a synthesis of the sexes."[44] In the climate of post-Stonewall New York City—*Bluebeard* premiered the year after the riots—the third genital was a less-than-subtle sendup of nontraditional sexual identity: gay or lesbian. Mac, on the other hand, uses their disfigured genital to represent the role of non-binary-based, fluid identity, and more specifically, transgender, gender-fluid, or gender-queer roles in the United States, where these categories continue to be underrecognized in gay and lesbian politics. Mac carries through the trope of their signature fool as one who is at the same time natural and artificial, both queerly born and made.

Red Tide Blooming marked the first time that the media equated Mac with Ludlam's work. Phoebe Hoban of the *New York Times* noted that they had "taken a page from Charles Ludlam's Theatre of the Ridiculous,"[45] and Martin Denton of nytheatre.com credited Mac for turning the Ludlamesque "upside-down and inside-out."[46] The critical and popular success of *Red Tide Blooming* secured Mac's identity as a contemporary Ridiculous performer, but it also gave them the confidence to bravely take their reinventive interpretation of the Ludlamesque beyond the site of its origin, attempting to expand the neo-Ridiculous community in New York City and beyond.

The Be(A)st of Taylor Mac *(2006)*

Following the run of *Red Tide Blooming*, Mac created a solo show that they could tour widely and easily, *the Be(A)st of Taylor Mac*. Borrowing from

Fig. 5. Mac in trademark sequined and glitter-bedecked makeup, c. 2006.
Photo: Lucien Samaha.

the form of a traveling carnival, they transformed their fool into a wandering troubadour, who was perhaps closest in character to Ludlam's Fool in *The Grand Tarot*. Mac's carnival world recalls Mikhail Bakhtin's theory of the "carnivalesque," where participants are invited to live in a topsy-turvy world of queer inversion.[47] Through touring, Mac extended the queer world they created in *The Face of Liberalism* and *Red Tide Blooming*, expanding the boundaries of their fool society beyond New York, where these earlier shows had taken place.

A cabaret that collages recycled songs from *Red Tide Blooming* with new songs and transitional monologues in an intertextual pastiche reminiscent of Ludlam, *Be(A)st* premiered at Edinburgh's Fringe Festival in 2006 and revolves around Mac with their ukulele, a trunk of draggy garments, and the war cry "the revolution will not be masculinized," which is also the title of the opening song. At various times during its two-year run in over forty theaters around the globe, Mac dedicated performances of *Be(A)st* to victims of hate crimes and violence spurred by their sexuality or sexual identity. For example, on Valentine's Day in San Francisco in 2008, they dedicated the show to Lawrence Forbes King, a transgender teenager who, two days earlier, had been shot and killed in a classroom at his high school in Oxnard, California. This sympathetic and jarring technique set the stage for an evening of life-affirming yet brutal honesty.

Exploring Mac's personal role within the vast and complicated globalization of the work, *Be(A)st* covers everything from past lovers to national security, masturbation, and manatees. At one point, attempting to express their own polysexuality, Mac reveals "I want to be a mermaid, merman, *mermanmaid*."[48] Not only does this intentionally connect back to Smith, the Mermaid Parade, and *Red Tide Blooming*, it also expresses a chimerical identity that is hypersexualized while also nonhuman, nongendered, and physically without genitalia. The mermanmaid symbolically represents the anti-identitarian action of ungendering, allowing Mac a freedom of choice to dictate a fluid identity, rather than one based on a normative binary of cissexuality; they colloquially refer to this act as the radical process of "embracing all pronouns."[49] In fact, following this period, Mac would begin to use the gender pronoun "judy" [*sic*], inspired in part by Judy Garland, in performance. In *Be(A)st* Mac theatrically embodies the concept of fluid and pluralistic gender by quickly peeling away garments onstage, transforming their body with various outfits that actively represent the possibility of playing with identity, as well as visually delineating different characters and scenes.

At the conclusion of the show, the space is littered with the garments and accessories that Mac has thrown off, creating a multilayered art-piece-cum-archive that ephemerally records each evening's unique performance. In transforming the theater into a *Wunderkammer* adorned with strewn-about costumes, props, and errant sequins and glitter, Mac marks the audience as an extension of the carnival space. By the end of the performance, audience members are no longer merely observers, but are invited to join a queer world that has been created, a diasporic society of fools with Mac as its liberator.

Be(A)st is altered from performance to performance with the addition of local and timely references and discussion with the audience, but Mac closes each evening's performance with their signature hymn, "Fear Itself."[50] The folk-style song recalls the community-forming anthem of Ludlam's era, as well as Bakhtin's notion that "folk humor" is a foundation of the carnival space.[51] Mac initiates community spirit by inviting audience members to participate in the refrain "we've nothing to fear but fear itself, fear itself, fear itself."[52] As the lights come up in the auditorium, the audience—now a chorus—is encouraged to view the attending others in a new light, as Mac attempts to ignite sparks of *communitas*. This act of transformation from distanced observer to engaged participant, which Jill Dolan describes as "moments in the perpetual present," marks the emergence of a new and fleetingly utopic community through a temporal queering, while still encouraging autonomy and individuality among audience members.[53]

The Young Ladies of . . . (2007)

Following their own initial exploration of their own experiences and emotions in *Be(A)st*, Mac evolved their Ridiculous fool by developing their most personal and autobiographical performance, *The Young Ladies of . . .*. The play was inspired by several boxes of letters that Mac's late father, Robert Mac Bowyer, received from women after placing a singles advertisement in the back of the Australian *Daily Telegraph* in 1968 when he was stationed in Vietnam. Bowyer died in a motorcycle accident when Mac was age four, and *The Young Ladies of . . .* was Mac's lyrical attempt at creating a tangible interpretation of their father through words and memories suspended in scores of letters. In this play about growing up both physically and emotionally, Mac wanted to "discover some common ground," and "[bridge] the gap between masculinity and femininity, fathers and sons and red and blue states."[54]

Young Ladies is set in a purgatory of postmarked envelopes and stage fog where Mac's fool persona matures during the course of the play, trading youthful abandon for a self-awareness born of experience. Mac's transformation from Pétit de Julleville *jeunesse* into an adult is set in motion when they are isolated from the society that they created for themself to inhabit in their earlier plays. The fool of this performance poetically reflects on their familial past, while the haunting refrain of "The Carousel Waltz" from Rodgers and Hammerstein's *Carousel* (1945) suggests Mac's displacement from the carnival they once called home. According to family lore, the film *Carousel* (1956) was Bowyer's favorite, causing Mac to equate their father with the rough-and-tumble character of Billy Bigelow: "I imagine my father's favorite character in the movie musical *Carousel* was the central character of the wife-beater. No, not the T-shirt but the actual person. Bill, that's his name. And Bill was a tough macho kinda guy, as wife-beaters tend to be."[55] Although the strained relationship between a hypermasculine father and son is a common aspect of the shared American gay experience, Mac was the first Ridiculous artist to tackle it in performance.

Young Ladies incorporates one of Smith's favorite theatrical conventions—the slideshow—to further demonstrate the schism between Mac and Bowyer. Mac shows a slide of "Dad with a boy toy"—an aged photograph of Bowyer holding a rifle—and then "Me with a boy toy," where Mac calls on an attractive young man from the audience to join them onstage. Mac continues to juxtapose pictures of their father in aggressively masculine situations with those of themself in drag and often in explicit and suggestive poses. Mac thus playfully uses this segment to comment on their own feelings of disconnection with their father regarding sexuality and generational codes. The slideshow features photographs that embody essentialist stereotypes around gender and masculinity for the audience to consider in relation to Mac's gender-fuck aesthetic. In contrast to the stereotypical cissexual traits projected, they wear opaque-white Pierrot-like face paint, a Baby Jane Wig, and a dirty tattered baby dress, reminiscent of a unisexual christening gown, which suggests an androgynous and desexualized identity. The juxtaposition of this almost childlike aesthetic with the aforementioned weary experience of the displaced fool makes for a complex and inherently queer figure, as the ungendered Mac inhabits both their past and present in one body. Whereas Ludlam employed gender-fuck in an attempt to move beyond gender in plays such as *Camille*, in *Young Ladies*, Mac uses it as a medium to switch genders repeatedly during midperformance, projecting a fluid queerness as they transform from their narrator-cum-fool persona into their father and the Australian women who wrote the original letters.

In true Ridiculous form, Mac relies on the letters not only for their concept, but also for their practice: the letters become puppets, masks, and finally a dress that Mac gleefully sports in a grand dance to the "Carousel Waltz." This approach brings Smith's and Ludlam's common practice of recycling trash into camp-infused beauty to a more sophisticated level rich in symbolism and sentiment. During the course of the run, Mac used a program note to invite audience members to send in letters to the theater, a proposal that was successful in exponentially increasing the piles of mail onstage and physically representing a network of collective belonging. This technique of creative recycling also forms a queer archive, which Halberstam defines as "not simply a repository; [but] also a theory of cultural relevance, a construction of collective memory, and a complex record of queer activity."[56] Mac actualizes this notion by creating a physical legacy of the voices in the text, but also of many who attended the performance. As a continuation of this trope, the climactic gesture of donning the paper dress of letters revives Mac's spirit from their state of melancholy reflection; draped in the epistolary correspondence of their queer family in the form of a garment bearing the handwriting of dozens of contributors, Mac escapes from the limbo-like world of the play in this new suit of armor, dragging the train of letters behind and reciting the mantra, "I hope. I hope. I hope. I hope."[57]

This optimistic final action and dialogue not only concludes *Young Ladies*, it also symbolically marks the end of the first stage of Mac's performative career. *The Young Ladies of . . .*, *The Be(A)st of Taylor Mac*, *Red Tide Blooming*, and *The Face of Liberalism* together form a body of work that is reflective of Mac's urgency to explore what it meant to be a queer American in the period directly following 9/11. The poignant coherency and quality of these works attracted the attention of New Dramatists, which awarded Mac a Playwright in Residency (2007–2014). This position ushered in a new artistic phase for Mac, providing an extended period of sustained funding that would allow them to subsist solely as a professional playwright and performer.

Conclusion

Mac's fool persona has matured into a sophisticated cultural mouthpiece through practice, growing popular support, and recognition of its artistic and political value. The development of Mac-as-queer-fool is fundamental to understanding their revival of the Ridiculous sensibility and practice by reshaping Ludlam's legacy as a reflection of the contemporary world. Although as a theatrical form, the Ridiculous broke down the walls of concealment through the act of public performance, at its origin, it constituted a safe space that allowed for freedom of expression without fear of homophobic discrimination. For this reason, the Ridiculous legacy has not been broadly accessible, but instead has been disseminated and transformed through internal channels of self-defined kinship.[58] Mac has extended such alternative channels of transmission by bringing their queer fool society to new locations and audiences, inviting a more diverse group of people into the neo-Ridiculous fold. Rather than trying to reproduce the work of its originators, Mac has used the queer legacy of the Ridiculous to pick up from where they left off. This approach has allowed Mac to maintain and transform the past within the present via performance, live and virtual, avoiding revivalism and upholding the Ridiculous as a genre with continued relevance as a mode for building a supportive community. In the Ridiculous theater, channeling predecessors in the present takes the shape of archival/temporal drag through the reinvention of the classical figure of the clown, layering it with the postmodern fool. Now well into the second stage of their career, Mac continues to grow performances out of the groundwork set by the plays written and performed in the fundamental period between 2002 and 2007, producing works that continue to open up new dimensions in their ever-evolving exploration of neo-Ridiculous performance.

Notes

1. An earlier version of this chapter originally appeared as "The Ridiculous Performance of Taylor Mac," *Theatre Journal* 64, no. 4 (2012). In this updated version I have changed Mac's pronouns to "they" to more consistently reflect their commitment to gender inclusivity. Because Mac did not introduce "judy" as a gender pronoun used in performance until after the period this chapter covers, I have avoided using it here.

2. Joseph Roach, *Cities of the Dead: Circum-Atlantic Performance* (New York: Columbia University Press, 1996), xi.

3. David Román, *Performance in America: Contemporary U.S. Culture and the Performing Arts* (Durham, NC: Duke University Press, 2005), 1, 3.

4. Román, *Performance*, 142.

5. Elizabeth Freeman, "Time Binds, or, Erotohistoriography," *Social Text* 23, nos. 3/4 (2005): 66. For a more detailed discussion of temporal drag, see Freeman, "Packing History, Count(er)ing Generations," *New Literary History* 31 (2000): 727–44.

6. When Mac started acting professionally, they dropped their surname, Bowyer, and began using "Taylor Mac" as their stage name.

7. Taylor Mac, personal interview with author, 11 March 2008. Unless otherwise attributed, information about Mac's views and personal history is based on this interview.

8. During this period, Mac trained with the San Francisco Mime troupe (his introduction to commedia dell'arte) and appeared in the juke box–style drag revue *Beach Blanket Babylon*.

9. Mac, interview.

10. Sean Edgecomb, "'Not Just Any Woman': Bradford Louryk, a Legacy of Charles Ludlam and the Ridiculous Theatre for the Twenty-First Century," in *"We Will Be Citizens": New Essays on Gay and Lesbian Theatre*, ed. James Fisher (Jefferson, NC: McFarland, 2008), 56–78. For more on Ethyl Eichelberger, see Joe E. Jeffreys, "An Outré Entrée into the Para-Ridiculous Histrionics of Drag Diva Ethyl Eichelberger: A True Story" (PhD diss., New York University, 1996).

11. Charles Ludlam, *Ridiculous Theatre: Scourge of Human Folly—The Essays and Opinions of Charles Ludlam*, ed. Steven Samuels (New York: Theatre Communications Group, 1992), 225.

12. Ludlam, Ridiculous Theatre, 225.

13. Marranca and Dasgupta, *Theatre of the Ridiculous*, 78.[We should have a full citation here. It's not listed in the bibliography, either.]

14. Enid Welsford, *The Fool: His Social and Literary History* (New York: Doubleday, 1961), 76.

15. Louis Pétit de Julleville, *La comédie et les moeurs en France au Moyen Âge* (Paris: Adamant Media Corp., 2001), 282.

16. Taylor Mac press quotes, available at https://taylormac.org (accessed 8 July 2021).

17. Mac, interview.

18. For a detailed history and analysis of this performance, see Sean F. Edgecomb, "Architecting Queer Space: Charles Ludlam's *Bluebeard* in the West Village," in *Readings in Cultural Performance*. eds. Suzanne McCauley and Kevin Landis (London: Palgrave Macmillan, 2017), 88–102.

19. Edgecomb, "Architecting Queer Space."

20. Jack Smith, "The Perfect Filmic Appositeness of Maria Montez," in *Wait for Me at the Bottom of the Pool: The Writings of Jack Smith*, eds. J. Hoberman and Edward Leffingwell (New York: Serpent's Tail, 1997), 26.

21. Smith, "The Perfect Filmic Appositeness," 18. For more on Smith, see *Flaming Creature: Jack Smith, His Amazing Life and Times*, eds. Edward Leffingwell, Carole Kismaric, and Marvin Heiferman (New York: Serpent's Tail, 1997); and Hoberman and Leffingwell, eds., *Wait for Me at the Bottom of the Pool*.

22. J. Hoberman, "Jack Smith: Bagdada and Lobsterrealism," introduction, in Hoberman and Leffingwell, eds., *Wait for Me at the Bottom of the Pool*, 17.

23. Tigger! Ferguson, personal communication with author, 11 April 2008.

24. Mac, interview.

25. Mac, interview.

26. Judith Halberstam, *The Queer Art of Failure* (Durham, NC: Duke University Press), 2.

27. Mac, interview.

28. Taylor Mac, personal communication with author, 19 July 2012.

29. Mac, interview.

30. www.taylormac.org (accessed July 14, 2021).

31. Taylor Mac, *The Face of Liberalism*. Unpublished manuscript (accessible through Morgan Jenness, Abrams Artists Agency, New York City).

32. Mac, *The Face of Liberalism*.

33. Mac, interview.

34. Victoria Pitts, "Visibly Queer: Body Technologies and Sexual Politics," *Sociological Quarterly* 41, no. 3 (2000): 443.

35. Thomas J. Csordas, ed., *Embodiment and Experience: The Existential Ground of Culture and Self* (Cambridge: Cambridge University Press, 1994), 12.

36. Taylor Mac, "Artist Statement," available at www.taylormac.net (accessed 11 August 2012).

37. Ludlam, who offered public *commedia dell'arte* workshops at the Evergreen Theatre in 1974, noted that the Italian genre also influenced his casting process within the RTC: "Actors were chosen for their personalities, almost like 'found objects'; the character fell somewhere between the intention of the script and the personality of the actor" (Ludlam, *Ridiculous Theatre*, 17).

38. Taylor Mac, *Red Tide Blooming*, in *Plays and Playwrights 2007*, ed. Martin Denton (New York: New York Theatre Experience, 2007).

39. Chris Baldrick, *In Frankenstein's Shadow: Myth, Monstrosity, and Nineteenth-Century Writing* (Oxford: Oxford University Press, 1987), 10.

40. Performance artist Ron Vawter also appeared as Jack Smith in Arabian drag for his solo piece *What's Underground About Marshmallows?* (1996).

41. Michael Atkinson, "Flesh Journeys: Neo Primitives and the Contemporary Rediscovery of Radical Body Modification," *Deviant Behavior* 22, no. 2 (2001): 118.

42. Hermaphrodites were common attractions in carnival sideshows in the latter half of the nineteenth century and beginning of the twentieth. Mac's portrayal of Olokun is a riff on the "half-and-half trick," which promised a figure whose gender was split down the middle.

43. Charles Ludlam, *Bluebeard: A Melodrama in Three Acts*, in *The Complete Plays of Charles Ludlam* (New York: Harper & Row, 1989), 119.

44. Calvin Tomkins, "Profiles: Ridiculous," *New Yorker* (15 November 1976): 83.

45. Phoebe Hoban, "Sea Creatures Spare Nothing, Especially Not the Glitter, in 'Red Tide Blooming," *New York Times*, 19 April 2006, available at http://theater2.nytimes.com/2006/04/19/theater/reviews/19tide. (accessed 14 August 2012).

46. Martin Denton, "Red Tide Blooming," available at http://www.nytheatre.com/Show/Review/5006355 (accessed 11 July 2021).

47. David Bergman notes that "[b]ecause camp likes to stand the world on its head, it is comparable to Mikhail Bakhtin's notion of the *carnivalesque*, a style noted for its gay

relativity and its mocking and deriding tone. The carnivalesque, like camp, is characterized by a licensed release of anarchic forces that tend to invert standard social hierarchies." See *GLBTQ: An Encyclopedia of Gay, Lesbian, Bisexual, Transgender and Queer Culture*, s.v. "camp," available at http://www.glbtq.com/literature/camp,2.html (accessed 12 July 2012).

48. Taylor Mac, *The Be(A)st of Taylor Mac*. Unpublished manuscript (accessible through Morgan Jenness, Abrams Artists Agency, New York City).

49. Mac, interview.

50. "Fear Itself" has gained a larger audience since Mac granted Broadway veteran Mandy Patinkin permission to perform the song at his concerts. Patinkin's non-Ridiculous interpretation of the song gives it a broader context and scope, although it also paradoxically dissolves much of the subversive anticommercialization behind Mac's original version.

51. Mikhail M. Bakhtin, "Folk Humor and Carnival Laughter," in *The Bakhtin Reader*, ed. Pam Morris (London: Edward Arnold, 1994), 195.

52. Mac, *The Be(A)st of Taylor Mac*.

53. Jill Dolan, *Utopia in Performance* (Ann Arbor: University of Michigan Press, 2005), 65.

54. *The Young Ladies of . . .* , Taylor Mac, available at http://www.taylormac.net/TaylorMac.net/The_Young_La-dies_Of.html (accessed 26 May 2012).

55. Taylor Mac, *The Young Ladies of . . .* Unpublished manuscript (accessible through Morgan Jenness, Abrams Artists Agency, New York City).

56. Judith Halberstam, *In a Queer Time and Place* (New York: New York University Press, 2005), 169.

57. *The Young Ladies of . . .* , unpublished script.

58. In recent years, a critical mass of scholarship has developed that explores notions of queer kinship. See, for example, Carolyn Dinshaw, *Getting Medieval: Sexualities and Communities, Pre- and Postmodern* (Durham, NC: Duke University Press, 1999); David L. Eng, *The Feeling of Kinship: Queer Liberalism and the Racialization of Intimacy* (Durham, NC: Duke University Press, 2010); Kath Weston, *Families We Choose: Lesbians, Gays, Kinship* (New York: Columbia University Press, 1997); Elizabeth Freeman, *Time Binds: Queer Temporalities, Queer Histories* (Durham, NC: Duke University Press, 2010); Gayle S. Rubin, *Deviations: A Gayle Rubin Reader* (Durham, NC: Duke University Press, 2011); and Esther Newton, *Margaret Mead Made Me Gay: Personal Essays, Public Ideas* (Durham, NC: Duke University Press, 2000).

TWO

Participation, Endurance, and the Pucker in Taylor Mac's *The Lily's Revenge*

Carrie J. Preston

"THIS! PLAY! IS! LONG!" the character, Time, speaks as a "*dire warn-ing*" in Taylor Mac's *The Lily's Revenge: A Flowergory Manifold* (which pre-miered in 2009 at HERE Arts Center): "No, really. LONG."[1] Enduring the time passing in the theater and the close contact with other spectators and actors, regardless of hunger, fatigue, discomfort, or disease, is a consistent feature of theater through the centuries. Taylor Mac loosely structured his nearly five-hour-long *The Lily's Revenge* on Japanese noh, a musical, drag theater performed in Japan since the fourteenth century; a full noh cycle features five plays interspersed with comedic kyogen interludes.[2] Mac's five-act play introduces the Lily, played by Mac, who ignores Time's warn-ings about the length of the play, emerges from the flowerpot and audi-ence, and demands to be the groom and the star of the play in act 1, "The Deity." The second act, "The Ghost Warrior," rearranges the proscenium theater into theater in the round filled with gorgeously costumed flower-characters, who ask Lily to travel to a factory farm in Ecuador, free the imprisoned Dirt, and lead a revolt against the wedding-industrial com-plex that butchers flowers. The third "Love Act" is a "Dream Ballet" (71) featuring various Brides and Grooms with wedding parties dancing their courtship antics while Lily travels to a factory farm in Ecuador, slowed by Wind's recitations of Susan Stewart's book *On Longing* (1992). A silent film appears for act 4's "The Living Person Acts: Part Four," which forces Lily to undergo various tortures at the factory farm in pursuit of becoming a man and perfect groom (85). Finally, the GARDEN of flowers plots to sabotage the WEDDING PARTY, but "The Mad Demon—Act V: Divine Madness" descends into orgy, reconciliation, and death.

These energetically raucous acts were interspersed with interactive intermission events that Mac called, following the Japanese noh tradition, kyogens, some of which were scripted, while others were devised by the company with the guidance of Mac's "Other Kyogen Ideas" list (116–19). When I saw *The Lily's Revenge* in October 2012 at American Repertory Theater in Cambridge, MA, a grill was tended by florally costumed performers to stave off audience hunger (and perfume the space). During one of the intermissions, I found myself in the open dressing room engaged in an exuberant and sweaty dance under a disco ball with the Tulip (Dereks O. Thomas), who asked about my opinions on marriage between humans and flowers or other vegetation. During another intermission/kyogen, I listened to an actor deliver a very fast theoretical lecture while writing notes on the mirrors in the men's bathroom, where it seemed perfectly appropriate for me to hang out given that I had received a paper mustache with some lines on the back. I recited these lines with the other wedding guests, moved my chair around to accommodate scene changes, slow-danced during the wedding, and, during act 2's haiku competition, presented my head to be licked by a performer.

Audience participation presents both physical and emotional risks to audience and actors alike, particularly when participation is eroticized as it is in *The Lily's Revenge*, and in most theater given that it demands the engagement of our bodies. Those who are ill or immunocompromised, survivors of gendered, sexualized, or racialized trauma, and individuals who are neurodiverse are, and always have been, particularly vulnerable in audiences and other groups. They are also both vulnerable in and marginalized by the various "institutionalized narratives" Mac explores/explodes in *The Lily's Revenge*, where Time threatens spectators who refuse to leave: "These Flower Girls, that lay about the stage in drool, were once AUDIENCE MEMBERS! . . . My eldest child, the malicious Great Longing Deity, God of Nostalgia, has trapped them in this cock-and-bull story with institutionalized narrative. INSTITUTIONALIZED NARRATIVE!" (16). By the end of *The Lily's Revenge*, and it took a long time to get to the end, Mac suggests that the inevitable failure of our endurance, brought about by disease and ultimately death, is one possible foundation for a renovated community. Mac provides room for the audience's nostalgic and seemingly flimsy attachments to traditions of all different kinds, from theatrical traditions to those of the wedding industrial complex. What we want,

Mac generously and generatively suggests, does not always align with our political beliefs. The institution of marriage might be rotten to its core, a wilted bouquet, but we still might desire it passionately. Weddings might be "bad community theater," and community theater might be *bad* theater, but Mac recognizes that we often want to be invited and to *actually participate* in both. Acknowledging our nostalgia and contradictory desires, then inviting our engagement with messy, incoherent, ultimately dying communities, Mac suggests, might transform them in a way that would invite the full participation of all.

I. Nostalgia

Why would we participate in rotten traditions, plays, and weddings, particularly when they have historically excluded us, made us uncomfortable, demeaned us, and even forced us to hide or change ourselves? The question was regularly asked during the campaign for marriage equality that raged during the creation of *The Lily's Revenge*; in 2008, California famously achieved marriage equality only to strike it down later that year with Proposition 8. A number of explanations for our desire to access problematic institutions have been offered, including the classic idea that we are *duped*, or (to put it more theoretically) "interpellated," in ideology and cannot know how oppressive institutions damage us.[3] "Reparative"[4] or at least somewhat more optimistic queer theories point to "disidentification,"[5] "feeling backward,"[6] "temporal drag,"[7] and "racial masochism."[8] *The Lily's Revenge* does not dismiss the damage of dominant ideologies or the potential for disidentificatory, backward, masochistic, or temporal drag from its bouquet of possible explanations. But the reason Mac explores at [great] length in *The Lily's Revenge* is "nostalgia," which Mac defines using the 1992 book *On Longing* by the critical theorist Susan Stewart, who gave Mac permission to use her work and name for a character in the play.[9] Mac's Susan has been forcibly cast as one of a bevy of flower girls all named Mary by the Great Longing, a character appearing in the play as a giant red theatrical curtain.

Near the end of act 1, Susan refuses the name Mary and proclaims, "I won't participate in nostalgic narrative any longer" (44). She then quotes from the real Susan Stewart's *On Longing*:

Fig. 6. The bridesmaids (Jing Xu, Margaret Ann Brady) press the Lily (Taylor Mac) into the Bible, as the Great Longing (Thomas Derrah) approves. Photo: Gretjen Helene; © APrioriPhotography.com.

"NOSTALGIA IS SADNESS WITHOUT AN OBJECT."

(Everything stops. Lights focus on SUSAN. She is allowed her moment
   in the spotlight and speaks to everyone.)

"A sadness which creates a longing that of necessity is inauthentic
because it does not take part in lived experience . . . the past it seeks
has never existed except as narrative." (44)

Lily's *longing* is to be the star of the show and so, following the usual
romantic wedding plot, it determines to become a man and marry the
bride. Lily realizes its own nostalgia in its desire to become the hero of
this established narrative during its long journeys to the factory farm in
Ecuador—made longer by the Wind's recitations of *On Longing*.[10] At the
end of act 4, Lily tells Dirt that it wanted marriage so that people would
love and value it, but now Lily understands that marriage is "[s]o large with
its billion dollar industry and century-old traditions . . . I couldn't possibly
understand it. And it is so small, [. . .] So small in its thinking, so limited,
exclusionary, and sexist[. . . .] And the miniature and the gigantic together
create a felt lack. A felt lack that is essentially . . . nostalgia" (89). *The Lily's
Revenge* honors that "felt lack," even if it is "sadness without an object," following Stewart's definition. The sought-after "past" might be a "narrative"
that "never existed" and is therefore "inauthentic," but it is also a story that
many find incredibly dear. Theater lovers tend to appreciate the narratives
performed on stage, even if they are, like the story of a Lily's journey to
a farm in Ecuador to free Dirt and become a man, seemingly far from
"lived experience"—and of course, the designation of "lived experience"
cannot be easily circumscribed if lives are almost infinitely diverse. This
is all to say that Mac makes room for, even celebrates, the Lily's nostalgia
and ours, suggesting that nostalgia is not merely a bad phase of dupedness
to be *rooted out* (so to speak). Nostalgia may also be full of pleasures to be
honored as part of a radical commitment to pleasure.

Mac's tolerant treatment of nostalgia and his politics of radical inclusion is most clear at the end of act 4 and throughout act 5: act 4's silent (but
in-color) film reveals Lily, in order to become "the perfect specimen" and
win the bride, submitting to horrific tortures at the factory farm, including physical exercise and team sports (even a pummeling on the football
field) with the "personal trainer John Paul," boot camp, waxing of his chest
hair, "perfection surgery," and electric-shock therapy (86–88). After Lily's

Fig. 7. The Bride (Davina Cohen) and the Lily, now the groom (Taylor Mac) with the flowers. Photo: Gretjen Helene; © APrioriPhotography.com.

"treatment," as it is "trapped in technology" of the film screen, Dirt and Lily have a frank conversation that helps Lily escape the cinematic prison (88). Dirt asks Lily: "But what would it be like if you stopped equating love with equality?" and "What would it be like to stop equating love with loving?" (89). At this point, the stage directions indicate that the actor playing the Lily appears in the theater (not on film) wearing a tuxedo without makeup or the Lily costume and answers, "It would be an all-day show" (89–90).

> LILY. (*On stage:*) I'd put on an all day show. With the help of friends. An all day show rehearsed in recreational centers, basements, and backyards. Performed for neighbors, strangers, friends who are family and family who are friends. People will sit in folding chairs, and there will be cardboard cut-out set pieces and mugging actors who sing songs on ukuleles, eat food, dance, drink too much, flirt with audience members, and genuinely think of the day as a special day. Not a perfect day but certainly a special one. One they won't

forget. One that strives to inspire them to make a commitment to each other. A commitment to be there on the days when there is nothing and no one.

DIRT. You're saying, to love others, you want to create community theatre?

LILY. Yes. [Which Mac said with a very cute, quite sheepish grin.] (90)

In this formulation, the long-pursued wedding is replaced by a day-long celebration that, as Dirt points out, sounds a lot like community theater and the ways such formulations of community demand rehearsal, participation, and commitment. The final stage transformation into act 5, the Mad Demon Act, presents a form of community theater, in keeping with its prescript: "'Weddings are bad community theater'—Anonymous" (91).

Act 5 stages an exuberant orgy with the entire cast, after which Master Sunflower claims, "(*Post-coital*) Now the Flowers are free to love who they wish to love" (106). With great joy, the Flowers plan a mass nuptial but pause to realize, "And isn't a group wedding one of the biggest clichés of all?" (106). Lily agrees with great pleasure, the pleasure of having realized the nostalgia within the wedding, embracing it, and beginning to transform it into community theater. Master Sunflower suggests, "But isn't it what you do with the cliché that elevates it?" and Brides and Grooms exclaim, with great relief, "You mean cliché doesn't have to be a reductive commodity?" (106). Everyone proclaims together, "Relativism has won the day," but the Pope screams, "NEVER" (106) and shoots them all with his machine gun (107). Before they die, the performers sing and dance, and everyone asks everyone else to marry them. Lily instructs:

I'll ask the question and then the lights will go dark. And in that moment of darkness, if you want to say yes, pout your lips like this. (*The Lily pouts.*) It is essentially a come hither pucker and it means, yes you'll make a commitment to *thinking* about marrying everyone and everything. And if your answer is no then leave your lips the way they are. And if your answer is no [. . .] that's fine. Because everyone understands having mixed feelings about marriage and commitment and . . . thinking. (110)

I puckered.

In this closing scene, the play acknowledges that its politics can "feel broad and simple," in the words of reviewer Jason Fitzgerald, who claimed, "*The Lily's Revenge* sometimes felt like too much fun, its potentially radical blow offered with a plastic sword."[11] The "plastic sword" is an apt image for any theatrical performance, and Mac would probably say that it is impossible to have too much fun. In fact, *The Lily's Revenge* makes fun of those who would refuse to have fun, whether that is characters like the machine-gun-toting, Twinkie-eating Pope (107), audience members who walked out or refused to return after one of the intermissions (there were always some), or critics who call it all "party shenanigans."[12] The play certainly makes fun of its own rambling plot and its self-conscious incorporation of noh conventions (which those serious critics might call orientalist appropriations) such as Master Sunflower's very slow walk across the stage:[13]

Master Sunflower.

. . . This play has been inspired by the Noh.

(She keeps going very slowly.)

The Noh who like Butoh, well, move so slow.

(She keeps going very slowly.)

Jesus Christ.   (50)

The Lily's Revenge performs and makes fun of noh conventions, weddings, and bad community theater. The play proclaims support for the politics of marriage equality and glories in the frills of wedding costumes, even as it, in seeming contradiction, critiques the institution of marriage in all its patriarchal and heterosexist exclusions. Why do we participate in such institutions, communities, and [bad] theater? For fun, *The Lily's Revenge* suggests. These institutions are riddled with garden-variety flaws, and we nostalgically (mis)remember the fun and imagine that we can do something different with the clichés, something that forces them to open wide enough to allow our . . .

II. Full Participation

Some theatergoers have great *fun* with the audience participation, whether encouraged or compulsory in *The Lily's Revenge*. Other spectators are annoyed and uncomfortable. In an interview, Mac claimed that one group, critics, are predictable in their response:

You know critics are socially awkward people—they just are!—so of course many of them have a problem with the participation because they can barely have a conversation with anyone. Right? So they always bring their bias to the critique of the participation, and then they say, "I didn't like it, but I did it, and it was really transformative and really great," or they dismiss it and say, "I wish there were less of those party shenanigans."[14]

Critics may not be Mac's ideal audience participants (or co-conversationalists), but some of us have been trying to understand Mac's approach to audience participation and how it differs from the experience economy of much immersive or site-specific theater—which deploys some of the same techniques. Several reviews and articles about Mac's approach to audience participation have quoted versions of the monologue at the beginning of Mac's epic 2016 *A 24-Decade History of Popular Music*, in which Mac's pronoun preference and personae, judy, claims to "hate audience participation" because it feels like "people forcing their fun on you"; judy then insists, "it's different when I ask you to do it . . . I *want* you to feel uncomfortable."[15] Of course, judy is a performer and not necessarily delivering Mac's "theory" of audience participation, which has in any case shifted with the aesthetic strategies and goals for each play and even from one production space to another: "while the marathon, twenty-four-hour performance in New York City emphasized community, fatigue, and coming together, the temporally and physically separated performances at the Curran [a proscenium stage] emphasized distance, hierarchy, and the work necessary to overcome disconnection."[16]

Mac's approach to audience participation is not fundamentally about shock, disruption, or discomfort (although it can do all of that); instead, participation serves the particular concerns and activist messages of the play. Participatory moments in *A Lily's Revenge* at A.R.T. encouraged audiences to acknowledge our complicity in and nostalgia for traditional, bigoted institutions such as marriage and to dislodge our carefully cultivated tolerance and complacency, partially through discomfort, uncertainty, and by literally making everyone *move* their own chairs. The production provoked the liberal pieties of many audience members, whose self-congratulatory beliefs might be (but rarely are) articulated as, "I'm so tolerant and good that I supported this A.R.T. drag show." At the same time, *The Lily's Revenge* extends audiences a radically inclusive invitation to the wedding party of our dreams, especially our secret, kinky, messy dreams.

The spirit of invitation is represented by the White Rose, "a host who hangs out with the audience during all the intermissions and pre-show, chatting them up" (112). She serves as a welcoming "guide" and support throughout the five-act performance, which requires the audience, at a minimum, to participate in the stage transformation for each act by moving their seats or finding new ones when the proscenium seating became theater in the round, then a church-like setup with audiences divided into "The Bride's Side" and "The Groom's Side," to a "cave of technology" with the audience surrounded by screens, and finally "back in the proscenium" for act 5 but "flipped" so "the audience sits where the performance was in the first act and the players primarily play where the audience initially sat" (8). The White Rose orchestrates these transformations and the audience's movements in and out of the theater with witty "banter" that, in the examples provided by Mac, takes on the spirit of an indulgent, somewhat acidic hostess, just a little put out by her guests: "Chatty Kathys in the back with the wine come on. Gather round . . . If you do not listen to this you will not be able to relieve your bladder for five whole hours" (112).

The White Rose embodies the strategies Mac learned for engaging, provoking, and shaping audiences in New York's drag-club scene—where Mac might face hecklers or find the audience distracted by a couple having sex: "Mac would descend the stage and waltz over to sing right near them, stealing the thunder back for himself: When he returned to the stage, all eyes were on him again. He called this strategy 'incorporating the calamity.'"[17] The "calamities" at A.R.T. were somewhat less distracting and more about rejection of the participation fun or the rules against cell-phone calls, surfing the web, and texting ("chimping" as the White Rose puts it, mimicking a chimpanzee texting) except during the third intermission: "For we are conducting an experiment: what would it be like if, during two out of three of the intermissions, you stayed engaged with the audience members, creators, and physical intimacy of the play?" (113). Some refused to participate in the experiment or other aspects of the play, and some were confused or angry, while others needed assistance moving their chairs or finding places to sit in the transformed auditorium. The White Rose needed to incorporate or deescalate any and all such calamities.

The White Rose also gave audience members instructions about how to engage with the kyogens or intermission performances. Although the kyogens may vary with each production, the script indicates that there should be an "open dressing room" where the actors do their makeup, chat, and dance with audience members as part of a "Discussion Disco"

(116). There should be a "Context Corner" or minilibrary that provides information and readings about, for example, "the history of myths, marriage, Susan Stewart, The Hero's Journey, Theater of the Ridiculous, Noh, Kyogens, The Act-Up ashes action, Flower farms, the various collaborators' earlier works, etc." (116–17). The most important piece in the "Context Corner" is the "Playwright's Monologue" or "video program note" that movingly describes Mac's experiences attending weddings as a guest and cater waiter, awakening sexuality, and longing for orgies to be more like weddings with "flowers and grandmas dancing and tuxedos and cake and cock all mixed together" (118). Mac also describes having an ambivalent reaction to the first gay wedding Mac attended in 2004; it was so "typical" as an "all day affair" with guests participating and/or observing silently, some of whom love or violently hate the day, although most "are trapped somewhere between" (118). The "Playwright's Monologue" reveals one possible origin for the "pout" Lily invites audience members to put on their lips in the last moments of the play (110). During Mac's first AIDS Walk in San Francisco, Mac wanted to be kissed by the "marching gays" and therefore held a pucker while walking along (117).

While the play ends with the possibility of a collective audience pout in the blackout, the play begins with the Lily in the audience, trying to get to its seat like any late theatergoer. The stage directions indicate: "*(The Lily finds its seat with great disturbance and blocks the person behind with its enormous petals.)*" The first line of the play is an apology to the person seated behind it: "Sorry" (15). The Lily maintains its fictional identity as an audience member while Time warns the audience about the length of the play: "Flee. I beg you. Make your escape now . . ." (16). The characters address audience members throughout the play, which comments on this act of breaking the imaginary fourth wall between the stage and audience when the Flower Girl who awakens into Susan Stewart "tries to stop herself from breaking the fourth wall but her momentum crashes her through it" and right out into the audience (23). Another moment where theatrical conventions are exposed and transformed is when the Great Longing closes its stage curtain on the wedding party in act 5 and is revealed to be "*made entirely of red cocktail napkins with dreams written on them*" (95). The stage direction continues:

The Curtain, which should be larger than the Act I Curtain, should not be partially covered in red cocktail napkins but completely so.

The magic of this moment is in seeing a massive stage curtain made entirely out of cocktail napkins. The audience, during the intermission, should be asked to write down their various dreams on red cocktail napkins. The illusion is that their dreams have been used to build the Act V Curtain. . . . I've seen it done full-out and it takes the audience's breath away and I've seen it done half-way and watched it do nothing for the audience, as it then becomes a gimmick rather than a wonder. I beg of you to choose wonder over gimmick. (95)

The Curtain, now literally composed of the audience's dreams, seems to have won the day and proceeds with the nuptial ceremony. The audience stands in for the guests at the wedding and recites from cue sheets (I got the mustache for the groom's side) distributed by a white-frilled and feathered Baby's Breath, who conducts them into responding to the Great Longing's provocative game of bride reveal (93):

THE GREAT LONGING. Do you want that Bride?
GUESTS. Yes Curtain.
THE GREAT LONGING. Do you really want her?
GUESTS. Don't tease us Curtain. Don't. Oh. Oh. Oh.
THE GREAT LONGING. Where do you want that Bride?
GUESTS. In the center! GET HER IN THE CENTER!
THE GREAT LONGING. Oh I'll get that Bride in the center.
GUESTS. OH CUUUUUUUURTAAAAAAAIN. (97–98)

The audience performs roles, and the performers break personal, bodily boundaries as they move through the audience, listen to their heartbeats (17), even lick and kiss them:

MASTER SUNFLOWER. (*Licking an audience member:*) Yes licks and love.
FLOWERS. Intimacy, the best of Dirt's creations.

(They all lick audience members.) (59)

In the long (seven-page) buildup to the play's final question asking us to pucker if we will "make a commitment to *thinking* about marrying everyone and everything" (110), the Lily introduces the question with kisses for the audience:

Fig. 8. Lily (Taylor Mac) after kissing an audience member in the final scene of the play. Photo: Gretjen Helene; © APrioriPhotography.com.

LILY. Yes. It all comes down to this, and I don't want you to answer now, because there's nothing worse than watching people say yes, under public pressure, when what they really mean is no, but I have a question for you all.

(LILY goes to an audience member.)

Even you.

(The LILY kisses the audience member.)

And you.

(The LILY kisses another audience member.)

And the ushers.

(The LILY kisses an usher.) (104)

Audience members were asked to consent to being kissed, licked, or touched and some seemed visibly annoyed; others may have been traumatized, a risk the play took in 2012 that feels much riskier to me a decade later.

III. Infection

Looking back on the audience participation in *The Lily's Revenge* from the period of Covid-19 produces a "Great Longing" in me (to borrow the name of the play's talking stage curtain). Back in 2012, I was a little nervous about the licking and kissing—primarily because I happened to be pregnant and felt my vulnerability to sickness more prominently at that time. Still, I was a willing participant. In the midst of the Covid pandemic, with theaters shuttered, required masks (not the gorgeous kind for floral costumes), and six-foot "social distancing" signs functioning like spike marks, my nostalgia is high for the carefree times of open theaters and other public gatherings—even weddings. Now it is hard to imagine plays that allow us to crowd into a sweaty disco party in an open dressing room and receive kisses and licks from performers. Such gestures, particularly when permission to lick or kiss was not requested, seem to stem from a time of innocence or naiveté, when fears of contagion and recognition of the scourge of sexual trauma were pressing less on our social interactions. In retrospect, we should have paid more attention. Many in our community have always needed to attend to the health risks that Covid-19 has brought to wider attention, and theaters may have never felt accessible to more-vulnerable groups. In participatory productions, theatergoers have less control over risks to immune systems compromised by age or health conditions. Audience participation is also more frightening to those with a history of trauma because they might fear that a theatrical experience could cause them pain or fear.

Covid-19 has encouraged able-bodied folks who generally enjoy good health to be more attentive to the accommodations needed by vulnerable members of their communities. The theater industry is also having important discussions about safety and consent, both for performers and audiences in participatory or immersive theater.[18] Safety is a complex negotiation for artists like Mac who must balance certain risks against their goal of using art for activism and offering aesthetic experiences that might make some in the audience uncomfortable. Just a year before the pandemic hit, Mac claimed, "Everyone expects to be safe in the theater—

maybe challenged a bit with an idea or two—but I say, well, maybe you're *not* going to be safe."[19] Ableism, white supremacy, and patriarchy have largely determined *who* has gotten to feel safe in the theater and other public places, as Mac recognizes. To navigate and undermine this disparity, theaters might redefine safety and adopt structures like those used by bondage, dominance, sadism, and masochism (BDSM) communities for communicating consent and desires for participation, including advance negotiation, safe words, and aftercare.[20]

Public health responses to the Covid-19 pandemic have severely curtailed BDSM practices as they have privileged forms of the (typically heteronormative) nuclear family. Shelter-in-place orders focus on and essentially define families as those sharing the same household, with little recognition of more complex or disbursed affiliations. *The Lily's Revenge* provides prescient guidance on how to face the normative influence of public health restrictions as it engages that other virus and ongoing pandemic, HIV/AIDS, which is incurable but manageable for those with access to quality medical care and antiretroviral drugs. Mac's pouting, puckering journey toward writing *The Lily's Revenge* occurred at Mac's first AIDS walk, where "a Sister of Perpetual Indulgence" passed on "an incurable disease called glitter" (117). The influence of HIV/AIDS on the play is evident in the first act when the Great Longing accuses the Lily of being "diseased" (26). A character named "the Incurable Disease" is introduced in act 5 as part of the flower army or "daisy chain of command" set to tear down the wedding (91).

The Incurable Disease is the character who lasciviously chases the Great Longing off the stage when it is defeated at last (106), and then leads it back onstage with a leash—in a nod to BDSM practices—allowing the Great Longing to deliver one last haiku (109).

While the Incurable Disease is not explicitly a personification of HIV/AIDS, the character is associated with sexually transmitted diseases. In one of the battle vignettes, "[t]he curtain closes and opens to GROOM LOVE getting a blow job," although his back faces the audience, which cannot see who is giving oral sex. GROOM LOVE orgasms, turns around, and looks down to see that "*his crotch is a giant pus infected sore*," after which, "*He runs off and the INCURABLE DISEASE wipes its mouth and chases after him*" (100–101). This moment is certainly a "shenanigan" played for shock and laughter, but just moments later, it sets up one of the play's more trenchant statements about inclusion. The Lily stops the war between flowers and wedding party by kissing the two brides, grooms, Time and Susan (they have fallen in love), and even Incurable Disease:

Fig. 9. The Cast after being shot by the Pope; Incurable Disease leads the Great Longing by a leash. Photo by Gretjen Helene; © APrioriPhotography.com.

INCURABLE DISEASE. What about me?

LILY. Yes. You too Incurable Disease. Because, if you live long enough you play all the parts.

TIME. And forgiveness is a way to love.

(The LILY tongues The INCURABLE DISEASE.) (104)

Lily is right. An incurable disease "plays" each of us if we live long enough. While gender, sexuality, race, ethnicity, class, species, and all the other identity categories are about difference and often divide us, the fact that we all face the onset of incurable disease is one of our few commonalities. Every living creature has the potential to become sick or disabled, and each will ultimately die.[21] Disease, disability, and death could be one basis for community, so Lily kisses, actually "tongues," the Incurable Disease before turning to kiss audience members, ushers, and techies (104).

If the new Incurable Disease of the novel coronavirus would keep lips and tongues in quarantine and certainly prevent the whole-cast orgy that Lily's kisses provoke at the end of the play (106), *The Lily's Revenge* anticipates the community that might be built around shared vulnerabilities to disease. The play also foresees how the forces of bigotry, represented by the machine-gun-wielding Pope, can use public health crises as an excuse to destroy communities and distribute racist, homophobic propaganda.[22] Mac's "Playwright's Monologue" reveals that AIDS awareness arrived for Mac "in the form of The Pope preaching abstinence to fight AIDS" (117). Mac's first orgy experience was on Halloween night, where Mac dressed as a "zombie cater waiter," with tuxedo around ankles. Mac recognized the power of claiming liberation while costumed as icons of repression: "Three people costumed as Princess Diana [the bride of the first (televised) wedding Mac attended], Ronald Reagan [whose homophobic administration disregarded HIV/AIDs], and Pope John Paul II [preacher of abstinence] are seen having a three-way. It seems to me the most perfect of days" (118).

Mac set out to make *The Lily's Revenge* one of those most perfect of days, where the Lily gets revenge for being thrown on the White House Lawn after the death of Ronald Reagan, and the all-day wedding actually becomes community theater. But this is a unique version of perfection in which the guest list for the party includes an Incurable Disease. Audiences are invited to the party too, even compelled to participate, without being forced to find that enduring the five-act production is their perfect day. Lily recognizes near the end, "Their butts are sore and they wanna go home" (105), and the Marys claim, "I love that some of you have to pee and some of you are crying at the manipulative nature of a key change modulation" (110). Whether crying or peeing or anxious to get out of the theater, we are all inevitably failing the endurance test and finally dying—so Mac seeks to infuse more pleasure, forgiveness, and fun throughout. Lily asks the audience to deliver the last gesture of the play, either by puckering and agreeing to think about loving and marrying everything, or by leaving our lips the way they are; and "that's fine. Because everyone understands having mixed feelings about marriage and commitment and . . . thinking. And you may not want to marry a man and a flower and an Incurable Disease" (110). Mac hopes we pucker for the imagined kiss, but the stage lights go dark, and we don't have to confess either way.

Notes

1. All play quotes are from Taylor Mac, *The Lily's Revenge: A Flowergory Manifold* (New York: Playscripts, Inc., 2013), 15.

2. Noh and kyogen are considered the oldest continuously performed theatrical

forms in the world. Of course, performance is never static; contemporary noh events do not typically include the full five-play cycle, and kyogen plays have been and continue to be performed in other venues outside of the noh context. For more on the international influence of noh performance, see my book *Learning to Kneel: Noh, Modernism, and Journeys in Teaching* (New York: Columbia University Press, 2016).

3. Louis Althusser, "Ideology and Ideological State Apparatus (Notes Towards an Investigation)" [1970], in *Lenin and Other Essays*, trans. Ben Brewster (New York: Monthly Review Press, 2001): 121–76. Forgive me for my note-dropping in this paragraph, but most readers will not need a summary of these theories to understand Taylor Mac's approach.

4. Eve Sedgwick, "Paranoid and Reparative Reading, Or You're So Paranoid You Probably Think this Essay Is About You," in *Touching Feeling: Affect, Pedagogy, Performativity* (Durham: Duke University Press, 2003): 123–52.

5. José Esteban Muñoz, *Disidentifications: Queers of Color and the Performance of Politics* (Minneapolis: University of Minnesota Press, 1999).

6. Heather Love, *Feeling Backward: Loss and the Politics of Queer History* (Cambridge: Harvard University Press, 2009).

7. Elizabeth Freeman, *Time Binds: Queer Temporalities, Queer Histories* (Durham: Duke University Press, 2010).

8. Takeo Rivera, "Do Asians Dream of Electric Shrieks? Techno-Orientalism and Erotohistoriographic Masochism in Eidos Montreal's *Deus Ex: Human Revolution*," *Amerasia Journal* 40, no. 2 (2014): 67–86.

9. Susan Stewart, *On Longing: Narratives of the Miniature, the Gigantic, the Souvenir, the Collection* (Durham: Duke University Press, 1992).

10. Although Lily longs to become a man, I use the pronoun "it" in keeping with Mac's stage directions, "*(The LILY finds its seat with great disturbance and blocks the person behind it with its enormous petals.)*" (15).

11. Fitzgerald continues, "Mac's desire to be liked bleeds into his politics, which, in their embrace-the-moment, love-for-all rhetoric, can feel broad and simple." See Jason Fitzgerald's review of *The Lily's Revenge*, in *Theatre Journal* 62, no. 3 (2010): 457–59.

12. "The Art in the Room: P Carl Talks with Taylor Mac," *Howlround* (24 September 2017): https://howlround.com/art-room

13. I explore how the critique of "orientalism" can be incisive as well as a sledge-hammer and describe the *suriashi* sliding step of noh in *Learning to Kneel* (New York: Columbia University Press, 2016).

14. "Art in the Room," https://howlround.com/art-room

15. David Bisaha, "'I Want You to Feel Uncomfortable': Adapting Participation in *A 24-Decade History of Popular Music* at San Francisco's Curran Theatre," *Theatre History Studies* 38 (2019): 133–48; 141. See also Ethan Philbick, "Ten Things I Learned About History from Taylor Mac," in *The Helix Queer Performance Network* (2015): https://www.helixqpn.org/post/110066363227/ten-things-i-learned-about-history-from-taylor-mac

16. Bisaha, "Uncomfortable," 137.

17. As discussed in the introduction to this volume, Mac's preferred pronouns are complex, with "judy" as a performance pronoun and they/them as perhaps the best for signaling Mac's fluidity; I prefer using proper names as much as possible. The "he/him" pronouns in this quote are used by Sasha Weiss in "Taylor Mac Wants Theater to Make

You Uncomfortable," *Times Magazine* (2 April 2019): https://www.nytimes.com/2019/04/02/magazine/taylor-mac-gary-broadway.html

18. Blair Cadden, "Unblurred Lines: The Role of Consent in Emmersive Theatre" (8 July 2020): https://howlround.com/unblurred-lines

19. Weiss, "Taylor Mac."

20. Cadden, "Unblurred Lines."

21. See Robert McRuer's related claim that we are all "virtually disabled" because we will experience disability if we live long enough; in *Crip Theory: Cultural Signs of Queerness and Disability* (New York: New York University Press, 2006).

22. US President Donald Trump, for example, refers to Covid-19 as the "kung flu." Alana Wise, "White House Defends Trump's Use of Racist Term to Describe Coronavirus," *NPR* (22 June 2020): https://www.npr.org/2020/06/22/881810671/white-house-defends-trumps-use-of-racist-term-to-describe-coronavirus

THREE

Between *Hir* and There
Considering Taylor Mac's Work as Bridging Genres

Kelly I. Aliano

Taylor Mac's[1] play *Hir* is one of the most significant pieces of American drama of the past decade, spouting numerous productions across the US since its world premiere in 2014 at the Magic Theatre in San Francisco. This is due in large part to two seemingly contradictory factors: the play is a deeply relatable and accessible portrait of American family life, while also being an experiment in dramaturgy, blending elements of Naturalism, Absurdism, and Theatre of the Ridiculous into an incisive commentary on gender roles and what it means be a member of a family. Mac has created a play that is a composite of dramaturgical forms, so it can operate on multiple dramatic levels, mirroring the complexities of how self-formation occurs. A person is never solely one thing or another; everyone exists in some sort of in-between space, at least when it comes to identity. So, too, is the structure of this play never singular. *Hir* is neither attempting just to depict life as it is, scientifically and objectively, nor is it simply wallowing in the despair of our existential crisis. Rather, as the play does those things, it also offers us a mode of subversion through its use of Ridiculous elements. This blended dramatic structure allows Mac to comment on the values of the contemporary American middle-class family.

Mac's play explores how gender and familial roles intersect with (or diverge from) finding one's own sense of self. The play is about the act of self-creation in a social structure that wants to dictate position, and thereby function, which is a challenge to navigate even for the most confident individual. Each of the characters struggles with becoming who

Fig. 10. (from L. to R.): Cameron Scoggins as Isaac, Daniel Oreskes as Arnold, Tom Phelan as Max, and Kristine Neilsen as Paige in *Hir*. Photo: Joan Marcus.

they need to be in light of who, based on their assigned role, they perhaps "should" be. Because of this personal slippage of identity for each of the four main characters, Mac allows the play to be crafted with a great deal of slippage between dramatic modes. Mac calls the style of *Hir* "Absurd realism," which judy defines as "simply realistic characters in a realistic circumstance that is so extreme it is absurd."[2]

On stage, it appears like a traditional family drama, set in a realistic American living room. In this way, it hearkens back to the traditions of Naturalist drama and its emphasis on environment as a factor in behavior. This was particularly true in the 2015 Playwrights Horizons production, directed by Niegel Smith with scenic design by David Zinn and costume design by Gabriel Berry.[3] All visual details signaled that this was going to be an exercise in realism. And yet, once the dialogue began, it was clear that something else was also happening here: while the Connor family speaks to one other in recognizable language, there is a way in which their style of speech is reminiscent of the kind of non sequiturs that populate Absurdist drama. Many things get spoken aloud, but it is hard to pinpoint exactly what these individuals are really *saying* to one another: communication between them feels strained. And even this element does not encapsulate all of what the play is offering; there are many moments of great humor, as in a Ridiculous comedy. Using the Ridiculous reminds us that perhaps this is meant to be a mockery of the forms and/or subjects at work here, as nothing is meant to be too sacred in a play of that genre. By blending aesthetic modes in creating *Hir*, Mac reminds the audience to look beyond the surface to understand who these people are and how they behave. This play exposes individuals in the process of becoming their truest selves, and Mac presents that narrative in a genre-fluid way in order to throw into relief the fluidity of identity.

Hir*Story: An Overview*

To accomplish this, *Hir* traps its audience in a single living-room space in order to observe this self-formation in process. We witness one afternoon in this family's life; there are no scene changes and no outside interactions. Each one of the Connors is trying to self-define both relationally—in terms of their unwritten social contract as members of the same family—and as individuals in control of their own destinies. Paige, the matriarch, has abandoned all of her housewifely or motherly duties and now indulges in museums, travel, and culture as ways to pass the time and to avoid caring for her now-incapacitated husband, Arnold. Arnold, once a powerful and cruel husband and father, has lost both his job and his mind, having suffered a crippling stroke. While he once served not only as breadwinner but as abuser of this family, he is now little more than a vegetable, dressed in clownish garb and makeup as a source of amusement for Paige. Isaac, a dishonorably discharged Marine, returns to this home of disarray, which is a shock for a young man desperate for a sense of normalcy and deeper meaning for his life as a member of his childhood clan. Finally, and perhaps most importantly for Mac's project, there is Max (pronouns are ze/hir), once known as Maxine, a trans male youth who is quite obviously embracing the process of self-discovery.

Max's identity is key to understanding what is at stake, both for this family and for the theme of the play more broadly. Of Max, Paige states, "Max is the root of who we are. Truly. The root of who we are and the cusp of the new. There has never been any such thing as men and women, and, Isaac, there never will be."[4] This new vision of human identity is the undercurrent throughout this play; rather than allowing their family roles to define them, Paige is pushing her children to self-identify, to become who they could be instead of being limited by who they are or where they were born.

Mac takes a similar approach to dramaturgy. Rather than forcing the play to fit one form or another, judy allows the content itself to dictate form, freeing the play to be what it is, without trying too hard to fit a particular theatrical or dramaturgical model. In prefacing the published text of *Hir*, Mac reminds us that "If at any moment it feels like your production is venturing into theatre of the absurd, theatre of the ridiculous, a Brechtian remove, or a metatheatrical deconstruction, then rein it in. Likewise, if it feels like realism is steering every choice, try to find the absurdity in that realism and turn the volume up" (ix). Productions of this play need to be a blend of forms; they are not meant to be too much (or more) of one genre than any other.

The dramatic lineage for *Hir* seems to takes us from the realm of turn-of-the-century dramatic realism to post-WWII Absurdism and on to mid- to late-twentieth-century Ridiculous Theatre. This trajectory mirrors the actual development of modern drama; in 1966, Ronald Tavel declared that "We have passed beyond the absurd: our position is absolutely preposterous."[5] This brought to life a new movement, the Theatre of the Ridiculous, in order to move past the Theatre of the Absurd. Absurdism had offered a different kind of "real" than Naturalism before it; rather than emphasizing the scientifically observable objective world, it embraced the metaphysical qualities of our human condition as the basis of human experience and identity. At the turn of the twentieth century, Naturalism had been experimental in its own right, breaking with the over-the-top and unrealistic emotional narratives of the spectacle-driven form of melodrama. By borrowing from each of these forms in stride, Mac is able to craft a play that accomplishes what these earlier genres did while also being fresh, innovative, and relevant to our contemporary world. For this drama to work, it must mirror Max's process of gender exploration: it must allow itself to operate in a transitional in-between space and to swap between identities, when necessary. Max's mother, Paige, claims, "Everyone is a little bit of everything" (22); whether or not this is true for all human beings, it is certainly true for this play.

Therefore, to make sense of the rich tapestry of this play, I begin by exploring the genre of "Absurd realism" that Mac has created for telling this story. I then lay out key elements of its three source genres: (1) Naturalism, (2) Absurdism, and (3) Theatre of the Ridiculous, to explicate how it is built. Finally, I analyze the significance of *Hir* and offer broader reflections on Mac's contribution to dramatic literature and the contemporary moment.

Telling HirStory: *The Queer Genre of "Absurd realism"*

The fluidity of genre that Mac employs in crafting this play emphasizes the play's interest in exposing the fluidity of gender: its form mirrors its content. In this way, it updates all of its ancestors of genre into the modern world, a world that is advancing rapidly and leaving old constructs of gender identity and presentation in the past. Max's assertion of self is not necessarily radical or progressive; for this family, it is totally normalized. As Max declares, "The world is going forward. There's no time to be worried about gender. Gender isn't radical. It's not even progressive. It's an everyday occurrence" (50). There is nothing strange about Max's identity; it is simply part of the world in which we all live. It is not revolutionary or subversive, as gender is no longer an either/or binary. It is something much more complex, and everyone else can either catch up to where Max is or be left to the past.

Mac mirrors this is in the collaged dramaturgical style judy uses for creating this play; there is no "either/or binary" for playwriting at work here, either. I argue that this is a queer approach to dramaturgy and that judy's work should be viewed as the inheritor of the rich collection of queer dramatic forms that preceded it, especially Theatre of the Ridiculous. In his book *Charles Ludlam Lives!*, Sean Edgecomb creates a lineage of artists who bring the "queer legacy" of Ludlam's Ridiculous work into our modern world. This "queer legacy of the Ridiculous theater tradition is delinked from more traditional forms of genealogical trace by its nature, hovering between a self-motivated exclusivity and socially imposed abjection," according to Edgecomb. Its remove from the mainstream was intentional, as "At its origin the Ridiculous manifested a safe space that allowed for freedom of expression without the fear of homophobic discrimination, but as a theatrical form, it also broke down the walls of concealment through the act of public performance."[6] In creating a safe space for queer artists to work, the Ridiculous also fashioned a theoretical creative "space" for queer work: a mode of playmaking and dramaturgy all their own. Clearly, with *Hir*, Mac is creating judy's own rules for how a play should be crafted, dramaturgically speaking.

To bring the Ridiculous into the twenty-first century, then, I argue alongside Edgecomb that the work must encapsulate the spirit of Ludlam's plays while also innovating that form for our contemporary era. Edgecomb asserts that works by Mac and others "all channel Ludlam's ghost, though I'd like to think their success is propagated by the ability to tame that specter by entertaining him through new, innovative works."[7] Indeed, as we see with Mac's *Hir*, judy is not simply following the guidelines for how Ludlam crafted a play in the last century. Rather, judy is blending other modes of dramaturgy with the Ridiculous to create something new and freshly relevant. It is this that has led to the success of many of Mac's works. Mac adapts the tradition of the Ridiculous to suit judy's own artistic purposes. For Edgecomb, this is key to what makes judy an inheritor of the Ridiculous, as such artists must be innovators in their own right. Edgecomb explains, "Because Ludlam's unspoken mission was to constantly evolve, his heirs must continue to develop work that honors the Ludlamesque tradition while also 'exploiting' his work."[8] Playwrights like Mac, and Charles Busch, another of Edgecomb's case studies in *Charles Ludlam Lives!*, have found ways to appropriate from the Ridiculous mode but move it from queer, downtown spaces into mainstream commercial theater.

Both Mac and Busch have succeeded at something that neither Ludlam nor his contemporaries were able to accomplish during their lifetimes: they have had plays break into the mainstream American commercial theater, by creating plays that include characters, themes, and plotlines that are both recognizable and accessible, even for those uninitiated in experimental or avant-garde theatrical modes. Consider Busch's *The Tale of the Allergist's Wife*, which is his perhaps least Ridiculous play. For John Simon, writing in *New York*, this lack of Ridiculousness was the play's best quality: "Who would have expected from a campy downtown playwright a nicely structured, intelligently funny, satirically relevant uptown comedy?"[9]

In many ways, I would argue that the label of "Absurd realism" would work as well for Busch's play as it does for *Hir*. It, too, has dialogue that often feels Absurdist in its usage of non sequiturs, but it ultimately offers a fairly realistic portrait of middle-aged married life in New York. It even has its fun with the experimental artistic scene; one of the characters implies that *she* inspired Warhol's most iconic Pop Art work. Lee states, "He [Warhol] used to come over and we'd share a can of soup. He got such a kick out of the way I used to pile the empty Campbell soup cans on top of each other. I guess you could say, I planted a little seed."[10] Busch's play was a commercial and critical Broadway success, suggesting that he had found a way to make the Ridiculous accessible to mainstream, commercial audiences. Why do *The Tale of the Allergist's Wife* and *Hir* feel relatable to mainstream audiences? Because, at their core, they are presenting realistic subject matter in a recognizable and accessible way.

Thus, both Mac's and Busch's innovations to the Ridiculous form bring in elements of realism in meaningful ways, but do so to better connect with their audiences. In this way, they still feel deeply in line with Ludlam's thinking about creating plays, because they embrace the reality that plays are written for the audience. Ludlam reminds us, "The theatre is a humble materialist enterprise which seeks to produce the riches of the imagination, not the other way around."[11] Theater is commercial—it is a product to be consumed—but that does not preclude it from being aesthetically interesting and certainly not from having a profound effect on its audiences. To ensure this meaningful affect for audiences, Mac crafts judy's contemporary Ridiculous work as a piece of "Absurd realism," meaning that both the Naturalistic and the Absurdist modes are essential for unpacking how judy is updating the Ridiculous. Valuing the presence of these dramaturgical modes is also necessary to make sense of what is at stake in *Hir* and how this play is meant to operate in performance.

Creating Hir*Story: Naturalism as a Source*

Taylor Mac's *Hir* owes aspects of its dramaturgy to a number of key dramatic genres of the twentieth century. In doing so, judy challenges many of our preconceived notions about what innovative dramaturgy should be—or even can be. This is because, at least for me, when thinking of innovative twenty-first-century dramaturgy, realism is not usually the form that first comes to mind. And yet, Mac is tapping into something prescient not only about American drama—whose greatest works often feature or center around a domestic space—but also about experimental drama. In "The Great American Living-Room Gets a Remodel," Isaac Butler argues, alongside Eric Bentley, that realism's greatest successes come from the degree to which it is, in fact, nonrealistic. Of *Hir*, Butler writes:

> Max's vexation could double for the play's own frustration at its inability to collapse the dramatic form of the living-room play. This in turn suggests a reason for the realist living-room play's stubborn

durability. It isn't just that theatres are conservative or that sub-scribers love them. It's that from the start naturalism has produced plays that rebelled against its strictures. Anti-realism has, it turns out, always been with us—today's playwrights are continuing a tra-dition, not overturning one.[12]

The blending of dramaturgical forms that Mac accomplishes, then, is part of a rich legacy of remixing realistic elements with characteristics and material usually more suited for antirealist and avant-garde forms. In this way, Mac's work is a continuation of artistic experimentation, recognizing that Naturalism may have always been avant-garde in some way. Natural-ism operates as a meaningful dramatic core for storytelling, but theme and purpose are best exposed when subtly deconstructed through the other dramaturgical elements with which it is paired.

It is not difficult to recognize at first glance what makes *Hir* feel like a play in the tradition of Naturalism. The plot is straightforward family-drama fare: a young man, Isaac, comes home to be with his dysfunctional family after facing the traumas of war, only to find that his childhood home may be as much a war zone as any he has just left. This realistic plot is reinforced in the play's production elements. For one, Mac insists on the casting of a transgender actor for the trans role of Max, ensuring that per-sonal reality for the character. In addition, the house set in which the play takes place signals a theatrical setting in which, as Émile Zola argued of Naturalism, "The environment should determine the character."[13] This liv-ing room clearly defines the interactions between these individuals; they seem crammed in among their many cluttering possessions and need to navigate this space to interact with one another.

Indeed, Zola's whole principle of Naturalism emphasized where people were, how they dressed and spoke, and what they owned as giving us a portrait of who they were and how they would behave. Zola writes of the modern playwriting of his day as needing "accurate scenery" so that it "immediately establishes a situation, tells us what world we are in, reveals the characters' habits."[14] We understand who these people are from where and how they live. The description for the Connor family home has this quality of revelation: it gives us a sense of their identity and relationship through its use of visual detail. As Mac describes it, "It is the kind of home that, no matter how hard you clean, will always seem dirty. Dishes are piled up in the sink; the cracking wallpaper bears decade-old stains; piles of laundry are strewn about to the point where it's difficult to walk; and

Fig. 11. (from L. to R.): Kristine Nielsen as Paige, Cameron Scoggins as Isaac, Daniel Oreskes as Arnold in *Hir*. Photo: Joan Marcus.

there seems to be a layer of dust on everything. It is an absolute disaster" (4). Just by seeing this scenic arrangement, we can make certain educated guesses about how this family lives and how they feel about that lifestyle. This general disarray gives us a sense of a family who has given up: they live in the illusion of the American dream, but do nothing to improve on or even maintain it.

The kind of "realism" that Mac is employing for his "Absurd realism," then, shares similarities with turn-of-the-century realistic plays. I use Henrik Ibsen's *A Doll's House* (1879) here as an example, because the opening stage directions of that play resonate with the kind of specificity of stage properties that we see in the scenic design for *Hir*, crafted by David Zinn for the 2015 Playwrights Horizons production. To open *A Doll's House*, Ibsen describes the setting:

Between the doors stands a piano. In the middle of the left-hand wall is a door, and beyond it a window. Near the window are a round table, arm-chairs and a small sofa. In the right-hand wall, at the farther end, another door; and on the same side, nearer the footlights, a stove, two easy chairs and a rocking-chair; between the stove and the door, a small table. Engravings on the walls; a cabinet with china and other small objects; a small book-case with well-bound books.[15]

We can already assume that the family who lives in the home described here cares about appearances, as they own many objects, such as china and "well-bound books," that feel as if they serve no function except for show. This sort of specificity of items also signals to the reader or viewer that every object on stage matters. The dirty laundry on stage in *Hir* also functions in this dual way. From a literal standpoint, it signifies that Paige no longer does laundry, so dirty clothes litter the stage; in addition, said clutter is clearly symbolic of the anarchy that marks this family's relationship to one another and to the space in which they live. In a realistic work, such attention to detail is necessary for the stage world to seem real.

In both Ibsen's play and Mac's, we have titles that fixate on location. Nora is entrapped in her "doll's house" living room, while the Connors have to make sense of what it means to be "hir." This title, which is also Max's chosen pronoun, should be pronounced "here," confirming that physical setting and location must matter to the play's action and meaning. We need to scrutinize where these individuals are to understand fully who they are in both of these works. For Mac, as for Ibsen, this consideration of location and identity might be structured with a difference: it is *where* the Connor family members are that is preventing them from fully becoming *who* they are. Like Nora's life in her doll's house, being here is being entrapped. This explains Paige's desperation for Max, like Nora before hir, to leave: ze will only be able to become hir fullest self beyond these four walls.

The realistic setting offers audiences a particular expectation, in terms of dramatic style, and for much of the play, Mac does not disappoint. Generally, the dialogue throughout this play is realistic: people talk to one another in much the same linguistic manner they would in day-to-day life. Indeed, for Zola, this was key for Naturalist drama. Zola writes, "We are moving toward simplicity, toward the exact word, spoken without bombast, quite naturally."[16] Generally, throughout *Hir*, this is how the Connors speak as well. While they often express themselves in non sequiturs, as is the case in Absurd dramas as well, there is a sense that this throws into relief the larger lack of communication that often exists in families:

we spend a lot of time speaking with one another, but in many families, we might actually rarely say anything of great consequence. Zola believed that the modern theater must realistically reflect the world in which it has been set: "The time has come to produce plays of reality," and "what is needed now is a broad and simple portrayal of men and affairs."[17] At its core, *Hir* offers a significant, resonant commentary on family life and the roles it offers its component members—mother, father, child, sibling— simply by being born into such a structure.

This play asks incisive questions, particularly about the relationship between fathers and children, as both Isaac and Max are forced to come to terms with how they feel about Arnold, because he is now the one in need of care and they are the potential caregivers. This resonates strongly as a realistic dramatic construct—think Arthur Miller's *Death of a Salesman* or Eugene O'Neill's *Long Day's Journey into Night*—as well with Samuel Beckett's Absurdist play *Endgame*. At the end of *Hir*, Max cares for Arnold, in spite of Paige's protestations, perhaps as a reminder that we go on simply because we must go on. It is the only way to exist. As Isaac relates, "Life is not the finishing of events. It is a continuation. Each day you do what needs to be done with the understanding that there is no end to the doing" (57). This throws into relief a sense of existential repetition.

Therefore, theories of realism in drama are useful for making sense of the play that Mac has crafted, but they can only take us so far. Mac's is a qualified realism, one that is also deeply influenced by the Theatre of the Absurd, a form that is "realistic" in a whole other manner: by boiling down the human experience to the essence of our human condition and the despair of our existential crisis, characters are often abandoned in settings with little to nothing to signal who they are or what they should do. In this way, Mac is manifesting a complex mode of dramaturgy, one that is both grounded in the real quotidian world and allows us to explore the depths of our metaphorical human experience.

Creating HirStory: *Absurdism as a Source*

While on the surface *Hir* appears to be a realistic snapshot of American family life (and indeed, much of what Mac presents in this play is very relatable and relevant), something much more complicated occurs in the dramaturgy of the play's dialogue. While characters speak to one another consistently during the play's two acts, they communicate very little to one another. By play's end, there is not a sense of a shared depth of under-standing one might encounter at the conclusion of a traditional realistic play. While the Connors all share the same living space, they each seem to be embedded in their own realm of loneliness and isolation.

In this way, while the play appears on the surface to be a Naturalistic work, the thread of Absurdism, signaled in Mac's genre description, is key to making meaning in this play. Consider Martin Esslin's "essential hall-marks" of the Theatre of the Absurd:

> the abandonment of the concepts of character and motivation; the concentration on states of mind and basic human situations, rather than on the development of a narrative plot from exposition to so-lution; the devaluation of language as a means of communication and understanding; the rejection of didactic purpose; and the con-frontation of the spectator with the harsh facts of a cruel world and his own isolation.[18]

In many ways, these qualities are present for each of the characters in *Hir*, and most definitely for Isaac and his father, Arnold. Isaac is on the preci-pice of an existential crisis; he has lost a clear sense of who he is or what he wants out of life after his wartime experiences. Arnold, too, is facing the "harsh facts of a cruel world and his own isolation," as his own mistreat-ment of his wife in earlier years has led her to reciprocally mistreat him now that he is incapacitated.

The relationship between Paige and Arnold feels especially grounded in the realm of existential cruelty. In Absurdist dramas, especially those by Beckett, there are often pairings of characters who both need one another to feel a sense of meaning or purpose in life but also recognize that their "other" may be their greatest source of torment. So, too, has Paige needed Arnold in order to define who she is—a wife, a mother, a victim—only to realize now, later in life, that she could have had agency over her identity if only she had left him years before. This throws into relief the degree to which this play, at its core, offers us commentary on the gender roles prescribed by American family life. Absurdist plays have always been linked to political imperatives, as they were reactions to the postwar era; Mac updates this dramaturgical mode to resonate with issues present in our contemporary world, especially those related to gender roles and social norms.

This commentary on the nuclear family feels most pronounced in the relationship between Paige and Arnold, a pairing marked by abuse and loathing. The representation of their married life resonates with Winnie and Willie in Beckett's play *Happy Days* (1961), as gender roles are necessary to understanding the self in that play as well. Winnie is trying to maintain some essence of her femininity, despite being "Imbedded up to above her waist in exact centre [*sic*] of mound," opening the play with an extended ritual of beautifying.[19] As she no longer has a full body on which to display her female self, she must emphasize the femininity of the parts of her still exposed, particularly her face. Winnie makes a point of putting on lipstick, an action that may seem entirely unnecessary under her current circumstances, yet that is essential to her selfhood. However, in Mac's play, it is not Paige but Arnold, the male-identified spouse, who is wearing makeup, which is progressively removed from his face over the course of the play. In *Hir*, makeup has a gender-signifying function similar to that in *Happy Days*, but it is used in the opposite manner: rather than empowering a woman through expressing her femininity, it is used with Arnold in order to emasculate him. As the "father," one might guess that he has all of the power, especially since their household setting seems to mirror a twentieth-century television-sitcom living room where dads were usually the dominant force in the family. But in this household, it is Paige who is in control. When Isaac questions why his father, a cisgender male, has put on makeup, Paige admits it was her doing: "It's what we do now. We play dress up" (11). Arnold is being forced to experience a performativity of identity; he no longer has agency over how he expresses or presents himself.

This anarchy of identity mirrors the chaos of the setting, reflecting the Absurdist tendency to strand characters in their circumstances with little sense of motivation or clear objective. In *Waiting for Godot*, Didi and Gogo must wait for Godot because . . . they must. "And if he doesn't come?" Estragon asks. "We'll come back tomorrow," Vladimir responds.[20] Beckett's protagonists are existentially trapped in their situation, much like Nora and Torvald were physically trapped in their dollhouse setting. By blending this Absurdist trope with the environmental realities of setting in Naturalism, Mac throws into relief the myriad ways in which humans imprison themselves, both literally and figuratively. Paige consistently mentions how her children can and should leave this household; she recognizes this home as the prison that it is, and desperately wants her children to become more than this setting will ever allow. Rather than being victims of existential despair, she wants her kids to assert control over their own fates.

Their positionality as children within a family, then, creates a great push and pull, in terms of self-identification and social role, for Isaac and then Max. Because of this, they each seem to face that quintessential Beckettian crisis of "I can't go on/I'll go on," in the midst of all this chaos. Each child feels moved to help Arnold—to do more or better than their mother has, in terms of compassion—but each is also enticed by the freedom and self-determination offered by the outside world. In the final moments of the play, Max's acts of caretaking hearken back to Beckett's *Endgame*, as ze takes on a Clov-like role, tending to Arnold as Clov cares for Hamm. "I love order. It's my dream," says Clov, as he tries to make sense of his life of entrapment with Hamm.[21] For both Clov and Max after him, there is a sense that the imposition of structure will somehow solve all problems. Yet Paige recognizes that this is not so; she says, "You lose things. Important things. And you can't get them back. And some of the things you say are lost, are actually gone" (88), a reminder that they cannot just go back to the "happy" way things were at some earlier, seemingly simpler, time because that happiness no longer exists (and may never have been real at all). This raises important questions about the relationship and dynamics between members of the same household: how we both help and hurt one another in our shared existences. Mac gives us a stirring and relevant portrait of the modern family, one that recognizes both the depth of kindness shared among family members and the inherent tragedy of being trapped in one's childhood home with no sense of independent selfhood.

This emphasis on the questions of self-determination resonates with the role prescribed by being someone's child. Both Beckett's and Mac's plays particularly consider the connection between fathers and children, asking serious questions about whether we should forgive our fathers their failings and whether they deserve our kindness simply for having raised us. Clov understands that his life was not necessarily marked by love in the way others might think it was. Clov proclaims, "They said to me, That's friendship, yes, yes, no question, you've found it. They said to me, Here's the place, stop, raise your head and look at all that beauty."[22] Things can seem, on the surface, to be much better than they actually are. Simply being safe from the outside world may not be enough for one to feel truly fulfilled; it may come with responsibilities too great to allow one to live one's fullest life. Max, too, like Clov before hir, has been forced, through the play's revelations, to recognize that hir family life was not all ze believed it to be: there was cruelty, abuse, and suffering. In the play's final moments, Max embraces a desire to leave, telling Paige, "I don't want to be here," which Paige validates: "You don't have to be" (88). Ze recognizes, as Clov had always wondered, that "There are places where it's easier. Where people aren't like this" (88). Max could leave and, in doing so, find a better life.

Until the events of the play have transpired, Max's plan is "to live on a Radical faerie commune," once ze turns eighteen (28). Yet while Clov consistently says he will leave and appears to be threatening to do so in *Endgame*'s final moments, Max wishes to leave, but it is Paige, the parent figure who says, "You'll get away. You'll do better" (88). Rather than selfishly trying to imprison Max with her, to avoid her own loneliness, Paige sees a different fate for Max. Interestingly, it is Max who, in the play's final moments, begins to care for Arnold: "MAX *takes his wet nightgown off . . .* MAX *brushes* ARNOLD's *hair down. Calms him, and starts to clean up the urine with a nearby towel*" (89). This shocks and upsets Paige, as she recognizes how this could entrap her child: ze might become a prisoner by becoming a caregiver. As much as this mirrors Beckett's *Endgame*, unlike Hamm and Clov, Mac's characters seem to have some agency over what happens to them. It is not as if "Outside of here it's death,"[23] as is the case in Beckett's play; Max *could* choose to leave, but does not. Whatever happens to hir, then, feels a bit more like a product of hir own actions, manifested by the social pressures of hir familial role.

This ending can have a tragicomic impact for the audience: it is hard to know whether there is meant to be any humor in what has happened or if it is just terribly sad. Absurdist plays, too, are funny, sometimes brutally so, and it is often impossible to separate when one should laugh from when one should cry. As Pozzo tells Didi and Gogo in *Godot*, "The tears of the world are a constant quantity. For each one who begins to weep somewhere else another stops. The same is true of the laugh."[24] *Hir* has a similar feeling to it—while it appears on the surface to be very comedic, its final moments can be seen as deeply painful.

Yet Max seems to have chosen hir final actions; no one is trapping hir in this situation. The commentary the play offers, then, is not just about the individual existential crisis; rather, it critiques the inherent tragedies of our middle-class American norms. Mac's play, then, takes us beyond the Absurd, as Tavel once said his Ridiculous work would. The play does not solely indulge in the despair or disillusionment associated with our human condition. Rather, it allows its characters to fight back against one another and their circumstances, just as Paige has in abandoning her assigned heteronormative role. In this way, *Hir* does not quite fit the

Absurd model perfectly; it is too active to be pure Absurdism while being too abstract to be pure Naturalism.

Creating HirStory: Theatre of the Ridiculous as a Source

In many ways, Mac's *Hir* seems to live up to Charles Ludlam's "Aim" in his *Manifesto* by "revaluing combat" in order "to get beyond nihilism."[25] While the characters often face, and even discuss, their own existential crises, Mac's play allows them a decent amount of agency over those forces of disillusionment and despair. Of course, Mac warns against allowing the play to become too Ridiculous, as doing so, I believe, would undercut the impact of the social commentary that its Naturalism offers and the contemplation of the human condition that its Absurdism provides. However, even when added together, these two genres alone do not fully encompass all of the qualities of *Hir*.

For one, the play is quite funny, marked by all sorts of Ridiculous-style physical comedy. Toward the end of the play, for example, Isaac teaches Max to make the bed, military style. Mac describes the action: "*They try to keep up but aren't that successful because* ARNOLD *undoes almost everything* MAX *does. It is essentially a bed-making lazzi.* MAX, *as the lazzi progresses, gets more and more frustrated with* ARNOLD, *to the point where ze is pushing* ARNOLD *and on the verge of violence with him*" (76). It is humorous, to be sure, but a kind of sinister humor—we are laughing at something that also exposes interpersonal cruelty within this family. This suggests a kind of revaluing of what we should—and even can—laugh at, which is at the core of the Ridiculous. As Ludlam declares, "The things one takes seriously are one's weaknesses."[26]

This sense of reversing the traditional valuation standards is a significant Ridiculous element. Ludlam writes, "I think the whole keynote of the Ridiculous and camp is a rigorous revaluing of everything. What people think is valuable ain't valuable. Admiring what people hold in contempt, holding in contempt things other people think are so valuable—it's a fantastic standard."[27] Consider all of the garbage the Connor family owns: in realistic plays, people are often defined by their material possessions, so they buy up lots of fancy stuff to prove their worth. But Paige has chosen to disavow that mindset. She reminds us that owning nice things does not necessarily improve one's life: "Tell that to all the neighbors who have had to get three jobs, never see their kids, and still can't make ends meet, all so

Fig. 12. (from L. to R.): Cameron Scoggins as Isaac, Kristine Neilsen as Paige. Photo: Joan Marcus.

they can keep their Formica countertops" (36). Clearly, this play is offering commentary on middle-class American family life: what it values may not actually be all that valuable.

This sensibility of revaluation extends to the thematic concerns of *Hir* as well. It would seem that maintaining the family should be the most important thing, but it is not. In fact, the journey of self-discovery, separate from one's assigned family role, is the more significant characterization: Max is the play's most fulfilled character. This profound sense of agency and selfhood has been shaped through Max's acceptance of hir nonbinary identity. Yet even this queer theme is marked humorously; Paige explains to Isaac, "There are no longer two genders. No longer simply a Y and X chromosome but an alphabet of genders. They call it the LGBTTSQQIA community. Or what I call the gender of [*pronouncing LGBTTSQQIA as if it were a word*] Lugabuttsqueeah" (21). This poking fun at the play's central theme regarding gender identity is reinforced in the scenic design—the refrigerator features plastic alphabet magnets spelling out this "word."

Therefore, humor is at the core of the dramatic construct of *Hir*. It is a tightly crafted satire that pokes fun at "high culture" in the same way that Ludlam once celebrated: "Theatre without the stink of art."[28] In his play *Le*

Bourgeois Avant-Garde (1983), an adaptation of Molière's commentary on upper-class life in seventeenth-century France, *Le Bourgeois Gentilhomme* (1670), Ludlam mocks the artistic elite where Molière once poked fun at the aristocracy. In Ludlam's play, Mr. Foufas's greatest wish is to be a member of the "avant-garde," and attempts to marry off his daughter to an artist to achieve this goal. While the plot of the play is delightful, the play's real purpose was "to illustrate [Ludlam's] opinion" that avant-garde art "doesn't really mean anything at all and is, more often than not, pure pretense."[29] Consider Mr. Foufas's "deconstructed letter": "'Beautiful—your—eyes—for—dying—am—of—I—fair—love—mistress.'"[30] It does read like a Dada poem, per Tristan Tzara's anarchic instructions,[31] but, in so doing, reaffirms that Dada poetry may not actually mean anything at all.

Paige's obsession with culture seems to have the same Ridiculous quality as Mr. Foufas's preoccupation with the avant-garde did in Ludlam's play. She insists that the whole family—minus Arnold, of course—go to the museum, declaring, "We love art," to which Isaac responds, "We've never liked art" (39). Max's fluidity of identity seems to extend to hir interest in this as well, as ze went to Paris with hir mother when Isaac was away, but now claims that "I always have comfort issues in museums" and that "old paintings full of . . . people pointing" are "fucking boring" (39). Ze even redefines the *Mona Lisa*, explaining, "the Mona Lisa is transgender" as "It's a self-portrait of da Vinci" (40). Max offers a modern interpretation of the work, and even of art in general, but eschews providing definite proof. As Mr. Foufas's letter is only poetic in the eye of the beholder, Max leaves this reading of da Vinci's painting in a similar subjective place, only claiming that "Lots of people. Scholar people" back hir up. Max defiantly advances, "History is conjecture so why can't *hirstory* be the same thing?" (41). Establishing objective truth is not a goal for the characters in Mac's play; they are instead embracing, willingly or not, a kind of ultimate fluidity and subjectivity for all aspects of their lives.

In fact, in their disavowal of fixed truths, Paige offers a direct critique of my chosen profession, commenting, "Academia is where people go who are too afraid to have uninstitutionalized discourse" (27). This is her and Max's justification for why Max will not be attending college. Now, they do admit to Isaac that they appropriated this idea from Sarah Schulman's *The Gentrification of the Mind*, and when pushed on the subject by him, Max reveals that ze may or may not have read it. Even if ze did, ze did not fully understand what ze was reading, a further commentary on intellectualism. Mac even goes beyond offering commentary on art and academia to implicitly critique judy's own dramatic work. While discussing Max's identity and pronouns, Paige asserts, "The youth don't understand. You can't mess with content and form at the same time" (24). Yet this is precisely what Mac's play does; to best encapsulate its subject matter, Mac created his own dramaturgical mode, appropriating and remixing a variety of elements from other recognizable dramatic forms.

Hir: *A Contemporary Portrait of the Modern American Family*

Hir's treatment of its subject matter is not a complete mockery of the issues at hand, however. Despite sharing some similarities with the campiness of the Ridiculous, this is not solely a "seriousness that fails," to quote Susan Sontag.[32] Rather, it goes beyond that construct, bringing the Ridiculous into the twenty-first century. Consider the play's representation of gender, particularly that of Max, which gives the play its title. The sincerity and authenticity with which Max's identity is treated advances the discussion of gender from the Ridiculous, which was principally interested in using drag to expose the complex performativity of gender identity, as well as cross-gendering performers exclusively for comedic reasons, or to take advantage of a particular actor's comedic talents and abilities.

In many ways, Mac's work, while displaying an inheritance from the Theatre of the Ridiculous, takes that form conceptually and ideologically far beyond what Ludlam and others were able to accomplish. This is because Mac's play engages with immediately relevant subjects such as the acceptance of trans and nonbinary identities into not only our understanding but our lexicon of gender and selfhood, something that did not figure prominently in twentieth-century Ridiculous Theatre. In fact, Ludlam, for one, gets this wrong, at least insofar as he attempted to make sense of Warhol "superstars" Candy Darling and Jackie Curtis. Of Candy and Jackie, he writes:

> You give a performance and come offstage, and you've got to get into yourself and rest, reconstruct your own true personality again, indulge it. Only then can you go back and play the role again. But once you start playing the fantasy twenty-four hours a day, you may have obliterated your personality on a more or less permanent basis. A mask can be a protection to preserve what's inside, but in the case of Jackie and Candy—particularly of Candy—they were always

being overly generous with others, giving so much they didn't leave anything for themselves.[33]

What Ludlam may be misunderstanding here is that Candy and Jackie were not giving a performance in their day-to-day lives. They were living as authentic versions of themselves, expressing their gender identities as they saw fit.

As a genderqueer individual, Mac understands that drama must embrace a more nuanced view of gender representation in contemporary plays, both on the page and in performance. This is directly relevant to *Hir*, as Mac insists on a trans actor for the role of Max. In an interview with Lisa Kron for *American Theatre*, Mac notes:

> I'm a big fan of duality on stage. I like to see the character and the performer at the same time. When you can cast somebody who actually is transgender performing the role, it's just deeper. You don't see the exact history of the actor, but you can bring a little bit of the reality into the theatre, and the theatre into the reality, and that's the great joy for me. Usually I don't decide what gender the characters are until the first draft is done, if ever, but from the get-go I knew Max had to be transgender or genderqueer. The characters are trying to figure out what to do with masculinity. To get at that, it was important to me that one of the characters come from the middle.[34]

This takes us well beyond the misguided lens with which Ludlam viewed the experiences of individuals like Candy Darling and Jackie Curtis. Mac uses the play's dramaturgy to explore the complexities of gender, and then maintains that focus with visionary casting of transgender and genderqueer individuals in representative roles, something that has only recently become commonplace in mainstream American theater.

In this way, the play offers a direct and specific challenge to traditional binary gender norms. This is not just a play about men and women, fathers and sons, mothers and daughters, with all of the traditional gender tropes intact. Rather, it is a contemporary portrait of the modern American family, embracing the idea that the narrative of self is a much more complex conversation than a simple distinction between "this" and "that" identity. Thus, the play also disavows the old gender norms of the American family: the straight cis-male father has become someone to be laughed at. As tragic as Arnold's condition and Paige's treatment of him seems, it may be justified. As Paige says, "Don't you pity him. Those who knew him, know of his cruelty, we will *not* rewrite his history with pity" (19). This centers the existential question at the core of the Arnold plotline. As Clov ponders in *Endgame*, "There's one thing I'll never understand. Why I always obey you. Can you explain that to me?" Hamm considers, "No . . . Perhaps it's compassion. (*Pause.*) A kind of great compassion."[35] Certainly, Clov could be acting from a compassionate place, but he also might be responding to a sense of obligation. He may feel it is his duty to care for this man at the end of life because he took Clov in and cared for him when he was a small boy. And because it is impossible to leave their little void, Clov will be trapped there forever. In *Hir*, this sense of duty is not only about the entrapment of the individual; rather, how they engage with Arnold has implications for our understanding of the dynamics of the American family overall. If men were held accountable for their actions, perhaps we could begin a new narrative of the American family, one that is more open, inclusive, and equitable for all involved.

For Isaac, this can be achieved by "honor[ing] what he was able to do and then you do better. At some point somebody has to stay home and do better" (82). His vision is one that looks toward the future, but Isaac conflates moving forward with going back to his childhood past, believing that being home will somehow give life, and even death, purpose. Isaac reflects, "All I've done for the last three years is care for blown-up limbs and intestines and pieces of brains. Half a heart. Knowing that if my body were to get blown to pieces, I'd want someone to care for them. To send them home" (83). The central questions of selfhood and identity were thrown into painful relief for Isaac because of his wartime experiences seeing people reduced to pieces of flesh that reflect nothing of their personal stories. Isaac laments, "You can't leave places. The only useful job you can have in the places where everything is blown up is to care for the pieces" (81). His journey is one of entrapment, and ultimately it is circular: he joined the military to escape this household, only to find a deep desire to return home once he was in combat. On returning home, he finds nothing the way he left it and is ultimately displaced once again, as Paige forces him to leave. This circularity of the connection between location and selfhood is contextualized by the pronunciation of Max's pronoun and the play's title: "hir," which would sound like "here." This is a play about the crossroads between identity and place, about the degree to which we think or hope that *where* we are will help us to make sense of *who* we are. Isaac's journey was not only a physical one; he was also on a quest to find himself. Because he has not yet formulated a unique sense of identity, his journey is not complete; no place can define him until he figures out how to define himself.

Max, on the other hand, has already defined hirself and is therefore freed to act how ze wants. Where hir is not all ze is; ze knows hir identity and longs to live it fully, out in the world. And yet, Max finds hirself in the caregiver position at the end of the play: ze has made the active choice to stay and care for Arnold. This may not be what Paige wanted for her child, but it is not up to Paige to decide. If we see, along with Paige, this final portrait of Max as tragic, it is not Max who is to blame for that tragic outcome, but rather American society and its emphasis on the nuclear family. The heteronormative family structure is what ruined Paige's life and what sent Isaac off to war, which disrupted his life. Now, it is threatening to poison Max's unique journey as well. Being members of this family has ruined hir mother and brother, but Max is determined to create another outcome for hirself, one that is more humane and more compassionate.

Ze is empowered to make a free decision for hirself—ze need not stay here—but chooses to stay because ze is trying to do the right thing. The issue here is that the right thing for one's family, by traditional American cultural standards, might not be the best thing for the individual. Max is showing a depth of humanity, which may ultimately be corrupted by the exact cultural system—the family—that it is trying to serve. In this way, *Hir* offers biting commentary on American family life and how its assigned roles can disrupt the pursuit of a meaningful sense of self.

Whose Story Is It? Hir *and Issues of Race in American Family Dramas*

Despite the depth of the commentary the play offers, there is one glaring omission: any specific discussion of race as it pertains to this "average American family." Indeed, when looking at *Hir* as whole, it would seem that these roles could be played by actors of any race, yet there is no particular textual material meant to draw attention to a racial or cultural identity for any of the characters particularly. However, it would still seem that the focus of the play is on white, Eurocentric culture, considering the influences I discussed here. In the Playwrights Horizons production, the version I saw, all of the performers were white and the language of the play, in its semi-absurdist nature, defies any sense of regionalism or identity markers in its turns of phrase, styles of speech, or dialect. On the one hand, it seems as if this family could be *any* American family. But, on closer inspection, it could perhaps be more clearly seen as being *any white* American family. It seems that, generally, recent productions have continued to cast white actors in the lead roles. Does this suggest that this play is racially limited? Or, is it meant to offer a critique of "whiteness" as a standard of American greatness by showing the cruel and corrupt side of the seemingly "perfect" white American family? What could be gained by casting BIPOC performers in some or all of the roles in this play? *Hir* may come across as if it is not about race at all; yet this depiction, if seen as throwing into relief the conflation of the American experience with the privileging of whiteness, offers a potential biting commentary on precisely that trope: maybe the white American ideal is not all it pretends to be.

Even if *Hir* is not specifically about race, by exploring the American experience, it must be, by extension, engaging issues of race inherent to that topic. As Che Gossett reminds us, "Visibility politics, or the kind of queer and trans politics we might call neoliberal, cannot account for the ways that blackness ghosts and haunts the normative, the way it exceeds representational fixity."[36] Even if the play is not directly engaging race as a factor in this family's situation, in its elision, the play, too, is drawing attention to the subject of race. To cast Black actors, for example, might be to offer a new perspective on the play's interrogation of "the American dream," one that intentionally and incisively considers the racial component of the failures of that American dream.

Hir makes no direct argument about the role that racial-identity or white-supremacy culture has played in these individuals' experiences. Implicitly, then, the play operates from a kind of "colorblind" position, which, as Alison Reed discusses in relation to theory practices, "satisfies an institutional need for multicultural representation and theoretical diversity, while perpetuating colorblind logics that foreclose possibilities for justice by denying the existence of white supremacy."[37] Because attention is not explicitly drawn to it, race is not a factor in the progression of events in this play. And yet, Isaac's situation in the military, for instance, would be much more complicated if the role were played by a Black actor, as this would offer a route for scrutinizing the experience of Black military members and their treatment in the armed services. Would he still just be a young man giving in to the nihilism of the interminable murder and torture that is warfare? Or would he instead become a representation of a flawed system, one that entices young BIPOC people into the military with promises of opportunities and training only to strand them in traumatizing work with no easy means of escape?

In terms of casting, perhaps even more provocative might be the role of Max, if played by a Black actor. What might this character offer, in terms of opening conversations about intersectionality, for example, if ze were not only trans but a person of color as well? In "Troubling the Waters: Towards a Trans* Analytic," Kai M. Green "explore[s] trans as a productive site of possibility relative to black [*sic*] sexual identity politics and theories of black [*sic*] gender and sexuality" in order "to mine trans for its use value as a method or optic, one that, similar to queer, refuses temporal or spatial fixity."[38] Considering the absurdist framing of this play—happening both anywhere and nowhere, at the present and for all time, simultaneously—this could be an evocative way to approach Max's trans identity, as a focal point for exploring selfhood and how, more broadly, it is constituted, shaped, and adapted. Green continues, "Moreover, I use it [trans] to articulate a unique relation between two or more identity categories where one marks the limits and excess of the other, simultaneously deconstructing and reconstructing or reimagining new possible ways of being and doing."[39] The play could become an exploration of the intersectionality of identity and exploit how the cultural influences on it shape or distort those identity experiences.

Mac's play offers space for contemplation of the "modern American family," in all of its grotesque realities. In this way, the play offers a biting critique of the façade many families put up in order to look perfect—i.e., like a white family on television from the 1950s—when in reality, their problems may be legion. Perhaps it is the revelation that dysfunction is the actual common state of the American family and perfect harmony and bliss are the aberration. The family members' inability to conform to a conventionalized "standard" is only a logical outcome of a flawed system. To look at this from the perspective of "queer of color analysis," per Roderick A. Ferguson's work, would highlight "an understanding of nation and capital as the outcome of manifold intersections that contradict the idea of the liberal nation-state and capital as sites of resolution, perfection, progress, and confirmation."[40] Perfect was never possible; the flaw was in seeking some form of it at all. Ferguson reinforces that "queer of color analysis presumes that liberal ideology occludes the intersecting saliency of race, gender, sexuality, and class in forming social practices."[41] The issues present in this play would resonate on new registers when race is considered. Future productions might benefit from casting nonwhite actors in these roles to bring to light the inherent critique on white American ideals already built into Mac's dramaturgy.

Conclusion

Hir offers a biting critique of the American family, but does so in a way that maintains the integrity of each its main characters, no matter who is cast in the roles. In reviewing the play for The *New York Times*, Charles Isherwood remarks, "What is remarkable about 'Hir' is not its woolly, dark vision of an American family run amok, but the flawed and real humanity that simmers beneath all the surreal comedy."[42] Mac has constructed the telling of this story so that it can be both funny and deeply affecting at the same time. In structuring the play the way that he has, Mac allows for commentary on family life (realism); for asking existential questions (Absurdism); and for the use of humor in deep and meaningful ways to poke fun at its own preoccupations (i.e., art and gender) (Ridiculous). In this way, the play is both subversive and progressive, opening key questions about the American experience and allowing room to imagine a better lifestyle.

This vision of a better future reflects the queer qualities of this play. While the Connors may not be living in an ideal situation, their reality throws into relief our own family lives, and through the presence of Max, offers a reminder to seek other ways of being besides those that society has assigned us. As José Muñoz states, "Queerness is a longing that propels us onward, beyond romances of the negative and toiling in the present. Queerness is the thing that lets us feel that this world is not enough, that indeed something is missing."[43] This play possesses this hopeful quality: the audience should want more than what any of these characters have come to accept as their reality. We can be better, truer versions of ourselves, and in this manner, find a kind of personal freedom.

Hir is a remarkable reminder of what makes Taylor Mac such a significant contemporary playwright. Mac's plays are deeply relevant to the issues of the day while always pushing the envelope in terms of dramaturgy and production elements. Mac, as a playwright, offers new and innovative models for storytelling and reinvents the tried-and-true genres in ways that make them feel fresh and resonant. In this manner, Mac's work goes beyond judy's earlier influences, capturing mainstream attention and thereby shining a light on important issues of gender, identity, and selfhood that offer us both a clear snapshot of who we are as a society, and more profoundly, what we are as human beings. This thematic complexity is only possible through a complexity of genre construction, which can only be manifested by a playwright willing to explore the possibility that "Everyone is a little bit of everything" (22).

Notes

1. When referring to Taylor Mac, I will be using Mac's chosen pronoun, "judy."

2. Taylor Mac, "A Few Notes from the Playwright," in *Hir: A Play* (Evanston, IL: Northwestern University Press, 2015), ix.

3. This was the production that I saw. Thank you to the New York Public Library for the Performing Arts, Theatre on Film and Tape division, for allowing me to review the production from their archive.

4. Mac, *Hir*, 21–22. All subsequent references to play text are credited with in-text parenthetical page number citations.

5. Ronald Tavel, quoted in "Ronald Tavel, Proudly Ridiculous Writer, Dies at 72," by Dennis Hevesi, in the *New York Times*, 27 March 2009. https://www.nytimes.com/2009/03/27/theater/27tavel.html#:~:text=In%20August%201965%2C%20two%20one,on%20short%20screenplays%20that%20Mr.&text=Tavel's%20manifesto%20for%20the%20movement,our%20position%20is%20absolutely%20preposterous.%E2%80%9D

6. Sean Edgecomb, *Charles Ludlam Lives! Charles Busch, Bradford Louryk, Taylor Mac, and the Queer Legacy of the Ridiculous Theatrical Company* (Ann Arbor: University of Michigan Press, 2017), 38.

7. Edgecomb, *Charles Ludlam Lives!*, 42.

8. Edgecomb, Charles Ludlam Lives!, 42.

9. John Simon, "'The Tale of the Allergist's Wife,'" *New York* (13 Mar 2000). nymag.com/nymetro/arts/theater/reviews/2317/

10. Charles Busch, *The Tale of the Allergist's Wife*, in *The Tale of the Allergist's Wife and Other Plays* (New York: Grove Press, 2001), 290–91.

11. Charles Ludlam, "Manifesto: Ridiculous Theatre, Scourge of Human Folly," in *Ridiculous Theatre: Scourge of Human Folly* (New York: Theatre Communications Group, 1992), 157.

12. Isaac Butler, "The Great American Living-Room Gets a Remodel," *American Theatre* (25 March 2015). https://www.americantheatre.org/2015/03/25/how-contemporary-playwrights-are-re-defining-the-living-room-play/

13. Émile Zola, "Naturalism in the Theatre" (1881), in *Theatre Theory Theatre*, ed. Daniel Gerould (New York: Applause, 2000), 365.

14. Zola, "Naturalism," 360.

15. Henrik Ibsen, *A Doll's House* (1879), (Project Gutenberg e-Book, 2001), 2.

16. Zola, "Naturalism," 366.

17. Zola, "Naturalism," 354–55.

18. Martin Esslin, *Theatre of the Absurd* (New York: Random House, 2004; originally published, 1962), 233.

19. Samuel Beckett, *Happy Days* (New York: Grove Press, 1961), 7–9.

20. Samuel Beckett, *Waiting for Godot* (New York: Grove Press, 1954), 10.

21. Samuel Beckett, *Endgame* (New York: Grove Press, 1958), 57.

22. Beckett, *Endgame*, 80.

23. Beckett, *Endgame*, 9.

24. Beckett, *Godot*, 22.

25. Ludlam, "Manifesto," in *Ridiculous Theatre*, 157.

26. Ludlam, "Manifesto," in *Ridiculous Theatre*, 157.

27. Charles Ludlam, "Camp," in *Ridiculous Theatre* (New York: Theatre Communications Group, 1992), 226.

28. Ludlam, "Manifesto," in Ridiculous Theatre, 157.

29. Rick Roemer, *Charles Ludlam and the Ridiculous Theatrical Company: Critical Analyses of 29 Plays* (Jefferson, NC: McFarland and Co., 1998), 124.

30. Charles Ludlam, *Le Bourgeois Avant-Garde*, in *The Complete Plays of Charles Ludlam* (New York: Harper Collins, 1989), 707.

31. Tristan Tzara, "How to Make a Dadaist Poem." https://www.writing.upenn.edu/~afilreis/88v/tzara.html

32. Susan Sontag, "Notes on 'Camp,'" originally published 1964. https://monoskop.org/images/5/59/Sontag_Susan_1964_Notes_on_Camp.pdf

33. Ludlam, *Scourge of Human Folly*, 22.

34. Taylor Mac, quoted in Lisa Kron, "Taylor Mac's 'Hir': Just Your Average Kitchen-Sink, Genderqueer Family Drama," *American Theatre* (26 November 2014). https://www.americantheatre.org/2014/11/26/taylor-macs-hir-just-your-average-kitchen-sink-genderqueer-family-drama/

35. Beckett, *Endgame*, 75–76.

36. Che Gossett, "Blackness and the Trouble of Trans Visibility," in *Trap Door: Trans Cultural Production and the Politics of Visibility*, eds. Reina Gossett, Eric A. Stanley, and Johanna Burton (Cambridge, MA: MIT Press, 2017), 183–90; 187.

37. Alison Reed, "The Whiter the Bread, the Quicker You're Dead: Spectacular Absence and Post-Racialized Blackness in (White) Queer Theory," in *No Tea, No Shade: New Writings in Black Queer Studies*, ed. E. Patrick Johnson (Durham, NC: Duke University Press, 2016), 48–64; 49.

38. Kai M. Green, "Troubling the Waters: Mobilizing a Trans* Analytic," in *No Tea, No Shade*, 65–82; 66.

39. Green, "Troubling the Waters," 66.

40. Roderick A. Ferguson, *Aberrations in Black: Toward a Queer of Color Critique* (Minneapolis: University of Minnesota Press, 2004), 3.

41. Ferguson, *Aberrations*, 4.

42. Charles Isherwood, "Review: 'Hir' Sorts Through a Family in Transition," *New York Times* (8 November 2015). https://www.nytimes.com/2015/11/09/theater/review-hir-sorts-through-a-family-in-transition.html

43. José Muñoz, *Cruising Utopia: The Then and There of Queer Futurity* (New York: NYU Press, 2009), 1.

FOUR

Queer Pussy Time

Taylor Mac's Lesbian Decade

Kim Marra

At the turn into hour 23 of *A 24-Decade History of Popular Music*, which is to say at around 10:00 a.m. on Sunday, October 9, 2016, in St. Ann's Warehouse in Brooklyn, New York, Taylor Mac, who uses the pronoun "judy" and has been aptly dubbed "Bedazzled Shaman, Social Critic, Radical Fool,"[1] stood strumming a ukulele clad in perhaps the most stripped-down nonbinary drag of the entire marathon performance: a sheer nude body stocking inscribed with the graffiti "Mother," "Goddess," "Sister," "Love," and "Her" in large rough black lettering while revealing male chest hair and genitalia beneath (fig. 13). A shaggy layer of pink satin breast-cancer-awareness ribbons pinned up and down the stocking calves suggested unshaven silky blond feminine leg hair. Bald-headed, face sad-clownishly streaked with the tear-splotched heavy black and sparkly eye makeup of the preceding AIDS decade, judy summoned self, ensemble, and audience through sleep-deprived exhaustion to honor us former caregivers of our dying brothers with an hour of music popular among radical lesbians from roughly 1996 to 2006.

I focus on Mac's Lesbian Decade not only because of how it paid homage to lesbians of my generation, but also because of how it culminated a performance strategy working through the whole *24-Decade History*. That strategy arose from judy's signature mode of appropriation for making incisive queer feminist historical reclamations and commentary. Throughout the marathon show, blue-eyed white male judy performed a dizzying array of appropriations of others' music, stories, identities, and perspec-

Fig. 13. Taylor Mac in the nude onesie base layer of the Lesbian Decade costume, *A 24-Decade History of Popular Music*, St. Ann's Warehouse, October 9, 2016. Photo: Lisa Freeman.

tives. But Mac managed to do this with such keenly ironic self-reflexivity and extraordinary openness and vulnerability to others' experience that the performance both mitigated the replication of dominant power dynamics and fostered utopic communal transformation. To an exceptional degree, the content, timing, and state of judy's body (and ours) *in extremis* in the Lesbian Decade compounded that vulnerability and openness as Mac spectacularly embodied "pussy" as both an adjective and a noun. The "naked" nonbinary Fool attire was but a first layer, to which much was strategically added over the hour's well-dramaturged, compellingly staged song list. By decade's end, in a stunning climax of costume and cultural critique, Mac donned a sumptuously lush fabric sculpture of ravaged receptive orifices writ large and queer where male, female, fluid, and trans sexualities, genders, and ethnicities all came together. Literally and figuratively enfolded in composite, intersecting labia, our Bedazzled Shaman led us through an ingeniously rigged, pointedly theatrical rebirth.

On that early October 2016 weekend, Mac's self-proclaimed "radical faerie realness ritual" glorification of pussy all too hopefully anticipated the historic possibility of the nation electing its first female president a month hence. Given that two decades earlier in the *24-Decade History*, the production had featured a giant missile-sized inflated penis balloon colored with the stars and stripes and passed overhead through the room and out the door into history like a dirigible, the scale of the Lesbian Decade's pussy rendering and rebirth signaled an emergence into a new order. This literally overblown utopic vision, already highly fraught, was further charged with the pivotal political events that broke immediately around the marathon: the releases in rapid succession of US security agencies' official confirmation of Russian meddling in our election, the "grab 'em by the pussy" Access Hollywood tape, and Clinton campaign manager John Podesta's hacked emails, all on Friday, October 7, as many of us were arriving in New York City to attend the performance the next day; and the second presidential debate (the one in which Trump stalked Hillary) on Sunday evening, October 9, which many of us would anxiously watch just a few hours after the performance ended. Barely ten minutes into the show, which commenced at noon on Saturday, October 8, Mac directly referenced the Friday events, exhorting the audience: "Gird your pussies!" Multiple times throughout the marathon, judy called out "Is America ready for Hillary Clinton?" to loud cheers from the St. Ann's audience.

Flagrantly defying a tenacious USAmerican value system where any deviations from straight white capitalist masculinity risk denigration as

Fig. 14. Two mannequins showing the pieces of Mac's costume for the Lesbian Decade in the exhibit "Costumes from Taylor Mac's *A 24-Decade History of Popular Music* Designed by Machine Dazzle," Hancher Auditorium, University of Iowa, Iowa City, Iowa, April 24–28, 2018. Author photo.

effeminate or "pussy," manifold forms of feminine valorization boldly marked Mac's overall queer aesthetic. In addition to hailing leaders endowed with vaginas, Mac voiced numerous references during the whole show to the mouth- and anus-pussies we all share regardless of identity. A highly diverse musical and special-guest ensemble and stage crew (the Dandy Minions) ramified the inclusive, queering vision of the event. Most spectacularly, judy continuously shape-shifted in and out of the extraordinarily inventive costume creations of collaborating artist Machine Dazzle, who fashioned a multilayered effeminizing design for each of the twenty-four decades. Through the costuming, songs, shtick, and patter of the Lesbian Decade, pussy became most graphically explicit, and even more clearly so in retrospect, illuminating of intersectional politics and phobias that played into the election and resounded in its aftermath.[2] As enacted in the one-time-only full marathon, the twenty-third hour marked a queer pussy time that bears a reckoning as scholars continue to take stock of Mac's epic achievement.[3] Drawing on an extended interview with Machine Dazzle during a subsequent traveling exhibit of all the *24-Decade* costumes on my home campus, as well as song lyrics, reviews, and multimedia documentation to flesh out my experience of the historic St. Ann's event, I analyze the performance dynamics of Mac's Lesbian Decade and reflect on their political ramifications before and since the 2016 election.

Packing and Unpacking

In the framework of the performance, the queer pussy time of the Lesbian Decade emerged from the show's historiographical approach to drag working in conjunction with solo and ensemble musical numbers and stories. When I subsequently interviewed Machine Dazzle amid the costume exhibit, he explained that he and Taylor do not really consider themselves drag queens, although the term "drag queen" sometimes becomes shorthand for what they do. "This isn't your typical drag. This is not 'RuPaul's Drag Race,'" he asserted. "This is embodiment of a story. It's not drag; it's embodiment of concepts and ideas." Highlighting the queer and marginal, the overall concept of the twenty-four-hour-duration concert traces a hopeful view of history that moves toward an intersectional feminist future through a pattern of oppressed diverse communities building themselves up as they are being torn apart. David Román clarifies that "While each decade has its own stand-alone logic and coherence, when experienced together they build to tell a story of ongoing cultural resilience in the midst of tragedy and catastrophe. The entire project is a radical revision of American history through popular song; and yet, there is so much more."[4] Machine Dazzle's costumes extravagantly play on this historical revisionism within each decade by bringing the past into the present through research and inspired whimsy.

Quoting period fashion while incorporating pop kitsch and Ziegfeldian flare, each of Dazzle's twenty-four designs uses female dress not so much as a glamorous façade but as a highly imaginative armature for interweaving dominant cultural repressions of and subversions by the feminine or effeminate. Still "genderfuck" in aesthetic but more elaborately crafted than some of Mac's earlier costumes, these creations both pack a visual punch from a distance and reward close scrutiny, with startlingly subversive elements often lurking in cleverly nested details.[5] Moreover, because deviations from straight white capitalist masculinity historically have been racialized as well as gendered and sexualized, racial and ethnic dynamics are also variously woven through these dresses and the accompanying musical and narrative repertoire. In Machine's and Taylor's mode of drag, the white male body comes to these creations "as is." Machine noted, "We don't tuck; we wear what fits. We don't change who we are." Wearing these costumes while voicing the songs and stories becomes a series of self-consciously intersectional political acts that merge identities, cultures, and eras. In Mac's embodied intersectional and historiographical performance, wardrobe "malfunctions," which happened a number of times at St. Ann's, far from spoiling an effect, provide opportunities for enhancing the immediacy of present connection and audience engagement.

During our conversation, Machine emphasized that although the Lesbian Decade gives special focus to lesbians, lesbian desire pulses through the show so that what happens in the 1996–2006 hour consummates a key motif of Taylor "trying to insert the lesbian." Most centrally, lesbian musicians provided the primary beat of the concert, in particular lead guitarist Viva DeConcini and drummer Bernice "Boom Boom" Brooks, who played, respectively, for seven and five of the show's eight acts, each act being comprised of three one-hour decades.[6] Several story and costume points also brought the pulse of lesbian desire to the surface. An early example accompanies the highlighting of the show's feminist historiographical roots in the second decade, subtitled "Women's Lib," with the distribution of paper copies and reading of Judith Sargeant Murray's landmark treatise "On the Equality of the Sexes" (1790). Machine costumed Taylor in a gown he describes as "The French Revolution meets the Industrial Revolution. Severed Heads in Cherry Tree disguises from the Guillotine float across the Atlantic and arrive on the American coastline. The steam engine played a major part in westward expansion . . ."[7] To the back of a gown made of dangling French Empire silk tassels intermixed with bloodied Styrofoam heads, Machine affixed two large steam-engine smokestacks belching repressed passion and emerging feminist power—with a lesbian twist. When Taylor sings "O dear, what can the matter be. . . . Johnny's so long at the fair," the problem is not Johnny's absence but his return, because it interrupts the lady's plan for a lesbian affair. That desire erupts again in Crazy Jane, the Temperance resister of the third decade, who dons a gown shaped like a whiskey barrel boldly emblazoned with lapping, shimmering purple-green tongues from red-lipsticked mouths and a belt hung with a pink battery-powered vibrator and a double-penetrator dildo.

Marking World War I and the suffragist generation a century later, Machine costumed Taylor in an Edwardian gown draped with clusters of coconut-sized, soft fabric fortune cookies with denuded-pussy-like folds. His note accompanying the costume in the exhibit reads "only her fortune cookie knows what's in her custom muff," a wildly hairy crimson heather accessory for hand warming. Below the muff, a fortune unfurls from one of the labial cookie slits on a strip of white cloth: "XOXOXOXOXO." Then came the Speakeasy Decade (1916–1926) characterized, according to Machine's notes, by "Androgyny as revolution. Masculine women and Feminine men! Happy Days Are Here Again!" The costume literally combined the genders with a flapper gown front belted over slim-fitting knickers that were fully exposed behind. In between songs, Taylor told us a graphic tale about women fisting each other, which judy punctuated with a wry quip "Bet you thought they were all like Ellen." Ultimately, however, the fulfillment of these lesbian desires was thwarted by the men coming home from the war. Following the show's historiographical arc, a similar interruption happened after World War II. Finally, after the male-centered caregiving of the AIDS Decade, explained Machine, "lesbians could have their story."

In the transition to the Lesbian Decade, Mac gave a multilayered lesbian salute to Viva DeConcini. Taylor had been letting one musician from the band go after each decade so that judy would be left alone for the final one, and this was the send-off for the show's lead guitarist. To original music composed especially for this show, Taylor sang the poem "I want a president" by Zoe Leonard, artist and founder of the 1990s lesbian activist group Fierce Pussy. The poem begins with the lyric "I want a dyke for president," which prompted cheers for the departing musician while "Viva for President!" stickers were passed around the room. Along with dykes, the poem demands empowerment for others who are intersectionally oppressed—from the person with AIDS and the pregnant teen who cannot access medical care; to those who have been sexually harassed, gaybashed, and deported; to the black resident who had a cross burned in their yard. Leonard had originally written the poem in tribute to iconic lesbian poet Eileen Myles's self-described "openly female" run for the presidency against Bill Clinton in 1992. When the poem resurged as a rallying cry in 2016 for more representational leadership, Leonard expressed concern that it would be taken as a call for a third-party candidate; she flatly declared "It's not. 'I'm with Her!'" invoking the Hillary Clinton campaign slogan.[8] HRC was now the candidate best poised to advance the cause of those named in the poem. Likewise, Myles endorsed Hillary and defended her candidacy in a passionately incisive *BuzzFeed* essay that concluded with insistent genital specificity:

> I actually trust a person who can change their tune. I trust her. I don't think Hillary has horns though she does have a vagina and wouldn't you want it sitting on the chair in the Oval Office (not to get all weird) because things will *never* be the same. She will see something no woman in America has ever seen before and then all of us will see it. She's like our astronaut. That's what I want that at the end of this world or the end of this race the end of this joke: America. It's why I ran (against her husband) in 1992. I wanted *my* vagina on that chair. Now I want Hillary's there.[9]

Myles also aspired to be the poet chosen to read an original poem at Hillary Clinton's inauguration. Taylor singing the Myles-inspired Leonard poem and all of us cheering "Viva for President!" at St. Ann's on October 9, 2016, channeled this lineage of dyke passion, poetry, and pussy power into support of HRC.

After Viva's rousing send-off, the Lesbian Decade wittily began with a delivery of boxes to be unpacked. Heralding the magnitude of loss from the disease, judy had let go of an especially precious collaborator at the top of the AIDS Decade (1986–1996), the costume artist who had so brilliantly dressed judy, mostly *a vista*, in a new creation for each decade. Barely an hour since we had bid him good-bye it was announced that a UPS order had arrived . . . from Machine! This clever ruse did much more than elicit a peal of delighted recognition and solve the practical problem of delivering the next costume to Taylor.

A hunky bull dyke, played by trans performer Becca Blackwell, wheeled a red hand truck stacked with several colorful boxes up onto the stage as Taylor, still wearing part of judy's one-legged, patchwork AIDS-quilt-inspired costume, signed the clipboard to receive the order. Blackwell's burly male demeanor and lace-up work boots evoked the hand-truck-wielding butch delivery woman of *Fun Home* fame who sparked young Alison's self-recognition, a reference made sweeter by Lisa Kron's presence in our St. Ann's audience.[10] Here this figure galvanized a more complex configuration of lesbian, queer, and allied identifications. Rather than a plaid shirt and jeans or overalls, Blackwell sported a vintage UPS chocolate-brown khaki delivery uniform, complete with logos and cap, on loan from a fetishist's collection, which injected different desires into the mix.[11]

Delivery accomplished, the male-passing Blackwell joined a group of dykes who appeared with lawn chairs, beer and soda cans, and a grill to set the scene of a Lesbian Tailgate at the Michigan Womyn's Music Festival (aka Michfest), this decade's example of a community that was building itself up more inclusively as it was being torn apart. Representing a diverse range of ethnicities and butch/femme personas, these Tailgaters, arrayed in a semicircle that opened onto the stage and into the audience, were played by out lesbian performers and writers known in Mac's New York performance scene, namely Madison Krekel, Mariel Reyes, Erin Markey, Pamela Sneed, Tanisha Thompson, and Drae Campbell.[12] While Michfest famously excluded men over its forty-year history (1976–2015) and was riven by arguments over transgender admissibility that contributed to its closure, its performance re-enactment expanded to embrace not only Mac as lead singer and all the male and trans members of the ensemble, but, in effect, the entire St. Ann's assemblage as Tailgaters. We were all invited into this Mich-mosh animated by music and drag choices that reveled in gender and sexual inversions and quite literally as well as thematically unfolded pussy-centered histories of pleasure and trauma.

The first box yielded the aforementioned sheer nude body stocking into which Taylor changed as the base layer for the set. The black graffiti lettering over judy's "nude" body followed the tradition of feminist punk bands of the late 1980s and early '90s, such as Bikini Kill, whose lead singer Kathleen Hanna famously performed in a lingerie-type bra with "SLUT" scrawled over her bare belly as an angry riposte to her violent, gun-toting alcoholic father and, more generally, to the demeaning male gaze and abusive male touch.[13] In queer sisterhood with Hanna, Taylor and Machine appropriated the convention to the complementary purpose of feminizing the male body and mooting a frontal riposte to judy's own gun-toting, alcoholic father, Lt. Robert Mac Bowyer, and his ilk.

These personal counter-patriarchal dynamics carry forward into the *24-Decade History* from the profile Taylor offers of Robert "Bob" Mac Bowyer in judy's earlier autobiographical play *The Young Ladies of . . .* (2007). Because Bob Bowyer died in a motorcycle accident when his son Taylor Mac Bowyer was just four years old, judy must reassemble his life through revealing bits of remaining knowledge, most tellingly: his father's favorite musical, *Carousel*, featuring the wife beater Billy Bigelow, whose song "Soliloquy" frames *The Young Ladies Of . . .* (and later forms a gut-wrenching centerpiece for Taylor in the *24-Decade History*'s World War II decade); boxes of letters Bob received from scores of young women in response to a singles ad he placed in a newspaper during his Vietnam service; and rites of manhood in the Bowyers' "tough Texan, conservative, macho, military, farm family." Along with profligate pursuit of female pussy, Bowyer rites of manhood inculcate effeminophobia, or extreme aversion to effeminate tendencies, in boy children.[14] This involves dressing the boys in baby-doll female garb and giving them girlie gifts at birthdays to pussify and shame them. The boys are then "baptized" in jeering laughter before receiving properly male toys to "remasculinize" them, a process Taylor memorializes with a projected photograph of Dad "smiling with a handgun," the "real" man's coveted personal bulwark against turning pussy. Ongoing remasculinizing rituals for the Bowyer men include "faggot-bashing stampedes" and abuse and denigration of women. Male relatives traditionally hire a female prostitute for each Bowyer boy on his sixteenth birthday for an initiation that instills quick selfish satisfaction and forecloses learning how to pleasure a woman. After the birthday boy has his turn, the male relatives, in ascending order of age, then partake of her pussy themselves, probably in that same quick, selfish, uncaring Bowyer male way. Because Taylor coincidentally was born sixteen years to the day after Bob's younger brother, judy deduces that judy's father was in line to grab some of that pussy when judy's mother was laboring to bring judy into the world.[15] Flagrantly still clad as an adult in the type of dress preschooler judy would have worn for effeminacy aversion therapy, which obviously did not take, Taylor wittily sets judy's own life and oeuvre in contradistinction to this family legacy.

If this early play pulls Mac's effeminophobic, misogynistic patrilineage into devastatingly clear focus while asserting judy's commitment to spectacular artistic and personal refutation of this heritage, *A 24-Decade History* at once hugely magnifies that commitment and reveals occasional pitfalls in the refutation. Along with racism and xenophobia, misogyny and effeminophobia are so ingrained in USAmerican social history and so insidiously internalized across the population that their dynamics can be felt even amid resistant and corrective cultural expressions, including within queer as well as straight cultures. Mac does not claim immunity to this; as a Bedazzled Shaman, Taylor embraces imperfection and failure, which are fundamental both to the genre of popular music and to what judy calls "the genius of performance art." At St. Ann's, the shaman took ownership of self-complicity in oppression even as judy led us in the radical faerie realness ritual to overcome it. Accordingly, when judy related certain anecdotes about women's anatomy and sexual practices for laughs as a privileged white gay man, such as the one about women fisting each other in the Speakeasy Decade, the effects were double-edged. An even more striking example came in the Backroom Sex Party Decade (1976–86), when Mac told of watching a woman pull chicken bones out of her vagina followed by a whole chicken, which she then proceeded to eat, after which judy had two thoughts: "One, she has no boundaries, and two, she must be really full." Taylor disruptively lobbed a graphic tale of outsized female genital capacity and appetites into a backroom sex scene associated with gay male desires. But such anecdotes, recounted with a drag-artist's campy wit, also vacillated across the line between skewering and pandering to vaginophobic gay male as well as heteronormative bourgeois obsessions with vaginal sanitation and fears of female hunger. My own nervous laughter bubbled up from the repressed residue of girlhood conditioning to plug up the Curse, douche, shave, and Nair the snatch. Yet the saving—and amazing—grace of judy's multiplicitous openness to others' experience grew in performance to embody and love the dreaded pussy, ultimately without cutting irony, to extravagantly lesbian levels.[16]

Hence the power of the base layer of the Lesbian Decade costume on which maternal and sororal pussy are reclaimed and honored with graffiti inscribed on a Bowyer male body. Along with the words MOTHER, SISTER, GODDESS scrawled in black graffiti down judy's limbs, the word HERSTORY ran across the tops of judy's thighs and groin. The letters R and

S were incorporated into a black heart-shaped female pubic triangle hand-drawn over judy's visibly untucked maleness in a tenderly hermaphroditic genital juxtaposition. Rather than slashing punk anger, although some of that would certainly erupt later in the set, something childlike and naïve emerged in the lettering and overall mien of the bald-headed, extremely drained but somehow still performing Taylor in this nude onesie without the full armor of drag. Judy was embodying a herstory in which the vulnerability of the effeminate boy-man, scourge of Bowyer heritage, merged with that of the masculine or feminine girl-woman and trans person in a violent, straight masculinist society where the pussy-grabbing propensities of a major presidential candidate had just been undeniably revealed.

From that place of intersectional vulnerability, Taylor defiantly opened the set, strumming a ukulele, with the feminist/lesbian anthem "Pussy Manifesto" (1999) by the white queercore duo Bitch and Animal. If dominant society would shame, silence, and sanitize the pussy, Bitch and Animal want her manifest in all her hairy juicy splendor and life-giving power, from the biological and spiritual to the political. The verb in "Manifesto" keys the song's structure as a series of in-your-face commands, e.g., "Manifest this motha fucka #1," 2, 3, etc. Given recent news, the upcoming election, and the pussy-inclusive address of the performance, certain lyrics resounded with a particularly satisfying punch, from "Manifest this Muthafucka #3: I'm sick of my genitalia being used as an insult. Are you? It's time to let my labia rip and rearrange this," to "Manifest this Motherfuckrr #6: Employ the Pussy! [as] *teacher / *whore / *philosopher / *president / Pay her well!" to "Manifest this Mothafucker #8: Let Pussy manifest and let freedom sing!"[17]

Taylor then let judy's pussy manifest freely in a graphic anecdote about a personal sexual encounter. This followed judy's earlier sharing, in the Back Room Sex Party Decade (1976–1986), of a penchant for anonymous sex and the deep gratification and intimacy one can feel through the act of pleasuring a fellow human being, even a stranger, with a truly excellent blowjob. The Lesbian Decade anecdote involved an encounter with an African American man in a van in Provincetown that ended with judy yelling "This pussy is gonna change your life!" That assertion of pussy power led into Taylor's rendition of the languorous lesbian R&B funk song "Barry Farms" from Meshell Ndegeocello's 2002 album, *Cookie: The Anthropological Mix Tape*, about which Arion Berger wrote in *Rolling Stone*, "Iconoclastic soul sister Meshell Ndegeocello once again laser-focuses on putting forward her agenda: that only revolution will save the black soul, not to mention black music. *Cookie*'s uprising takes place in the bedroom, the streets and the studio, and Ndegeocello's supreme control over the tone and texture of her sinewy vibe is the sound of a woman in charge of her body and mind."[18] The song's title refers to the neighborhood in Washington, DC, where Ndegeocello (née Michelle Lynn Johnson) grew up and where she sets her black soul-saving bedroom revolution in the form of an on-again-off-again love affair with the young woman, "Shorty," at the center of the song's narrative. The lyrics address "All the shorties in the room" with the seductively repeated proffer "Let me wind ya up" before telling of the desire the singer awakened in Shorty, the resulting shame Shorty felt around her friends, and Shorty's culturally induced preference for a boyfriend who "liked to take her out and buy her things." By chance Shorty runs into the lesbian lover/singer again and can't help telling her she misses her because "can't nobody eat my pussy the way you do." But the lesbian lover/singer knows Shorty can't love her without shame and only wants her for that one thing, and so tells her "You should teach your boy to do that" (an education lost on Bowyer men until Taylor's queer mastery of the art) and moves on, concluding: "When I play, I watch the crowd. / I watch the women, women party / Chain reaction" The tone is wistful, but the ambiguity of the last two words, which are printed in the lyrics without final punctuation, is suggestive: a chain reaction of what—of the injunction to conform, or of unfulfilled desire roiling change?[19] Singing this song, Taylor reached across gender and ethnicity not only to honor often invisible or sidelined lesbian experience but to further Ndegeocello's "bedroom revolution" by percolating that force of historical change into the present through judy's own desiring, dexterously pussified performing body.

The revolution exploded into the electric-guitar and drum-powered punk energy of "Butch in the Streets/Femme in the Sheets" from the Tribe 8 album, *Fist City* (1995), in tribute to the raging '90s riot grrrl band that took its name from "tribade," an antiquated term for lesbian. Distinguishing themselves from the overwhelmingly white world of punk rock, Tribe 8 featured a multiethnic membership, including African Canadian bassist Lynn Payne and Asian American guitarist Leslie Mah, as well as Euro-American drummer Slade Bellam, guitarist Lynn Flipper, and lead singer Lynne Breedlove. Their legendary first appearance at Michfest in 1994 shook up the usual scene of folk music and *Our Bodies, Ourselves* values with fighting words and style: "We are San Francisco's own all-dyke, all-out, in-your-face, blade-brandishing, gang-castrating, dildo-swingin', bull-shit detecting, aurally pornographic, Neanderthal-pervert band of patriarchy-smashing snatchlickers."[20] Although organizers had invited the band to participate, many attendees protested, fearing that Tribe 8 fostered violence toward women because they practiced s/m. But controversy abated through workshops and conversation once protesters understood that Tribe 8 quoted male abuses in their performances purposefully to call them out, deconstruct their power dynamics through gender inversion, cathect anger and aggression, and resist.[21] Band members had personally suffered queer bashing, incest, and rape, including gang rape in Breedlove's case, so their rage was visceral, but not without irony and humor. As Flipper noted, paraphrasing Gloria Steinem, "Women's worst fear is rape, men's is being laughed at, so I try to laugh at them as much as possible."[22] Satirically mocking the phallic prerogatives of male rockers, Tribe 8 members stripped off their shirts and performed bare-breasted. Breedlove famously performed in boxer shorts with a long rubber dick that she would pull through the fly, stroke, and summon an audience member, preferably a straight man when at more mixed venues, to suck on bended knees.

Whereas Breedlove tended toward the extreme masculine in her butch persona, and Mac tended toward the extreme feminine in much of judy's drag, Taylor's costume for the Tribe 8 number constituted a criss-crossing of the two on the sex/gender spectrum. Taylor unpacked from the UPS boxes and pulled on over the graffitied nude body suit a pair of cutoff women's denim short-shorts hung with biker/punk wallet chains. Judy's feet slipped into a pair of what Machine described as "cherry-flavored combat boots," black Doc Marten–type boots dolloped with pink sparkly paint (fig. 14). Like Breedlove, Mac remained "naked" on top, although still male flat-chested. Rather than extruding a material penis, Mac brought out some sensational narrative dick by reading aloud a friend's first-hand account of the infamous Michfest moment when Breedlove severed and speared her rubber dildo with a hunting knife, held it triumphantly aloft, and flung it from knife point into the moshing audience.[23] This gender criss-crossing of Mac's costume and invocation of Breedlove's performance highlighted the butch/femme inversions of the chosen Tribe 8 song about tropes of topping and bottoming that play across queer identities and sexual practices: "She's a walking paradox in her jeans and her docs, / sporting big ugly tattoos, / She goes home throws her legs in the air, / Hoping no-one's heard the news. . . . / She wants to get plowed like everyone else . . ."[24] The tough, crew-cut, steel-toed butch and the effeminate Mac merged in this performance of pussy desires, while the castrating revenge fantasy gained power amid fresh outrage over the Access Hollywood tape in the woozy wee hours of that October weekend.

Engendering Empathy

Mac's butch/femme inversions ramified in the ensuing medley of k. d. lang's "Miss Chatelaine" (*Ingenue*, 1992) and Courtney Love's "Doll Parts" (*Live Through This*, 1994). If drag queens have been accused of reinscribing conventional feminine ideals, Mac combined two songs from the large oeuvres of these two popular artists that variously deconstruct those conventions and tap into nonconforming women's angst under gender tyranny. Named for the Canadian women's magazine *Chatelaine*, whose cover lang graced in 1988, the song begins: "Just a kiss just a kiss / I have lived just for this / I can't explain why I've become Miss Chatelaine . . ." For many lesbians of age at the time, the song is inseparable from lang's unforgettable performance of it, now memorialized on YouTube, on the *Arsenio Hall Show* as part of her promo tour for the *Ingenue* album in January 1993. She appeared in high femme drag, sporting a voluminous yellow chiffon gown, matching heels, full makeup, long painted nails, and a glamorous up-do, and swooned around the stage amid the sparkle of soap bubbles, à la the Lawrence Welk Show. Stunned at the butch lang's transformation, Arsenio exclaimed, "Is that k.d.?!" Gathering his wits as they settled onto the couch for conversation, he noted, "You look good; you've given up cleavage and everything tonight," to which lang sharply retorted, "I have so much gaffer tape under here!" She chose that costume "because there's a little bit of Doris Day in each and every one of us, especially when it comes to love." She said this mostly tongue-in-cheek, with a nod to the wishful queer subtext of Day's hit song "Secret Love" from *Calamity Jane*, but her performance nonetheless engaged the excruciating dominant cultural injunction that women need to embody the prevailing 1950s Doris Day ideal in order to be loved.

Without lang's veneer of campy humor, straight but queer-allied Courtney Love goes right for the pain of degrading objectification in "Doll Parts." Her critique aligns with riot grrrl feminist protests against Barbie Doll culture with hard-hitting lyrics such as "I am / Doll eyes / Doll mouth / Doll legs / I am / Doll arms / Big veins / Dog beg . . ."[25] In contrast to lang's artificially bubbly yellow chiffon waltzes as Miss Chatelaine, Love moves lethargically in a red baby-doll lingerie slip, singing in a seemingly drugged-out monotone in a junkie's bedroom with a bare mattress. But for both singers, as for so many other women, aspiring to an impossible ideal necessitates fakery and propitiates feelings of pain and emptiness. "I fake it so real I am beyond fake," sings Love, backed by her trenchantly named group Hole. Hopelessly seeking reciprocal affection and validation of her own personhood, she repeats the heart-wrenching refrain "Someday you will ache like I ache" thirteen times.

For Mac's performance of these two women's songs, judy and Machine manipulated the flagrant fakery of male drag artistry to connect with women's culturally induced artifice and longing even while provoking laughter. Judy unpacked from the boxes the next layer of costume accoutrements: a set of nude women's breasts and a wig made of neon green, pink, and yellow nylon mesh elastic tube cord (fig. 14). Inspired by Bitch's colorful kitsch prop designs for her "Pussy Manifesto" video, the wig also evoked Courtney Love's shaggy, bleached-blond, bed-tousled grunge do. The breasts, far from cheap drag stuffing or stack-ons, were high-end ($400) silicone prosthetics in a fulsome but proportionate cup size made for cis-women to wear after radical mastectomies, or for transwomen. Machine explained that he was going for a more realistic aspect of women's bodies amid the more fantastical artifice of other parts of the costume. Close examination in the exhibit affirmed that these breasts not only look fairly real, but their weight and softness to the touch are also quite life-like. That softness, coupled with the rawness of Taylor's voice in hour 23, added a layer of vulnerability to judy's humorous self-reflexivity when, in this whimsical femme/butch ensemble, judy sang with pointed inflection, "I don't know why I've become Miss Chatelaine." Laughter erupted more raucously when judy's wig fell off during the medley. But its absence also left Taylor bald and sad-clownish again, a mien made oddly more poignant by the softly feminine breasts.

From the mixed tone and ironic critique of the lang/Love medley, the set segued into folk-music community-building, as Anais Mitchell joined Taylor on stage to lead vocals and guitar in a collaborative rendition of Ferron's classic lesbian ballad "Girl on a Road" (*Impressionistic*, 1994). This was Mitchell's first appearance center stage in the marathon, but she had stayed up for the entire twenty-three hours in order to harmonize fully with Taylor and all of us assembled for this song, the longest of this decade's list and one of the longest of the whole 246-song concert. Though not lesbian-identified, Mitchell has long credited Ferron as a major inspiration for her own music, and this proved a quintessential moment to honor and pass on that influence.[26]

For this joint number, Taylor added to judy's sartorial ensemble a long,

Fig. 15. Mac wearing the prosthetic breasts, Macy Gray–esque vest, and butterfly wings on top of the nude onesie and denim cutoffs during the Lesbian
Decade at St. Ann's Warehouse, October 9, 2016. Photo: Lisa Freeman.

gray/black shaggy vest unpacked from Machine's boxes. During our interview, Machine showed me how he had made the vest with latch-hooked
strips of cloth ripped from old plaid cotton flannel shirts associated with
butch style. In this clever fashion appropriation, a stereotype of the lesbian
community was literally torn apart and rebuilt to create what Machine
described as a "grungy, big, rock 'n' roll, Macy Gray–esque" sleeveless fur
coat (visible on the rear mannequin in fig. 14 and on Taylor in fig. 15).
Machine's lovingly making it and Taylor's wearing it became forms of
materially honoring and opening lesbian culture to others, gestures that
Mitchell's female presence and voice powerfully amplified.

Long a staple at Michfest, Ferron's music delves into some of the most
buried and complex legacies of women's and lesbian experience with
extraordinarily rich and illuminating poetry, likened to that of her Canadian compatriot Leonard Cohen. This autobiographical song tells of a
girl's runaway journey from a sexually abusive upbringing; another rape

Fig. 16. Rear view of Mac in the butterfly wings during the Lesbian Decade at St. Ann's Warehouse, October 9, 2016. Photo: Lisa Freeman.

in a highway truck stop "by a man they all called Tiger boy . . . who just had to show me why"; the withering damage of this history to subsequent intimate relationships—"Does this terror know no end?"; and sustenance through writing music and moving on "as a girl on a road." The act of singing the ballad through its many verses performs that sustenance, especially with its invitations to others to join in its poetic refrain. The bleary-eyed St. Ann's crowd of 650 lent their voices, many humming and groping to learn the words for the first time:

> . . . Rain upon the water
> makes footprints sunk in sand. Anger upon angry
> hurt, take me by the hand. Take me by the heartstrings
> and pull me deep inside and say I'm one with your
> forgiveness and separate from my pride.

In effect, Mac and Mitchell's cover of the song answered Ferron's refrain, engendering empathy across straight-queer lines by pulling her resonant lesbian experience deep inside and inciting the rest of us to do the same. This personal-is-political kumbaya conjoined sufferers in the audience with those around them in sympathetic recognition both of sexual abuse itself and of societal complicity in perpetuating it. With awareness of the coming end of our uniquely shared marathon encroaching, the sing-along offered a balm against the glaring outer world of pussy-grabbing politics.

Butterfly Effects

After the final chords and hums of this folk interlude faded, Mitchell invited all the female musicians from earlier in the show back onto the stage for the riot grrrl–inspired indie rock band Sleater-Kinney's "One Beat" (*One Beat*, 2002). During the set-up, Taylor added the pièce-de-résistance layer to the Lesbian Decade costume: a set of giant pink butterfly wings (figs. 14 and 15), which outlandishly realized a metaphor used powerfully by both Ferron and Sleater-Kinney. In the retrospective *Thunder: A Film About Ferron* (2013), with "A Girl on a Road" playing on the soundtrack, the singer comments that "being plowed every night" by her stepfather indeed "was horrible, and it was also . . . the moth that turns into the butterfly" of her music.[27] That transformation of sexual repression, pain, and internalized ugliness into artistic expression encapsulated specifically in the butterfly image links lesbian Ferron to a queer lineage going at least as far back as Baudelaire, the Decadents, and the drawings of Aubrey Beardsley and extending through generations of modern visual and drag artists down to Mac and Machine. A monarch butterfly had keyed Machine's design for the Underground Railroad Decade (1836–46) "about change via time, direction, and migration," and rising desire for social transformation impelled this decade's butterfly as well.[28]

Specifically, the wings materialized the "One Beat" lyric "Take me to the source of chaos let me be the butterfly" and references to the "butterfly effect" (coined in 1987) wherein small movements can catalyze huge changes. "Does the Flap of a Butterfly's Wings in Brazil Set off a Tornado in Texas?" asked famed meteorologist and chaos theorist Edward Lorenz.[29] "One Beat" affirmatively applies that power to cultural acts, no matter how small or underrecognized. In spite of longevity and critical plaudits, Sleater-Kinney have never broken through the world of rock with a top hit. Comprised of singer-guitarists Carrie Brownstein and Corinne Tucker and drummer-singer Janet Weiss, and named after the street corner in Olympia, Washington, where they originally rehearsed in the mid-1990s, they have been heralded by music critics as among the best of indie rock bands. Greil Marcus even proclaimed them the best American rock band, period, in 2006. However, their feminist/queer politics, critical engagement with divisive social issues and world events, and the visceral physicality and aggressive style of their all-women-made music have kept them marginalized. Mac and ensemble's cover of the song magnified Sleater-Kinney's commitment to the Butterfly Effect, along with the queer butterfly genealogy of transforming sexual oppression and abuse into glorious art.

With the scale and physical, functional power of the butterfly costume in the performance of "One Beat," Taylor also enacted judy's own vision of using the past in the present to affect the future. As Mac articulated during the long development of *A 24-Decade History of Popular Music*,

> One of the things I like to do in these concerts is honor [the song] by actually singing what it is and trying to figure out why did the people really sing this song and then why did they actually try to sing it this way and care about it and honor those choices. And then to deconstruct them all and say, 'Well okay, how is this applying to our lives now?' and then find a new way of doing it that helps us kind of dream the culture forward. So, we honor the past by acknowledging it, we honor the present by acknowledging it, and then we take all that information and we dream the culture forward with it.[30]

Through Taylor and Machine's particular incarnation of the butterfly, the performance of "One Beat" materialized a wildly explicit dream of pussy power and physically beat it forward. As Machine explained in our interview, the original inspiration for the wing design came from the angel wings used on models in Victoria's Secret fashion shows, but he radically deconstructed that straight latter-day Ziegfeldian commodification of cis-female glamor and pulchritude. Instead of an airy feathery expanse, he fabricated a thick, solid pair of wings, each with a larger upper and smaller lower elongated guitar-shaped lobe pointing diagonally away from the spine. The wings spanned roughly six feet across from upper tip to upper tip, and four vertical feet from upper to lower tip on each side. The back of the wings was cut out of hefty poster board and painted hot pink. Each lobe was inscribed with a large female gender symbol in heavy black paint with the circle near the spine and the cross extending out to the tip. Affixed to the front sides of each lobe were deep, luxurious folds of satiny pink rimmed with lavender fabric with a softball-sized metallic magenta ball nestled near the tip. Taylor appeared to be enfolded in four enormous vulvas, each complete with clitoris and labia minora and majora. Amid that framing, the long, shaggy black vest read proudly like the dark pubic hair Victoria's Secret models would have to remove (fig. 15).

Moreover, this entire ensemble appeared not only explicitly genital but "turned on"—literally with strings of tiny lights nestled in the folds of glistening fabric, and figuratively by invoking another famous butterfly effect, that of the Venus Butterfly. This sexual arousal technique combining cunnilingus and fingering went mainstream on network TV dramas such as *LA Law* (1986) and *Rescue Me* (2005), which scripted it between heterosexual partners, but of course lesbians had been enjoying it for eons. If the Venus Butterfly famously centers pleasure in the female pussy, Machine's costume on Taylor's body enfolded other queer practices. On the back side, the four female gender symbols converged on a large, loose round rim of yet deeper folds of satiny lavender fabric, with irregularly bulbous clusters of magenta and lace fabric extruding from the center like hemorrhoidal tissue out of a prolapsed anus (fig. 16). From front to back, female to male, Machine made ravishingly graphic art out of otherwise culturally denigrated pussies.

With this massive construction strapped onto judy's body like a backpack, Taylor was able to stomp and bob with all the force the hardrock rhythm of "One Beat" inspires and let the wings flap mightily amid a stage filled with musicians and the dancing dykes assembled for the Michfest Tailgate. The rhythm and dancing took Taylor far down stage right, so that by the time judy sang the lyric about "oscillating energy on high," our Bedazzled Shaman was literally towering over where I and my partner were seated in the front row beating all that awesome pussy power right at us. Thus embodied, the song's "sonic push for energy" created palpable, material impetus for dreaming the culture forward.

At song's end, with the stirred-up waves of energy still circulating in the room, Taylor beckoned Sarah Schulman to the stage to read her Lesbian Avenger's "Dyke Manifesto," a clamorous call to action from the Dyke March on the eve of the 1993 March on Washington to combat lesbian invisibility in the gay rights movement as well as the larger society: "Wake up! Wake up! Wake up! It's time to get out of the beds, out of the bars, and into the streets. Time to seize the power of dyke love, dyke vision, dyke anger, dyke intelligence, dyke strategy. Time to organize and ignite, time to get together and fight . . .".[31] Dozens of purple balloons inscribed with "Ask About Lesbian Lives," like those the Lesbian Avengers had created, were released into the room, and we batted them around overhead before all but one disappeared as souvenirs. After Schulman finished, the remaining one hovered oddly still in midair high overhead, pulling focus from Taylor, who addressed it with feigned annoyance. That balloon's disruptive suspension magically would not let the question drop, furthering Schulman's call to action.

The intersectionality of oppressions resounded in the title and refrain of the last song of the marathon's Lesbian Decade, Lauryn Hill's "Everything Is Everything" (1998).[32] Having shed the massive butterfly backpack, Macy Gray–esque vest, and breasts during the Schulman reading, Taylor did this song with only the cutoff denim shorts over the "nude" graffitied onesie that left judy more vulnerably androgynous. The song's soft tone fit its message about the cyclical slowness of progress:

> After winter, must come spring
> Change, it comes eventually
> Sometimes it seems
> We'll touch that dream
> But things come slow or not at all
> And the ones on top, won't make it stop
> So convinced that they might fall
> Let's love ourselves and we can't fail
> To make a better situation
> Tomorrow, our seeds will grow
> All we need is dedication[33]

These words of the song set up Taylor's moving embrace with music director Matt Ray, the last and most vital collaborator to whom judy bid goodbye in the show. Certainly the two had shown superhuman dedication in arranging and performing this marathon creative intervention, which nurtured seeds of change that many of us, in October 2016, felt were in the offing. Thus our hazy sense of awe and hope witnessing the spectacular rebirth cum coup de théâtre into the twenty-fourth decade: alone in the spotlight, Taylor reached for the giant rolled fabric womb that had been pre-hung from the ceiling and encompassed the whole room with long white streamers draping outward, tentlike, from its pseudo–cervical ring. As this ring descended, Mac's arms extended upward through the center, stopped it at waist level, hooked it over the belted cutoffs, and unfurled rolls of shimmering red fabric that ingeniously became judy's final gown topped by a golden sunburst headdress. In the exhibit, Machine captioned Costume 24 "The Future Is Female," or, as he put it to me in person, "Time for the Pussy."[34]

Of course, in Hill's prescient and ever-more-resonant verses, the cautionary notes about "the ones on top" not stopping oppression for fear of falling prevailed. Although a sea of pink pussy hats at women's marches in DC and around the nation and the world on January 21, 2017, dwarfed Trump's inauguration crowds, the president's power in office enabled an onslaught of sexist, racist, and homo/transphobic rhetoric and policies— from inhumane restrictions on nonwhite immigrants and rollbacks of transgender rights, to blockage of common-sense gun policies in the face of epidemic mass shootings, to misogynistic epithets against "nasty" women challengers and gender-straightening style dictates that women who work for the administration "dress like women."[35] Trump's obsession with undoing his predecessor's legacy enacted white-supremacist male grievance against the equal rights of racial and sexual others. Rush Limbaugh, king of right-wing talk radio, to whom Trump awarded the Presidential Medal of Freedom during his 2020 State of the Union speech, repeatedly voiced that grievance in explicit terms of sexual domination. About courting black and gay voters, Limbaugh disdainfully queried: "Democrats will bend over, grab the ankles, and say, 'Have your way with me,' for 10 percent and 2 percent of the population?" Whether decrying the Hillary Clinton–led health-care reform initiative in the 1990s or the Obamacare mandate in 2010, Limbaugh intoned: "Bend over, America."[36] Such a pussyphobic alarm rang loud for patriarchal white corporate capitalists and Texas Mac Bowyer types alike. Now Covid-wary mask wearers in red-state America must brace for the epithet "liberal pussy."[37]

Thus, if I experienced Taylor as Bedazzled Shaman and orchestrator of communal transformation during the October 2016 marathon, I have come to appreciate judy even more as Radical Fool in the time since, a Joker who incarnated the dominant culture's worst nightmare of the pussified white male, a phobia lurking even in supposedly friendly quarters. When Hillary Clinton made her first postelection appearance on the *Late Show* as part of her 2017 *What Happened* book tour, Stephen Colbert

Fig. 17. Still shot of what Stephen Colbert showed to Hillary Clinton and then the camera on the *Late Show*, September 19, 2017, of an act his staff had prepared for election night 2016 had she won. Laura Bradley, "Colbert's Gift to Clinton: Naked-Man Butts Branded with 'I'm with Her,'" *Vanity Fair*, September 20, 2017. https://www.vanityfair.com/hollywood/2017/09/clinton-what-happened-election-colbert-late-show-naked-men

startled her with a picture of an act his staff had prepared to air on election night had she won: a line of five naked men standing with backsides to the camera, butts emblazoned one character per cheek with the "I'm with Her!" slogan, ready to bend over now that "the Femitariat was taking over"[38] (fig. 17). As long as taking it up the ass remains the prevailing interpretive paradigm for ceding power to a feminized Other, the prospect of full gender and racial equality remains distant, and the market for guns—the more lethal the better—as personal bulwarks against pussification more insatiable than ever.

Notes

1. The San Francisco Curran Theatre, January 4, 2016, so named Taylor Mac in its promotional video for the first six decades of *A 24-Decade History of Popular Music*. https://www.youtube.com/watch?v=wgind5eAjwQ

2. Derived from black feminist theory, intersectional politics seek to overcome interlocking oppressions based on categorizations such as race, ethnicity, class, gender, and sexual orientation under straight white patriarchal capitalist dominance for the achievement of social equality. See, for example, Disch, Lisa, Mary Hawkesworth, and Brittney Cooper, "Intersectionality," in *The Oxford Handbook of Feminist Theory* (Oxford: Oxford University Press), accessed 8 May 2022. https://www-oxfordhandbooks -com.proxy.lib.uiowa.edu/view/10.1093/oxfordhb/9780199328581.001.0001/oxfordhb -9780199328581-e-20

3. Because this decade's performance occurred in the twenty-third hour of sleeplessness, and personal memories have grown hazy, a number of sources have proven especially valuable in reconstructing and analyzing what happened. Some excellent reviews published in the weeks and months immediately after the event, of course, offered useful overviews and perspectives (e.g., David Román et al., "Subjective Histories of Taylor Mac's 'Radical Faerie Realness Ritual' History," *Theatre Journal* 69, no. 3 [2017]: 403–15; Erick Neher, "The Brooklyn Marathon: Taylor Mac's *A 24-Decade History of Popular Music*," *Hudson Review* 69, no. 4 [2017]: 631–42, 700; Suzy Evans, "A Trip Around the Sun with Taylor Mac's '24-Decade History,'" *American Theatre Magazine*, accessed October 14, 2016. www.americantheatre.org). But to zoom in on this particular decade with requisite specificity, I have supplemented my own record-keeping with conversations, time-stamped blogs, photographs, video snippets, and notes generously lent by colleagues who likewise attended the marathon, especially Meredith Alexander, Jennifer Buckley, Lisa Freeman, Andrew Goldberg, Jennifer Parker-Starbuck, and Kalle Westerling. Very fortuitously, my home institution, the University of Iowa, which had commissioned the Whitman Decade in 2015, invited Taylor Mac back in April 2018 to do the abridged version of the *24-Decade History*. For the week leading up to that performance, all twenty-four of the original costumes for the full marathon were on exhibit in our spacious and beautifully lit new performing arts center (Hancher Auditorium), and Machine Dazzle himself was in residence to give workshops and lead community arts events. Willa Fomar, production assistant for Pomegranate Arts, producer of the *24-Decade History*, accompanied him and helped arrange for me to formally interview him, which I did for nearly two hours in the exhibit, where he invited me to handle and talk about the costumes at intimate range. Willa herself answered a number of my questions informally, especially with respect to clarifying the Lesbian Decade song list that was used for the October 8–9, 2016, performance in St. Ann's Warehouse, because the set has varied slightly over different performances. I am most grateful to Machine and Willa for their generosity.

4. Román, *Subjective Histories*, 404.

5. For more on the development of Mac's "genderfuck" aesthetic through judy's earlier career, see Sean F. Edgecomb, *Charles Ludlam Lives! Charles Busch, Bradford Louryk, Taylor Mac, and the Queer Legacy of the Ridiculous Theatrical Company* (Ann Arbor: University of Michigan Press, 2017), especially 8–9, 141–42.

6. Author's interview with Machine Dazzle, Iowa City, Iowa, April 25, 2018. David Román, email correspondence with author, 7/14/2020.

7. Description from "Notes by Machine Dazzle" accompanying the exhibit "Costumes from Taylor Mac's *A 24-Decade History of Popular Music* Designed by Machine Dazzle," Hancher Auditorium, University of Iowa, Iowa City, Iowa, April 24–28, 2018.

8. "Zoe Leonard responds to and reads her text 'I want a president' (1992) on November 6, 2016." http://bit.ly/ZoeLeonardResponses. Accessed 8/8/2020.

9. Eileen Miles, "Hillary Clinton: The Leader You Want at the End of the World," *BuzzFeed* (February 23, 2016), accessed 8/8/2020.

10. See Alison Bechdel, *Fun Home: A Family Tragicomic* (Boston: Houghton Mifflin, 2006), 117–19. Lisa Kron wrote the book and lyrics for the Pulitzer-nominated and Tony-winning musical version of *Fun Home* that premiered on Broadway on April 19, 2015. Young Alison's sighting of the butch delivery woman occasions the song of lesbian self-recognition "Ring of Keys."

11. In the San Francisco production of *A 24-Decade History of Popular Music*, which was done as four six-hour "Chapters" on separate dates in September 2017, Marga Gomez did a dual cameo as the butch delivery woman and the reader of the Lesbian Manifesto; in the LA production (March 2018, also in four Chapters), Margaret Cho did the dual cameo. Author's interview with Machine Dazzle, Iowa City, Iowa, April 25, 2018.

12. These were credited as "Tailgaters" in an "Additional Credits" insert in the program for the show, "St. Ann's Warehouse and Pomegranate Arts present Taylor Mac, *A 24-Decade History of Popular Music*" (2016).

13. Ilana Kaplan, "Why Kathleen Hanna Spoke Up About 'Violent Alcoholic' Dad on New LP," *Rolling Stone*, July 6, 2016. https://www.rollingstone.com/music/news/why-kathleen-hanna-spoke-up-about-violent-alcoholic-dad-on-new-lp-20160706 (accessed June 1, 2018). See also the documentary "The Herstory of Riot Grrrl (Don't Need You)" (2005). https://www.youtube.com/watch?v=be5YcNT7jVk. I am indebted to Chris W. Henderson, former punk zine editor and filmmaker and 2020 graduate of the American Studies PhD program at the University of Iowa, for sharing information and original recordings from the movement with me.

14. See, for example, Niall Richardson, "Effeminophobia, Misogyny and Queer Friendship: The Cultural Themes of Channel 4's Playing It Straight," *Sexualities* 12, no. 4 (2009): 525–44.

15. Taylor Mac, *The Young Ladies Of . . .* , typescript from Morgan Jenness, Abrams Artists Agency, New York, New York, 2007.

16. I am especially grateful to Meredith Alexander, my partner with whom I shared the marathon experience, and with whom I engaged in numerous discussions about these issues that helped me clarify my own point of view.

17. http://www.songlyrics.com/bitch-and-animal/pussy-manifesto-lyrics/

18. Review of Meshell Ndegeocello's album, *Cookie: The Anthropological Mix Tape*, by Arion Berger, *Rolling Stone*, May 22, 2002. http://www.rollingstone.com/artists/meshellndegeocello/albums/album/168030/review/5946087/cookie_the_anthropological_mix tape (accessed June 1, 2018).

19. Songwriters: Me'shell Lynn Johnson / Meshell Ndegeocello, Barry Farms lyrics © Warner/Chappell Music, Inc., available at https://www.google.com/search?q=ndegeocello+barry+farms+lyrics&ie=utf-8&oe=utf-8&client=firefox-b-1 (accessed June 4, 2018).

20. 1994 Michigan Womyn's Music Festival Directory quoted in Evelyn McDonnell, "Queer Punk Meets Womyn's Music," *Ms.* (November/December, 1994): 78–79.

21. For firsthand accounts of Tribe 8's 1994 Michfest appearance, see McDonnell, "Queer Punk," 78–82; Gretchen Phillips, "I Moshed at Mich," *Village Voice*, September 6, 1994: 41–44; Ann Cvetkovich, "Sexual Trauma/Queer Memory: Incest, Lesbianism,

and Therapeutic Culture," *GLQ: A Journal of Lesbian and Gay Studies* 2 (1995): 351–56. McDonnell and Phillips offer more journalistic accounts, whereas Cvetkovich uses her rich description, including iconic photos, to lead into a complex and illuminating analysis of the relationship between incest trauma, therapeutic culture, and lesbian identity.

22. Lynn Flipper, quoted in *Rise Above: The Tribe 8 Documentary* by Tracy Flannigan, Red Hill Pictures, 2004.

23. Author's interview with Machine Dazzle, Iowa City, Iowa, April 25, 2018.

24. http://www.songlyrics.com/tribe-8/butch-in-the-streets-lyrics/ (accessed July 21, 2018).

25. See the riot grrrl documentary *Don't Need You—The Herstory of riot grrrl*, written and directed by Kerri Koch. Urban Cowgirl Productions, 2005. https://www.youtube.com/watch?v=a9G45K6FgaI (accessed August 14, 2020).

26. See, for example, "Guest Blog: Anais Mitchell," *American Songwriter* (February 28, 2012), https://americansongwriter.com/2012/02/songwriter-u-guest-blog-anais-mitchell/ (accessed July 24, 2018); Mike Ragogna, "Who's Feeling Young Now? Chatting with Blues Traveler's John Popper, Punch Brothers' Chris Thile, and Anais Mitchell," *Huffington Post, The Blog*, February 29, 2012. https://www.huffingtonpost.com/mike-ragogna/emwhos-feeling-young-nowe_b_1308484.html (accessed July 24, 2018).

27. *Thunder: A Film about Ferron* by Billie Jo Cavallaro, Bitch, and Ferron (2013) (Clawson, MI: Short Story Records). The quoted excerpt is available at https://www.youtube.com/watch?v=CSMK7DGPBsI (accessed July 29, 2018).

28. "Notes by Machine Dazzle."

29. At a 1972 conference of the American Association for the Advancement of Science, Lorenz presented the paper "Predictability: Does the Flap of a Butterfly's Wings in Brazil Set Off a Tornado in Texas?" which introduced the butterfly image. The term "butterfly effect" was coined by James Gleick and reached a wide readership with his best-selling book *Chaos: Making a New Science* (1987). See Peter Dizikes, "When the Butterfly Effect Took Flight," *MIT Technology Review*, February 22, 2011, https://www.technologyreview.com/s/422809/when-the-butterfly-effect-took-flight/ (accessed July 26, 2018).

30. "Taylor Mac: An Abridged Concert of the History of Popular Music," promotional interview, Museum of Contemporary Art, Chicago, October 2, 2013. https://www.youtube.com/watch?v=NfcmIPYSy0M (accessed September 15, 2018).

31. For a verbatim transcript of the "Dyke Manifesto," see Penny A. Weiss, ed., *Feminist Manifestos: A Global Documentary Reader* (New York: New York University Press, 2018), 339–41.

32. I am grateful to Jen Buckley for taking me deeper into the music of Lauryn Hill and Sleater-Kinney and providing me with copies of their respective albums, *The Miseducation of Lauryn Hill* (1998) and *One Beat* (2002).

33. Source: LyricFind. Songwriters: Lauryn Hill / Lauryn N. Hill. Everything Is Everything lyrics © Sony/ATV Music Publishing LLC, BMG Rights Management. https://www.google.com/search?q=lauryn+hill+everything+is+everything&rlz=1C1GCEB_enUS879US880&oq=lauryn+hill+everything&aqs=chrome.0.0j46j69i57j0l5.13597j0j8&sourceid=chrome&ie=UTF-8 (accessed 6/22/2020).

34. Author's interview with Machine Dazzle, Iowa City, Iowa, April 25, 2018.

35. "Dress Like a Woman? What Does that Mean?" *New York Times*, February 3,

2017. https://www.nytimes.com/2017/02/03/style/trump-women-dress-code-white-ho use.html (accessed 7/3/2020).

36. Gabriel Winant, "Rush Limbaugh's race to the bottom: Bend over, grab your ankles and submit to a mind-blowing rundown of the radio bully's obsessive butt talk!" *Salon*, May 21, 2009. https://www.salon.com/2009/05/21/limbaugh_obsession/ (accessed 7/6/2020).

37. Margaret Renkl, "What It's Like to Wear a Mask in the South," *New York Times*, June 1, 2020. https://www.nytimes.com/2020/06/01/opinion/coronavirus-face-mask-so uth.html (accessed 7/4/2020).

38. Laura Bradley, "Colbert's Gift to Clinton: Naked-Man Butts Branded with 'I'm with Her,'" *Vanity Fair*, September 20, 2017. https://www.vanityfair.com/hollywood/20 17/09/clinton-what-happened-election-colbert-late-show-naked-men (accessed August 14, 2020). Image also viewable at: "Don't blush, Hillary! Clinton's slogan gets a VERY cheeky makeover when Late Show host reveals NSFW photo of naked men wearing nothing but 'I'm With Her' painted on their butt cheeks," by Marlene Lenthang for dailymail.com,
published 23:52 EDT, 20 September 2017, updated 09:32 EDT, 21 September 2017.
Image address: https://i.dailymail.co.uk/i/pix/2017/09/21/14/4486F64300000578-4904 238-Just_cheeky_The_greatest_joke_of_all_was_the_plan_to_reveal_nake-a-1_150600 0728812.jpg (accessed August 14, 2020).

FIVE

Too Slow
Taylor Mac and the Rubs of Time

Lisa A. Freeman

Dressed in a (Machine) dazzling flapper outfit, Taylor Mac opened the fifteenth decade (1916–1926) of *A 24-Decade History of Popular Music* with a startling rendition of "Happy Days Are Here Again." The song begins at its normal tempo, celebrating the end of World War I; the casting off of conflict, deprivation, and worry; and the slide into decadence that has come to be associated with the roaring '20s. But gradually and then not so gradually, Mac speeds up the tempo to a frantic pace, practically spitting the words out in a clamorous rush.

As the audience, at Mac's direction, joins judy (Mac's preferred pronoun) in song and tries to keep pace with the increasingly frenetic accompanying gestures, the reiterative insistence that now is the time to be happy rapidly causes discomfort and anxiety instead.[1] I take this moment to be emblematic of the kinds of affective and temporal rubs that Mac repeatedly generates throughout judy's exuberant, probing, and exhilarating, one-time only, twenty-four-hour performance of American song and American history at St. Ann's Warehouse in Brooklyn, NY, October 8–9, 2016. Kicking off the narrative arc of this decade a bit ahead of schedule at approximately 1:40 a.m., this familiar, opening song, and the estranging bodily discomfiture it generates, participate in the dynamic push against complacency and pull toward activism that organize the performance event as a whole. While we are meant to celebrate each and every moment of utopian exuberance in this epic, overnight journey, the nagging feelings, and the ambivalent awareness that accompanies those unsettling feelings,

Fig. 18. Taylor Mac sings "Happy Days Are Here Again" at the opening of the fifteenth decade (1916–1926) in *A 24-Decade History of Popular Music*. Photo: Teddy Wolff.

are also meant to remind us that we have not yet arrived at utopia itself and that there has always been, and still is, much work to be done beyond this space to bring that perfect world into existence. Through the series of critical interventions that judy enacts in the hour-long spans that stand in for each decade, Mac literally reorchestrates, via the genius of musical director Matt Ray, the meaning of popular songs from each period and hence reconstrues and redirects the history they bear. In this manner, judy not only examines the shape that happiness supposedly takes in each era, but also to whom it could be said to have belonged and how it might or might not be attained—in what manner and in what tempo, particularly for those who have been marked across time as either queer or other and for whom happiness historically was meant to be out of reach.

For Larry and Barry, the closeted gay couple that Mac situates at the center of the narrative of this post–World War I decade, these are pertinent questions. In our introduction to this fictional duo of war veterans, played by audience members carefully selected and brought onstage by Mac, we are made to understand that while joined by love, they differ conspicuously in their emotional responses to the traumas they have experienced on the battlefield. Where Larry seeks to push down horrific memories of war and immerse himself in the after-party, Barry, paralyzed by equally traumatic memories, wishes only to sit quietly and console himself by reading James Joyce's *Ulysses* (1922). This literary selection is no arbitrary choice on Mac's part and adds yet one more rich and evocative point of reference to the dense veins of cultural citation and meaning that run through the work in its entirety. For just as we have immersed ourselves, perhaps in search of our own form of absorptive consolation, in a twenty-four-hour experience that synecdochally spans twenty-four decades, *Ulysses* is a novel that dramatically spans a twenty-four-hour period. Indeed, just as Joyce's postwar, modernist novel raises questions about how to represent a day and how to represent both the qualities of time and the consciousness of a time, so too does Taylor Mac's *History* reflect on the warps and woofs of the texture of time, its curious capacity to speed up and slow down, and the problem of how to represent and to make consciously felt the story of 240 years of American history.

For Mac, moreover, this storytelling is necessarily a partial project, and not just because he cherry-picks his way across 240 years of American song and American history. Rather, he also insists throughout the performance on the legitimacy of an adamantly queer perspective on those songs and that history. Brandishing the prerogative of a queer partiality and refusing all of the usually obligatory gestures of consolation for the heteronormative, judy points early on in the show to one of the fabulously referential outfits designed by costume artist Machine Dazzle and exclaims, "What about any of this says objective?" In this manner, Mac delineates a shared alternative framework, and from that queer perspective, works throughout the performance to excavate the archive that has formed the nation's history and songbook. Moving from one decade to the next, beginning with 1776–1786, judy insistently identifies traces of the queer that have always been inextricably woven into the lyrics, melodies, and stories of American song, waiting in plain sight to be discerned, teased out, and pulled forward by an unapologetic drag queen. In a performance that moves adroitly between the spectacle of drag and the intimacy of cabaret, Mac thus engages in what David Román terms a profound "reorientation of cultural memory" that opens up "a space in the national culture for a set of alternative sentiments and practices."[2] Accordingly, as I will demonstrate, the question of storytelling here is one neither of sufficiency nor of exhaustiveness but rather of creating and producing a performative doing that will push against the rubs of time and give rise to what I would term an affectively bound "body public" committed to moving queerly forward in time together.³

Working loosely from memory, this essay takes up parts of the narrative and action of the decade spanning 1916–1926 as a way to illustrate the "rubs of time" through which Mac not only draws us, amid this "radical faerie realness ritual sacrifice," into what anthropologist Victor Turner would term the experience of *communitas*, but also thrusts us outward into a space where we are meant to understand that complacency is not an option and that activism is a constant imperative.⁴ Any sense that we might be moving forward in this performance experience is not untroubled, nor does Mac intend it to be so. As much as we might want to say, or even believe, that Mac traces an historical arc toward greater justice—racial, sexual, and social—the rubs of time, those repeatedly nagging reminders, as we look backward in time from our present position, that we haven't made as much progress as we like to think, always remain palpable in judy's performance. Over and over again, we are made to feel, not only that the march toward justice and equity, as the Nina Simone song "Mississippi Goddam" reminds us later in the show, is "too slow," but that it does not move forward unerringly in a straight line or, alternatively, if it does move forward, it often does so in all *too straight* a line.⁵ Hence, even as the durational aspect of the performance immerses us in time and provides us with a sense of forward momentum, Mac repeatedly draws us into an experience of cognitive dissonance that pits this illusory sense of progress against the adamantly elusory nature of palpable change. The rubs of time, those moments in the performance when our awareness of our immersion in *a* time rubs up against the intractable movements and moments *of* time, remind us that there is still much work to be done. Thus, as Mac exhorts us again and again to sustain or repeat a vocal, verbal, or physical gesture, making it "go on longer than [we] think it should," he simultaneously produces in us both a timely awareness of rankling discomfiture—a sort of physiological correlate to the interminable persistence of oppression and discrimination—and the exhilarating high of what critic Jill Dolan terms "utopian performatives," those equally physiological "moments in which performance calls the attention of the audience in a way that lifts everyone slightly above the present, into a hopeful feeling of what the world might be like if every moment of our lives were as emotionally voluminous, generous, aesthetically striking, and intersubjectively intense."⁶

For Dolan, utopian performatives offer us a hopeful glimpse, in the context of a shared and embodied performance experience, of a more just future. They are ephemeral and fleeting, but they also leave behind a residue of desire for what could be. Taylor Mac's twenty-four-hour performance is redolent with such ecstatic moments, moving the audience forward to see beyond the horizon of the present to what might be possible. But he does not stop there, nor is his glance only forward-looking. Instead, Mac engages in a practice that constantly requires us to look backward and sideways, and perhaps even more importantly for the queer aesthetic he cultivates, to look obliquely or slantwise. Time rubs, as it were, in Mac's performance, as we come to feel through his queer rehearsal of American history not only how the past enfolds the present but also how it provides the substrate out of which a new sense of the present and future might be effected if we look at that past with a more tenacious and awryly wry eye.

Indeed, as performance theorist Rebecca Schneider reminds us, the past is not a settled thing. It is not frozen in time, and it never fully disappears. More particularly, the theatricalization of the past in and through reenaction—especially when such reenactments involve riffs or parodies—provides an opportunity to draw out the tensions between "history proper and its many counter-constituents," that is, "the resilience of the seemingly forgotten (that nevertheless recurs)."[7] Thus, for example, as Mac guides the audience through a raucous series of reenactments of monumental battles supposedly past—Civil War battles, World War I battles—we come to experience those performances not only as the repetition of contests between historical combatants but also as live contests over the stories that are told about those events. We are meant both to consider and to re-consider which bodies are represented and which bodies are marginalized in those stories, and whose memories are venerated and whose memories are reduced to mere traces. In this kinesthetic performance of what Schneider terms the "recomposition of remains *in and as the live*," we come to see the transformative potential of an active re-encounter with the past and in particular with those rubs against time that Schneider terms "irruptive 'counter memories.'"[8]

The utopian performative is thus produced in Mac's extraordinary performance not simply by propelling us toward a liberatory vision of a possible future, but rather, as queer theorist José Esteban Muñoz might have it, by offering a rehearsal of the past in which the latently queer is understood as not yet here but always already there, available to us and only waiting to be made legible in the past as a prospect of the future. This reconfiguration of the past as a time-space in which "[c]ertain performances of queer citizenship contain . . . an anticipatory illumination of a queer world," provides us with a revelatory way to read Taylor Mac's narrative of variously queer figures in American history.[9] In particular, it helps us to discern how Mac's embodied performances of gesture and song not only build on the ephemeral "remains that are often embedded in queer acts," but also enact a "refusal of a certain kind of finitude" out of which continual "tales of historical becoming" might emerge.[10] Through a narrative that is chronological but not necessarily linear, a narrative that repeatedly bends back on itself and is rife with anachronism, and a narrative that is replete with characters who refuse the normative, Mac willfully resists the impetus of national forgetting and makes those historical becomings present as part of our future remembering.

In our approach to the tale of Larry and Barry, we should not then forget their past or ignore both its tender and its horrific returns. Mac typically selects a white, normative-appearing, middle-aged gay couple to play these fictional avatars of a decade's consciousness. To highlight the effect of vulnerability where we don't usually think it can be found, they are made to remain on stage, objects of the audience gaze, oftentimes awkwardly so, through almost the entire hour. Larry and Barry, as Mac tells us, met and fell in love amid the trench warfare of World War I, a site of both violent trauma and intense intimacy for all those soldiers who fought and feared for their lives. And it is precisely that intimacy at the intersection of unremitting violence that provides the focal point of the reenactment of war that takes up most of the hour devoted to that prior decade, 1906–1916.

Over the course of that preceding hour, Mac gathers on the stage as many forty-year-old and younger male (self-identified) bodies from the audience as the space will allow. Those bodies are then packed tightly together and banded by prop barbed wire, mimicking both the sense of bodily threat and entrapment that soldiers might have felt as well as the absolute closeness of their bodies in the narrow trench spaces. The night before "battle," those men, many of them strangers to each other, are made to spoon one another, providing the comfort of human warmth and touch, even as they assume postures of intimacy among men, particularly heterosexual men, that are usually proscribed. Once the battle erupts, chaos ensues, and by the end of the hour the stage is strewn with all kinds of detritus, including a variety of bloodied, prosthetic body parts, the macabre remnants of bodies torn asunder by bombs and shrapnel. All of the action, including the work of a number of female audience members who "volunteer" as nurses to attend the wounded, is carried out under Mac's direction with an air of laughter, hilarity, and even comedy, as if it were all just in play, as to some extent it is. Yet as Mac works judy's way through the selected songbook for that decade, songs that were sung both by soldiers as they marched across Europe and by those who remained on the home front, and that we have come at a great distance to enjoy as part of our American songbook inheritance, take on a rather disturbing hue. The rueful rub of time is deeply felt here, as Mac discovers haunting omens of human fragility in songs that were meant to be about love and courtship. We come to realize, for instance, that even as lovers might meet "By the Light of the Silvery Moon," that same silvery light also prolonged battles and enabled enemies at night to target one another across the killing fields of Europe.[11] Even more appalling, "K-K-K-Katy," a Geoffrey O'Hara song that was meant to convey the nervous excitement of a suitor about to propose marriage before marching off to war, becomes instead an awful foreboding of the stutter that came to be emblematic in World War I literature as a symptom of the aftereffects of trauma and injury, the shattered word an embodied symptom of shattered inner lives.[12]

This is the traumatic past that Larry and Barry carry with them into the next decade, even as they also carry with them the deep bond of queer love that they had forged amid so much horror. And even as we are entertained by the party that celebrates the end of war, Mac ensures that we too are jarred by that past and reminded of its ongoing and persistent present. The balloons that we exuberantly passed along through the air during our frenzied rehearsal of "Happy Days Are Here Again" at the opening of the decade come back to haunt us by bursting at irregular intervals over the course of the ensuing hour. Each time a balloon pops, we are startled by a viscerally felt perturbance, a distant imitation of what a soldier suffering the effects of posttraumatic stress might feel. In this experience, we are reminded that time rubs, that no matter how far along we are in the narrative, no matter how far we believe we are moving forward and away from pain and violence, the traumas of the past remain under the surface, waiting to burst through at any moment to make a mockery of our present enjoyments. This dissonant reminder of previous traumas punctuates our pleasure, even as Larry and Barry each struggle to suppress or at the very least to move beyond that seemingly unremitting past.

As Mac takes care to explain, each decade in the twenty-four-hour performance is organized around the idea of showing how various communities "built themselves as a result of being torn apart." The impetus for

Mac was judy's own witnessing of the first AIDS march in San Francisco at which judy saw an entire community—literally besieged not only by a debilitating disease but by the hateful moral politics that cast them as diseased—coming together not only to celebrate its life but also to claim its right to be. In this spirit, the narrative of the post–World War I decade is devoted to exploring how best to cope with a traumatic past, how to reintegrate oneself into peaceful times, and how to embrace a queer life and queer living amid overwhelming memories of so much death.

Over the course of the hour, Mac stages a series of vignettes, each designed to work through that sense of alienation and dislocation. Two of those vignettes in particular stand out in memory—the first, a dance, and the second, a battle. While the two are of a vastly different proportion and tenor, neither ultimately provides either sufficient consolation or the desired cathartic release from the past. In the first vignette, Larry convinces Barry to set down *Ulysses* and join him for a dance. Alongside Larry and Barry on stage, Mac also directs a dance between the oldest audience member and the youngest audience member, with the older member leading. In this poignant manner, Mac creates a moment of physical intimacy between generations, a literal touching of bodies across the measure of time that we delineate by age and hence a kind of kinesthetic performative or object lesson on how to make times touch. It's moving to witness these juxtaposed touches between bodies in love and between bodies at such different stages of life. But at length the dance ends, and the bodies move apart, both Larry's from Barry's, and the oldest from the youngest. Time can touch lovingly here, but it cannot heal the breach.

The second vignette promises at least on its surface to provide for a more sensational resolution. With Larry and Barry still at odds with one another, Mac sets in motion a queer battle of absurd proportion. Giving full rein to what Sean Edgecomb has termed judy's "neo-Ridiculous" aesthetic, Mac stages a scattershot battle between an army of Tiny Tims—as in the ukulele-playing artist—and a gaggle of toga-clad Ulysses figures, each played by a supporting ensemble of burlesque performers who appear in various guises throughout the twenty-four-hour extravaganza.[13] If Larry and Barry can't resolve their differences, then perhaps having their surrogates fight it out in spectacular fashion might provide some modicum of release from those pent-up traumas and anxieties and, at the very least, allow Barry to come out of his shell. Where the World War I battle of the previous hour was fought in the key of tragicomedy, this new simulation of war is fought in the key of farce. It operates thus as a hilarious effort to nullify the material effects of bodily dismemberment and to dislodge the psychic traumas of violence through exaggerated playacting. The frenetic battle, however, ends in a draw, leaving us exhausted with laughter by the effort, but ultimately unsatisfied by the outcome. While the enjoyment of the spectacle may have lifted the burden of the past momentarily from our shoulders, it cannot purge or clear the mind of its experience of horrors. Memory persists and time still rubs not only for Barry but for us as well.

What then? How might this breach be healed? In a talk delivered at the Association of Performing Arts Professionals and subsequently at the Humana Festival in Louisville in the months following the twenty-four-hour performance, Taylor Mac recounted, "there's a moment in the decade we were performing that I'm particularly fond of. It's a reading of the last page of James Joyce's *Ulysses*. It's certainly one of the more beautiful passages of any piece of literature and I love using it as catharsis: as an example of something reaching beauty because it goes on longer than it should."[14] This may sound like a kind of oddity. How could reading aloud from the last page of this notoriously long and difficult novel be "used" as catharsis? But in the context of the queer aesthetic that Mac cultivates throughout his performance, it makes perfect sense. Where the staged dance relied on conventional understandings of the flow of time—from youth to old age—and where the staged battle relied on a conventional understanding of release or expiation through propulsive action, a sustained reading from the concluding pages of *Ulysses* not only provides for an experience of time's suspension but also provides for an experience in which our very notion of what constitutes an action becomes much more plastic.

In these moments, which apart from the very closing minutes are perhaps some of the most quiet moments across the entire twenty-four hours, Mac sits alone downstage on a stool. The audience members playing Larry and Barry have returned to their places in the room, and the stage lights are now concentrated solely on Mac's figure. As Mac reads, the room settles into an uncanny stillness. Almost as a body, the audience strains motionlessly to catch each and every word. Where the pitched battle we just witnessed depended on broad spectacle, this new moment requires that we bear down with concentrated attention on the sound of this one steady, almost incantatory, voice. Through an act that seems to resist the very notion of what it means to "act" and that seems to arrest the narrative progress of the performance and resist the forward motion of time, Mac thus plunges us into the absorptive experience of "queer time," where what Elizabeth Freeman has termed "chrononormativity,"

Fig. 19. Taylor Mac reads from the last page of James Joyce's *Ulysses*. Photo: Teddy Wolff.

or "the use of time to organize individual human bodies toward maximum productivity," no longer holds sway.[15] As Mac's voice comes to take on the stream-of-consciousness rhythms of Molly Bloom's mind's memory in the extended interior monologue with which Joyce concludes his novel, he engages in a performative doing that resists modern definitions of effective action in the present tense and instead engages us in the luxurious play of poetic language and time that wafts across those final moments of the text.

Thus it is no accident that Mac chooses to conclude the reading not with the rise in voice that one might predict from the series of "yeses" that punctuate the text's final lines—which some critics are apt to read as a kind of ecstatic release—but rather with a quiet fall in voice, almost to the level of a murmur. In so doing, he subtly conveys an understanding that the "yes" with which Molly's monologue concludes should not be read as a final point of closure, but rather as a "yes" that gathers past remembrance into present consciousness in anticipation of an affirmed future and the hope of what may still be yet to come. Surrendering, at this late early hour, to an embrace of the muted exhale of Mac's voice, we, too, are unconsciously absorbed by the animating possibilities of a utopian performative whose potentiality lies paradoxically in the electrifying fullness of stillness. In a manner that is equally effective, then, for those who know and those who do not know the text, Mac thus embeds a proleptic glimpse of a future in what would otherwise stand as an act of completion. Counterintuitively, we are meant to understand, as Barry has all along, that catharsis lies not in the exultant achievement of "Happiness," the normative demand that marked the beginning of the hour, but rather in the wondrous and queer beauty of continual acts of collective *poesis*, that is, in the embrace of an open-ended making, a making that goes on longer than it should amid time's rubs.

• • •

From the opening of the twenty-four hours in which we are exhorted to worship an audience participant, Heather, as a verb, to the somber conclusion in which judy serenades us with the repeated refrain that reminds us that we can either "lie down or get up and play," Taylor Mac seeks to leverage performance into a performative doing that will reach far beyond the space and time of our shared utopian moment. Throughout the performance, then, the audience is treated not merely as a passive partner but rather as an active collaborator in the making, that is, in the production of a ritual experience that will not only transform us, but also, judy hopes, will transform how we move through the world beyond. We should "fall in love with verbs more than nouns," Mac told us at a twelve-hour workshop performance at the Powerhouse Theater in the summer of 2016, offering us, in effect, a profoundly activist and adamantly queer articulation of the necessity not only of the utopian performative but of the performative doing. This sentiment, of course, proved all too prescient in the wake of the November 2016 presidential election, which itself loomed so ominously over the horizon of our twenty-four-hour experience, and which, both before and now amid this global pandemic, has only emboldened the ongoing harm enacted on vulnerable Black, Brown, and Queer bodies. Our work, the work of social justice, has gone on longer than it should and will continue to go on longer than it should. Yet, as Mac writes, "The facts show us, living in a chimera doesn't work; no matter how many metaphors we dismantle to convince us otherwise. We do have to grapple with calamity."[16] We have always, in other words, to push against complacency, to see through and past the cool palliatives that lull us into mistaking change for progress, and to engage in a queer *poesis* that will bring us ever closer to that not yet here.

Notes

1. All citations for *A 24-Decade History of Popular Music* are taken from memory and, where possible, backed both by photographic time-stamps at the twenty-four-hour performance and by notes taken at the twelve-hour performance workshop conducted at the Powerhouse Theater at Vassar College, July 30, 2016. judy is Taylor Mac's preferred pronoun and I use it throughout this essay.

2. David Román, *Performance in America: Contemporary U. S. Culture and the Performing Arts* (Durham: Duke University Press, 2005), 179.

3. See Lisa A. Freeman, *Antitheatricality and the Body Public* (Philadelphia: University of Pennsylvania Press, 2017), esp. 3–5.

4. See Victor Turner, *From Ritual to Theatre: The Human Seriousness of Play* (New York: PAJ Publications, 1982), 45–51.

5. Nina Simone, "Mississippi Goddam," 1964.

6. Jill Dolan, *Utopia in Performance: Finding Hope at the Theater* (Ann Arbor: University of Michigan Press, 2005), 5.

7. Rebecca Schneider, *Performing Remains: Art and War in Times of Theatrical Reenactment* (London: Routledge, 2011), 6.

8. Schneider, *Performing Remains*, 98, 174.

9. José Esteban Muñoz, *Cruising Utopia: The Then and There of Queer Futurity* (New York: NYU Press, 2009), 49.

10. Muñoz, *Cruising Utopia*, 65, 67.

11. "By the Light of the Silver Moon," music by Gus Edwards, lyrics by Edward Madden, 1909.

12. "K-K-K-Katy," music and lyrics Geoffrey O'Hara, recorded 1917, published 1918.

13. Sean F. Edgecomb, "The Ridiculous Performance of Taylor Mac," *Theatre Journal* 64, no. 4 (December 2012): 550.

14. Taylor Mac published the transcript for this speech on his website: https://www.ta ylormac.org/whats-gonna-happen/. The speech was first presented at the APAP conference in January 2017, and also at the 41st Humana Festival on April 1, 2017. It can be found in full on YouTube at https://www.youtube.com/watch?v=P5AFDirdDUU

15. Elizabeth Freeman, *Time Binds: Queer Temporalities, Queer Histories* (Durham: Duke University Press, 2010), 3.

16. Mac, "What's Gonna Happen?"

SIX

Taylor Mac, Walt Whitman, and Adhesive America
Cruising Utopia with the Good Gay Poet

Jennifer Buckley

The simple, compact, well-joined scheme—myself
disintegrated, every one disintegrated, yet part of the scheme,
The similitudes of the past, and those of the future,
The glories strung like beads on my smallest sights
and hearings—on the walk in the street, and
the passage over the river,

The current rushing so swiftly, and swimming with
me far away,
The others that are to follow me, the ties between me
and them,
The certainty of others—the life, love, sight, hearing of others.
. . .

Who knows but I am enjoying this?
Who knows but I am as good as looking at you now,
for all you cannot see me?
    Walt Whitman, "Crossing Brooklyn Ferry," *Leaves of Grass*
    (1860–61)[1]

On receiving the Edwin Booth Award at the City University of New York's
Graduate Center on April 28, 2017, Taylor Mac chose neither to give a
speech nor to sing a tune, but rather to read aloud Walt Whitman's poem
"Crossing Brooklyn Ferry." Several minutes into the recitation, he inter-
jected, "Don't worry, just twenty-five more pages! Because Walt Whitman,

like me, likes to make something go on a little bit longer than it should."[2] Delivered with sorry-not-sorry aplomb, it was a line guaranteed to charm the audience—and perhaps also to recapture the attention of minds wandering away from a twenty-six stanza poem written in the mid-nineteenth century. But it also calls attention to what I argue is Whitman's aesthetic and political place in the *24-Decade History of Popular Music*: at its center.

That Whitman is one of the *History's* heroes is obvious to anyone who has heard and seen Mac recite portions of *Leaves of Grass* during performances of the 1846–56 segment. In "Whitman vs. Foster: Songs Popular Near the Breaking Point," Mac champions the poet as the true "Father of American Song" in the first moments of what is supposed to be a knock-down, drag-out battle for that title. Whitman's opponent in this unabashedly rigged contest is Stephen Collins Foster (1826–64), the composer and lyricist who is usually granted the accolade. Staged during the twenty-four-hour St. Ann's Warehouse performance (October 8–9, 2016) as a mock wrestling match conducted in and around a red, white, and blue–roped ring, "Whitman vs. Foster" argues that the aesthetically innovative and politically progressive *Leaves of Grass* is the "song" we *should* have heard America singing since its initial publication in 1855 (fig. 20). Historically, of course, what much of America was actually singing during that decade—and long after—were Foster's indelible tunes. A wide readership was still out of Whitman's reach; his eventual canonization as America's "Good Gray Poet" would have seemed impossible, perhaps even to him, during the period encompassed by the *History* segment.[3]

I will take up the implications of Mac's decision to cast these two canonical nineteenth-century artists as opponents, but first I want to make clear the main points, as well as the stakes, of my argument about the show's uptake of Whitman's poem and his initial persona. Whitman's vision of America—aptly described by Thomas Yingling as a "homosexual utopia"—and his poetic practice of superabundance permeate the *History*. Like Whitman, Mac not only "hear[s] America singing," but also is singing a specifically queer America into being. It is a capacious, various, and perpetually emergent utopia—a poetic entity that gives its people an extended duration in which they can feel what the nation has been, is now, and might become if we all "get up and play" with and for one another.[4] I call up Yingling's circa-1992 essay here because he was one of the first publicly out American scholars to recognize that the forms of same-sex attachment articulated in *Leaves* are integral to its politics. Before he could complete that essay Yingling died of AIDS, like the many thousands of gay people whose relentless activism in the face of widespread illness and murderous government indifference inspired not only the *History*, but also the commitment to queer community-building evident in all Mac's work.[5] Yingling helped seed a thriving field of Whitman scholarship that has shaped Mac's understanding of the poem and his performance of its politics, whether or not we believe judy's jokey disavowals of academic standards. (Calling the audience's attention to the history-inspired details of designer Machine Dazzle's intricate costumes, Mac asked, "What about *this* says more than Wikipedia?") I draw on that Whitman scholarship, sparingly but pointedly, to show how and why Mac's very contemporary American *History* elevates the nineteenth-century bard of democratic bonding.

In Whitman's American utopia, and in Mac's, what binds the nation is not the state, much less its elected officials. (So skeptical is Mac of all leaders that the *History* disperses his own authority in its first minutes, when judy bids the audience to "worship the act of creation, not the creator."[6]) It is not the land that lies between its perpetually contested borders. It is not even a shared culture. It is love—a very particular type of love that Whitman called "adhesive," using a term of his era. This is not the love of the heterosexual reproductive pair privileged by church, state, and nearly all mass cultural products. Adhesive love is erotic, but not necessarily genital; it is of the body, yet it transcends the flesh. It is intimate, but not personal; indeed, adhesive lovers can be strangers. Though some "comrades" are closer than others, the union they build is nonexclusive and nonproprietary. "In Whitman's homoerotic vistas," Betsy Erkkila explains, "the love of strangers models the public culture of male love that he imagines as the future of democracy: the stranger exists as an unknown figure, a foreigner in public space, outside the prescribed intimacies of home, marriage, and family."[7] Both Whitman and Mac present queer, public sexual expression as the ground on which they and their audiences are creating an American utopia that remains always on the horizon. Whitman's poem privileges cruising in New York City's streets, while Mac's performance exalts anonymous sex in its nightclubs. Both artists offer up their exceedingly open, adhesive, absorptive, multiplicitous, temporally transcendent bodies and works as exemplars of queer, utopian, democratic world-making. Hearing that reading of "Crossing Brooklyn Ferry," I could not help but think about how Mac's choice of text, like the selection of that particular waterfront location for the New York City *History* performances, ties into what Jose Esteban Muñoz identified as an exceptionally "dense connective site in the

Fig. 20. Taylor Mac and ensemble, "1846–1856: Whitman vs. Foster: Songs Popular Near the Breaking Point," *A 24-Decade History of Popular Music*, St. Ann's Warehouse, October 2016. Photo by Teddy Wolff. https://client.teddywo lff.com/taylormacact3/h13394ad1#h3e001c89

North American queer imagination"—a cruising ground, in many senses.[8] For both Whitman and Mac, the waterfront pulses with what Muñoz so influentially described as "the possibility of queer transport, leaving the here and now for a then and there" that enfolds the turbulent past while enabling a freer future.[9] It is the possibility of that future to which the nineteenth-century poet and the twenty-first-century performer dedicate themselves, their audiences, and their maximalist works.

Sentimentalist versus "no sentimentalist": Mac's Whitman Contra *Foster*

Throughout the *History*, Mac unearths the queerness Americans have "dismissed, forgotten, or buried," starting with the would-be fabulous fop of "Yankee Doodle Dandy."[10] That said, he never hesitates to supplement the historical record by imagining characters such as Barry and Larry, the

World War I veterans whose trauma tests their love in the 1920s. However, neither historical excavation nor imagination is necessary to establish Whitman's sexuality, though it took American academics decades to fully acknowledge it.[11] Mac's performance of Whitman's famously free verse stresses *Leaves's* forthright celebration of human bodies—including the poet's, the performer's, and your own, dear reader, "whoever you are"—merging with one another and all living things in an erotic, ecstatic, and exorbitantly inclusive union that is both physical and spiritual. The first passage Mac performs is a credo-like excerpt from what would later be titled "Song of Myself," in which the speaking "I" and "you" become an us that "shall be" the US:

> I believe in the flesh and the appetites,
> Seeing hearing and feeling are miracles, and each part and tag of
>   me is a miracle.
>
> Divine am I inside and out, and I make holy whatever I touch or am
>   touched from;
> The scent of these arm-pits is aroma finer than prayer,
> This head is more than churches or bibles or creeds.
>
> If I worship any particular thing it shall be some of the spread of my
>   body;
> Translucent mould of me it shall be you,
> Shaded ledges and rests, firm masculine coulter, it shall be you,[12]

Declaring himself "a kosmos," the poet offers up his body as a medium that can not only "contain multitudes" but also connect them to one another on equal terms.[13] Notably, this multitude includes African Americans and Indigenous people, as well as women. It is true that Whitman's published writings before and after the 1855 *Leaves of Grass* reveal white-supremacist beliefs coexisting with sympathy for—and even identification with—enslaved Black people.[14] The fullest expression of that sympathy appears in the first *Leaves* edition, in which Whitman's song asserts the selfhood of every person, extending each an invitation to join the joyful union of limitless lovers.

This is the Whitman whom Mac puts in the ring with Stephen Foster. Even with a *lucha libre*–masked Tigger! playing referee, it seems clear by the end of Round 1 that Whitman will win the title of "Father of American

Song." Such an outcome would have astonished their contemporaries. During his brief lifetime, Foster gained unprecedented fame as the writer of so-called "Ethiopian" songs, including "Oh! Susanna" (1848), "Camptown Races" (1850), and "Old Folks at Home" (1851). Written mostly in blackface dialect and performed around the country and the world by minstrels, notably including E. P. Christy's famous cork-covered troupe, Foster's sentimental "plantation" songs have been said to encourage sympathy with enslaved Black people by attributing to his Black characters recognizably human emotions.[15] What they actually do is soft-pedal slavery's violence, thus enabling white-supremacist thought and behavior well into the twentieth century.[16] Having entered the public domain in the nineteenth century, Foster's music became ubiquitous in American mass media. Joseph Carl Breil's score for *Birth of a Nation* (1915) features three Foster melodies; these include "My Old Kentucky Home, Good-night!" (published 1853), which remains that state's official song despite the fact that the original lyrics include a racist term[17]—and despite the slimness of the evidence that the Pennsylvania-born Foster ever visited the Federal Hill plantation now known as My Old Kentucky Home State Park.[18] Max Steiner's soundtrack for *Gone with the Wind* (1939) incorporates no fewer than ten Foster melodies. Generations of cartoon-watching children, including my own, have absorbed Foster's music—probably unconsciously—while watching the escapades of Bugs Bunny and his friends and foes in Warner Brothers' *Looney Tunes* and *Merrie Melodies* series.[19]

Foster apologists argue that his personal stance on slavery is unclear, noting that Black activists including Frederick Douglass, W. E. B. DuBois, and Paul Robeson detected in some songs what Douglass described as "sympathies for the slave, in which anti-slavery principles take root and flourish."[20] It is true that Robeson's 1930 recording of "My Old Kentucky Home" remains a singularly powerful performance of a memorable melody, and that the lyrics draw on Harriet Beecher Stowe's *Uncle Tom's Cabin* (1852).[21] But as Mac's trenchant performance stresses, the song is not the straightforward "anti-slavery ballad" it is sometimes said to be: the idealized "Home" from which the enslaved speaker has been forced is itself a plantation. Whatever sentiments Foster expressed through the voice of a character sold down the river to labor in "the field where the sugar canes grow," they did not stop him from writing campaign jingles for proslavery "doughface" Democrats in 1856.[22] Perhaps the racial politics of his music were best expressed by Giuseppe Moretti, whose Pittsburgh public sculpture depicts Foster writing down a plantation melody while the barefoot "Old Uncle Ned" sits at his feet, playing a banjo. (The sculpture, completed in 1900 and long criticized as racist, was removed from public view in 2018.)

Mac's performance of Foster's minstrel songs makes it clear that neither he nor Matt Ray, the *History*'s musical director, is much interested in drawing out whatever sympathy Douglass, Du Bois, and Robeson once found in them. Indeed, Ray's arrangements of several blackface dialect songs come across as flat-out aggressive. At St. Ann's Warehouse, Mac hate-sang a couple of verses of a breakneck "Camptown Races" before declaring that enough was enough (and it really was). Ray remade the chorus of Foster's mournful ballad "Massa's in De Cold Ground" (1852) into a bracingly upbeat, celebratory jig, "appropriating" (Mac's term) the song by musically retrofitting it to the show's purposes.[23] Mac's performances of the minstrel songs are musically adept and entertaining, but also alienating enough to convince the audience that Foster deserves to lose the battle—and to have hundreds of ping-pong balls launched at the onstage audience volunteer gamely standing in for the songwriter. In sharp contrast, it is the resplendent Mac who embodies the figure of Whitman, and the poet's "songs" elicit from judy some of the *History*'s most exhilarating renditions. Whitman's famously long lines, delivered with verbal wit and vocal panache, reverberate manifesto-like throughout the rest of the show—and, it turns out, the Trump era that followed very hard upon it:

> Whoever degrades another degrades me. . . . and whatever is done or said returns
>   at last to me,
> And whatever I do or say I also return.

> Through me the afflatus surging and surging. . . . through me the current and index.

> I speak the password primeval. . . . I give the sign of democracy;
> By God! I will accept nothing which all cannot have their counterpart of on the same terms.[24]

Whitman wins hearts and minds—if not the actual title—at least in part because the *History* establishes an almost total opposition between him and Foster.[25] Mac and Ray do offer a sensitive, beautiful rendition of "Hard Times Come Again No More," which is now the best-known of the dozens of parlor ballads Foster wrote, hoping to attain a higher cultural status than "Ethiopian" tunes could afford. Even his loveliest ballads, though, reveal Foster as what Mac calls a "sentimentalist"—a designation judy contrasts with Whitman's self-identification as "no sentimentalist."[26] This antithesis serves as a foundation for the *History* segment as well as Mac's monologue "The Dying Sentimentalist," which judy performs toward the end of the "decade" as a rejoinder to Foster's "Beautiful Dreamer."[27] Drawing on the historical Whitman's wartime service caring for wounded Union soldiers in Washington, DC, Mac stages the poet as a "bedside mannerist," counseling Foster as he lies unconscious after a fall, the effects of which, compounded by alcoholism, would kill him. Speaking in Foster's ear, or perhaps within his mind, Whitman castigates the songwriter for selling romantic dreams of the antebellum South—dreams from which white-supremacist America has yet to awaken. At this point in the St. Ann's Warehouse performance, Mac had recast the part of Foster, who was now played by the entire audience, a large majority of whose members appeared to be white, as I myself am. (I recall judy looking over the 700 or so attendees early in the show and exclaiming in mock delight, "There's so many different *kinds* of white people here!") As we lay on the floor, Mac-as-Whitman urged us to "get up" and shake off the sentimentalist's racist reverie.

It does not matter to Mac that the elderly Whitman is on the record expressing admiration for Foster's songs, and I think it need not.[28] For my purposes here, it also does not matter that Foster—who looks wan in photographs, and whose parlor ballads were played by young ladies at home—appears far less conventionally manly in presentation than the strapping working-class "roughs" whose muscular masculinity Whitman extols as the foundation of a robust, adhesive America. However homoerotic one finds that famous 1855 frontispiece engraving of Whitman in laborer's clothes, the image looks very (very) dissimilar from Mac's gender-nonbinary performance persona, who sports in this decade a wig piled high with buttercream-y waves and a hooped skirt bedecked with glossy pages torn from gay porn magazines, among many other items.[29] (Despite judy's own visual difference from the "roughs," scholars of American literature and culture would catch the costume's nod to Whitman's participation in the massive expansion of print at midcentury: for his day job, the poet trained as a printer.) The differences between Mac, Mac-as-Whitman, and Whitman himself are not merely cosmetic. For example, both artists present their queerly permeable bodies as conduits for the voices of marginalized others: as Whitman writes, and Mac recites, "through me many long dumb voices" speak.[30] Yet Mac acknowledges his difference from those whose voices judy channels, especially when that difference confers privilege, in ways that Whitman does not.[31] The political (and of course historical) gaps between them are substantial, as Mac knows. Yet by giving Whitman's "sign of democracy," embracing Whitman's maximalist aesthetic, and adopting a Whitmanesque "body electric," Mac advances a queer utopian vision of an America that requires us all not just to "get up," but to "get up and play."

Queering Democracy, Cruising Utopia: Strangers and Lovers in Adhesive America

Although the *History*'s title does not specify the *Popular Music*'s country of origin, the start date of 1776 immediately suggests the work's national focus, as does the costume in which Mac enters. "Maybe you noticed, by the way I'm dressed, that I'm not exactly an unironic patriot," said judy in the opening moments of the St. Ann's Warehouse show. Gesturing toward the paniered explosion of rainbow-colored sequins, streamers, and sparkling foil stars that designer Machine Dazzle made for judy to wear during the 1776–86 segment, Mac drew approving laughter from the audience.[32] The line confirms the complex political stance toward America expressed in the show's first song—the hymn "Amazing Grace" (1779)—and much of what comes afterward. Anglican priest John Newton penned the lyrics in 1772, recalling the seemingly miraculous rescue at sea he experienced as a young man. In the centuries to come, the song's salvation narrative would make it a staple of the abolitionist, civil rights, and antiwar movements. Mac's performance suggests this, as judy concludes with the verse that begins "When we've been there ten thousand years / bright shining as the sun"—a verse that appears to have originated in African American worship traditions, and that Stowe documented in *Uncle Tom's Cabin*. Neither that aspect of the song's performance history, nor the lyrics, nor the major-key tune to which Americans have sung the song since the 1830s suggests that Newton perpetrated the slave trade for decades after the rescue, and would not publicly reject it until the 1780s.[33] But Mac and Ray might imply it, if you know how listen: Ray has re-set Newton's lyrics to the minor-key folk standard "The House of the Rising Sun," which describes the "ruin" of a young person at what is either a brothel or a prison in the slave-trade hub of New Orleans.[34] The irony in Mac's patrio-

Fig. 21. Taylor Mac and Timothy White Eagle. Costumes by Machine Dazzle. Photo by Teddy Wolff. https://client.teddywolff.com/taylormacact1/h39753f6a #h146a8bc

tism extends from a verbally up-front, musically minor-key recognition that America was founded on stolen Native land, built by stolen Black labor, and sustained by the systemic oppression and marginalization of people who are not white heterosexual men. The show makes those points early and often, beginning with "Grace" and with Mac's relinquishment of his grandmother's banjo to Timothy White Eagle, a performing artist who is of White Mountain Apache heritage.[35]

Irony of this kind is nowhere to be found in Whitman's poem. He sets his American song in a major key. Especially in the first three editions—the ones dated 1855 (which Mac's show privileges), 1856, and 1860–61—*Leaves* acknowledges but does not fully denounce the economic and racial (and to some extent, gender) disparities that existed in Whitman's beloved America. The poem accords some human dignity, and the poet's sympathy, to all the marginalized people living in the land: to laborers working in the most dangerous occupations, to free and enslaved Black people, and even to drunken female prostitutes "(Miserable! I do not laugh at your oaths nor jeer you)."[36] A universal "comrade" to all Americans, the poet-speaker declares, "I make appointments with all, / I will not have a single person slighted or left away," no matter how degraded.[37] Like Mac, who voices the strains of destitute Lower East Side tenement-dwellers, among many oppressed others, Whitman not only embraces but also *embodies* those pushed to American society's margins: "I am the man. . . . I suffered. . . . I was there."[38] Yet the poet refuses to condemn those who hold power, no matter how brutally they wield it. From his earliest known drafts for *Leaves*, dating to the late 1840s, Whitman casts the poet-self as a figure that is both all-encompassing and interstitial.[39] Through the sheer force of his desire, he draws all America's people, including those enacting evil, toward his end-lessly multiplicitous self. Further, that self stretches between those who are opposed to one another, binding them all within a new, radically leveled, fully democratic union that is both physical and spiritual.[40]

What enables the poet-speaker to build this union is love—specifically, "adhesive" love, Whitman pulled the term from the unlikeliest of sources: phrenology. Phrenologists posited that the cranium indicates essential biological, psychological, and moral divergences between individuals and groups. Reading the skull's curves, ridges, and bumps to determine subjects' capacities for "amative" (heterosexual) and adhesive (comradely, often same-sex) love, phrenologists provided pseudoscientific "evidence" that supported the long-standing claims of racists and the newly formal-izing discourse of homophobes. Executing what might be described as an act of pre-emptive appropriation, Whitman took up a term that would be used to demean people who loved as he did, not only valorizing same-sex desires and behaviors but making them the foundation of his whole theory of democracy, and thus of his American utopia. For Whitman, cruising is the democratic practice par excellence, as scholars including Yingling, Erkkila, and Peter Coviello affirm. I concur with Coviello, who goes so far as to claim that "virtually every strand of Whitman's utopian thought devolves upon, and is anchored by, an unwavering belief in the capacity of strangers to recognize, to desire, and to be intimate with one another."[41] *Leaves* acknowledges that pairing off with one lover has its charms—especially in the much-discussed "Calamus cluster" of poems first pub-lished in 1860–61—but anonymous erotic exchange is where it's at. By *it*, I mean utopia, which, as Yingling stresses in his account of Whitman's "perfectly homocentric world," is in fact "not a place but a practice" of perpetual deferral and displacement akin to Roland Barthes's *jouissance*.[42]

The relish with which Mac delivered these lines from "Crossing Brook-lyn Ferry" suggests his endorsement of Whitman's approach: "Gaze, loving and thirsting eyes, in the house, or street, / or public assembly!"[43] So, too, does the force with which the *History* proclaims the political power of anonymous sex. "They want you to think we're all like Ellen [DeGeneres], but we queers are some *kinky motherfuckers*," Mac insists early in the show, while describing the men's room action at the Mineshaft, a legendary leather bar that closed in 1985.[44] "They" are presumably those who promote the assimilationist gay political agendas Mac critiques in the *History* and in previous shows.[45] Like Whitman, Mac has in mind something far less domesticable than same-sex marriage. For Mac, the act of retelling prior generations' NYC cruising-site memories—including Whitman's—serves as a crucial resource for his own utopian world-making efforts.[46] Mac devotes an entire decade of the *History* to the memory of the 1970s "backroom sex party," during which judy serenades the Dandy Minions' energetic, prop-heavy performance of said festivities with an up-tempo rendition of David Bowie's "Heroes." Responding to this crucial inflection point in the *History*, Rob Onorato wrote, "It is so important to me that this show was about sex, that it spoke about it, spoke sex to power. You are powerful because you have sex—queer sex, anonymous sex, backroom sex. . . . Those who have gay sex in public . . . and talk about it are, judy suggested, heroes."[47] Moreover, the power to which these self-described "kinky motherfuckers" speak sex is nationalist (which is to say, cis-het) America, a point made overwhelmingly obvious by the giant, starred-and-striped, cock-and-balls balloon the Minions launched into the audience from the "Dandy Boudoir" balcony designed to spectacular excess by Mimi Lien. However much the audience delighted in batting that enormous penis around the room (it was so fun), the monster inflatable suggests an eroticized ambivalence toward America running even deeper than Bowie's. Recall that America more or less destroys Ziggy Stardust, the early Bowie persona whose songs Mac has performed; that a 1970s stay in Los Angeles nearly killed Bowie himself; and that a fully developed familiarity with US society and mass culture impelled him to write the 1997 song "I'm Afraid of Americans."[48] Mac's critique of US imperialism is every bit as pointed as it was in earlier works like the post-9/11 show *The Face of Liberalism* (2003), which Mac concluded by singing the lyrics "I'm afraid of patriotism, and nationalism, and jingoism," while wearing Machine Dazzle's American flag makeup design that replaced the stars with thumbtacks.[49] Yet as Sean F. Edgecomb writes, it is precisely the pointedness with which Mac critiques America's past and present that reveals "his belief in a democratic society that supports the expression of individual freedoms across 'a range of humanity.'"⁵⁰ Like *Leaves*, the *History* imaginatively founds that democratic society on unrestricted sexual expression either uncoupled from, or actively destructive of, heteronormative institutions. And like Whitman, Mac casts himself as the artist-medium cruising documented and imagined American pasts and presents to discover pathways that lead through sex club backrooms and gay-friendly basement bars (like Whitman's beloved Pfaff's) to a better future for all people.⁵¹ Mac knows well Whitman's famous description of the poet-as-medium, which emphasizes his powers to transcend not only space but also time: "The greatest poet forms the consistence of what is to be from what has been and is. . . . He says to the past, Rise and walk before me that I may realize you. . . . He places himself where the future becomes present."⁵² It is just this ability to see and demonstrate how "past and present and future are . . . joined," in Whitman's words, that Edgecomb identifies in Mac's performances as a "traveling subjec[t]."⁵³ Neither the poet nor the performer presents a detailed plan or path forward; rather, both envision *and also demonstrate* modes of queer world-making that invest deeply in futurity without ever proscribing a particular future. Mac's version of "Heroes"—the lyrics of which Bowie wrote mostly in the conditional tense—lets us feel the possibility of a love-filled future while also reminding us of the past's pain and the present's precariousness. So, too, did Mac's singing: after twenty hours of almost uninterrupted performance, in the context of a segment dedicated to the first generation ravaged by AIDS, Mac was just barely capable of launching his voice into its upper register at the top of Bowie's fourth verse. I felt that famous octave leap far more clearly than I heard it, but it resounded loudly enough to pull me up into Bowie's ephemeral fantasy realm, in which every subject is a "king" or "queen," and the only function of a wall is to separate people from their "shame."⁵⁴

By this point, readers familiar with theater and performance theory are likely to have linked this vocabulary of feeling, potentiality, and hope not only to Muñoz's thinking, but also to Jill Dolan's *Utopia in Performance*.⁵⁵ Dolan's equally influential argument is that theater, as a collective and ephemeral art form, can enable "moments in which audiences feel themselves allied with each other, and with a broader, more capacious sense of a public, in which social discourse articulates the possible, rather than the insurmountable obstacles to human potential." By emphasizing the "fleeting" nature of those moments, which offer necessarily "partial" visions of a "better later" that we might find "beyond this 'now' of material oppression and unequal power relations," Dolan calls attention to the temporalities of performance and of utopia.[56] In one obvious sense, performances of the *History* are ephemeral, having existed in a supercharged present of co-presence that lasts a maximum of twenty-four hours. The phrase that follows Bowie's line "we could be heroes" is, after all, "just for one day." Yet in its long-form versions, and in its overall concept, the *History* is also a durational performance, and for Mac's purposes the implications of the Latin root matter: its verb form is *dūrāre*, "to last."

Mac's own utopian thinking about the *History* consistently stresses both its evanescent and its enduring qualities. As he said about the twenty-four-hour show in a 2017 interview, "The goal was to make something tangible out of an ephemeral art and it worked." That tangible creation—here in one sense, gone in another—was and is a community, built by strangers and made of "love."[57] In an earlier interview, Mac stated the utopian aspirations of the project even more clearly: "We didn't really say this is the world that we want, onstage, but we were making it with the Dandy Minions and the audience and the music and everybody participating."[58] Moreover, the erotics of this ephemeral yet extended encounter are about as Whitmanian as one could imagine. What's most revolutionary about Whitman's democratic world-making efforts is his "steadfast refusal" to make the adhesive "attachments" described in *Leaves* "legible as simply or conclusively sexual," Coviello states. "Genital sexuality is simply at one end of a continuum that for Whitman is not divided according to the presence or absence of an erotic dimension, but scaled according to intensities."[59] Was it sexy when we fed each other grapes? When we laughed at each other's wigs? When we dozed against each other's backpacks? When we slow-danced to "Snakeskin Cowboys"? Both yes and no are insufficient answers to questions about the activities Mac sees as crucial to the show's tangibility. It is that erotic undecidability, amplified by the fact that we had never met before—a condition dramaturgically ensured by the regular physical shuffling of the audience—that afforded us the kind of "stranger-intimacy," which is, Coviello states, "just what Whitman means to refer to when be broaches the word 'America.'"[60] Speaking in terms that align closely with those of his poetic predecessor, Mac offers up his own "quee[r] body as a metaphor for the entire country," with judy serving as the infinitely supple "bridge" connecting audience members as the show shifts them from era to era, from place to place, and from partner to partner.[61]

"Longer than it should": Superabundance and Queer Aesthetics

Having discussed how Mac and his audiences are cruising an American utopia, I now return to his assertion that the *History*, like Whitman's poem, must go on "a bit longer than it should." Among the many arguments that scholars and artists have made about durational performance is that its relatively extreme length disrupts the late-capitalist—which is also to say heterosexist—temporal regime that Elizabeth Freeman calls "chrononormativity."[62] For Mac, a major benefit of durational performance is that its jarring length dislodges audience members from their regular, work-oriented schedules and releases them into an altered state in which they can become "deranged in their emotional availability." He believes that this distinctly queer temporality makes it possible for all audience members to "transform"—or, at the very least, to glimpse alternatives to the distressing day-to-day and historical timelines in which they live.[63]

While the *History* is Mac's longest produced work to date, it is not the only one that can be described as durational. Near the top of *The Lily's Revenge* (2009), a character informs the audience that "This play is LOOOOOOOOONG"—and it is, by anyone else's standards. Over nearly five hours, across five acts, a cast of forty performs an allegorical and boisterously theatrical destruction of modern Western dramatic structures that contain social problems—often resolved with a wedding—within an easily digestible two-hour time frame. "Culinary theater" is the dismissive term given to these dramatic forms by Bertolt Brecht, whose *Good Person of Szechuan* Mac performed to such piquant and poignant effect in 2013 with the Foundry Theatre.[64] However, in the absence of other aesthetic qualities, temporal indigestibility does not a queer performance make. Forced Entertainment also does twenty-four-hour shows; they, too, are messy, metatheatrical, and marvelous. But they are not queer. *The Lily's Revenge* and the *History* are *queer* durational performances because Mac and company complement those extended running times with other forms of aesthetic extremity, including a distinctive style that Jason Fitzgerald describes as "camp extravaganza" inflected by an "adorable, comic self-deprecation," a keen intelligence, and a deep ethical commitment to community-building.[65] Edgecomb persuasively links this style to Charles Ludlam's Ridiculous Theatre, with its blatant theatricality, its formal multiplicity, and its outsized intellectual and political ambition. In Ludlam's plays and in Mac's durational work, genderfuck meets genrefuck; excess—hyperbole, even—is crucial to the art and essential to its politics. Too-muchness of too many kinds is what makes Mac's durational art queer.[66]

Too-muchness is also a prime Whitmanian trait, as Mac acknowledged explicitly at CUNY and implicitly during *History* performances. Among Whitman's many formal innovations is the famous "long line," that primary unit of his free verse that is so very capacious and so fully flexible that it sometimes feels like disquisitory prose. (Indeed, in the 1855 edition, much of the poetry *looks* very much like prose, too.) Not only are the lines long; the poems within *Leaves* can themselves feel endless, especially when Whitman goes into catalog mode. As metapoetical as Mac is metatheatrical, Whitman writes that he "Know[s] my omnivorous lines and cannot write any less."[67] Mac delivers those omnivorous lines with vocal virtuosity, but even he has to push so far toward the end of his breath while reciting them that the audience whistles and applauds in appreciation of what they recognize as a feat of mental and physical endurance. Moreover, Mac's selection shows a preference for Whitman's longest poems, including "Song of Myself," "Song of the Open Road," and "Crossing Brooklyn Ferry." It is these poems that James Perrin Warren cites when he writes that "the long line captures the expansive freedom of Whitman's poetic style and evokes his vision of an expansive American culture," adding that "it is nonetheless an orderly poetic practice."[68] Both *Leaves* and the *History* are as capacious as they are because they must make room for disorder as well as order, for disintegration and integration, for gathering and dispersal—in Mac's words, for "falling apart" as well as "building up."[69] The artists build imperfection and failure into their respective projects, arguing strenuously that it is *because* they depart from normative aesthetics that they can do real democratic work.

Mac's refrain, "Perfection is for assholes," is a quip worthy of another queer apostle of aesthetic excess, Oscar Wilde, however far its sentiment departs from Wilde's own penchant for polished surfaces. Imperfection affords an accessibility that both Mac and Whitman link to the popular. Explaining the choices he made when compiling the *History*'s set list, Mac said that "classical song is about reaching for perfection—touching the hem of god. Popular song is about reaching the people, and it uses its imperfection in order to do that."[70] Mac, like Whitman's "American bard," knows that "the pleasure of poems is not in them that take the handsomest measure and similes and sound," and the people's pleasure cannot be sacrificed if the art is to do its work.[71] That work is nothing less than making a fully democratic world, the form of which is as unfixed as the East River, whose unceasing ebb and flow Whitman and Mac present as a vision of a queer utopian aesthetics that encompasses the poem, the poet, and the people: "The simple, compact, well-joined scheme—myself / disintegrated, every one disintegrated, yet part / of the scheme."[72]

The Archival "body electric"

You, too, are part of the scheme. Yes, *you*, reader, whoever and whenever you are. Whitman's poem insists that he is cruising you right now as you read his lines, and was cruising all of us gathered on the East River's bank in October 2016, who caught glimpses of the "flood-tide" and "ebb tide," on which he'd built so much of his poetry and democratic theory, as we took breathers or smoke breaks or made calls or looked across at the bridge or the skyline or up at the stars or the dawn or the rain or all of the above during the St. Ann's Warehouse shows.[73]

> I am with you, you men and women of a generation,
>   or ever so many generations hence;
> I project myself—also I return—I am with you, and
>   know how it is.[74]

The medium that ensured Whitman's access to you is the book, which he knew how to design, compose, print, bind, and advertise. His poems are replete with language that creates a complex erotic bond between writer and reader that extends across time and space because *books do*. The poet might not know your name—indeed it's more properly adhesive if he doesn't know—but he knows that when you read his lines you will be "holding me now in hand."[75] It gets sexier from there on. It's not only Whitman's body that is the "electric" conduit for the charges of affection that will adhere the nation; it's also the book, as an object, which he believes will carry those pulses across time and space and into an American future inhabited by the American lovers whom his all-encompassing vision already embraces. Mediation is no barrier to this form of stranger-intimacy.

In Mac's work, too, written and printed objects transmit not just knowledge but also affect, across bodies and across time. Bundles and suspended streams of typed and handwritten written letters are central to Mac's solo autobiographical play *The Young Ladies Of . . .* (2005), which takes its title from a 1968 call for correspondence that his late father sent out while stationed abroad with the US military. In one of the play's most poignant images, Mac's performance as "archival inquirer" takes on the form of a dance with the letters, which are animated by Basil Twist's puppetry before settling into the shape of a wearable dress.[76] If anything, bodies, archival documents, and objects are even more firmly and pleasurably entangled in the *History*. Many of the songs, most of the costumes, and more than one menu were reconstructed from research the creative team conducted using archival documents, some of which (like *Miss Beecher's Domestic Receipt Book*, 1871) they take pains to cite directly.

And then there are the mannequins. In a review of the twenty-four-hour show, Kalle Westerling described the "living costume installation" in the St. Ann's Warehouse lobby, which designer Machine Dazzle created over the course of the show by dressing twenty-four mannequins with the costumes that Mac removed at the end of each hour. (The installation subsequently toured to other venues.) Westerling, who emphasizes the ritual aspects of the performance, rightly calls this installation a "reliquary," stressing the transformational potential of the objects in the installation and those that spectators took away from the theater. These objects, he argues, "continue to move the performance's time and space into our everyday lives. . . . Who is to say that the transformation is not still going on?"[77] It is: I know it, I feel it (the ping-pong ball that made its way from the St. Ann's Warehouse floor to my pocket to an airplane to my desk tells me so), it hasn't ended, the American utopia we glimpsed in that ecstatic time is possible, in spite of everything, I can never un-see what we saw, we'll never arrive but we have to keep going, having felt what we felt we are just as Mac said we were, saying Whitman's words: "we are insatiate henceforward."[78]

Notes

1. Walt Whitman, *Leaves of Grass* (Boston: Thayer and Eldridge, 1860–61), 379–80, 385. All citations of *Leaves of Grass* refer to the digitized US editions available on the Walt Whitman Archive, whitmanarchive.org

2. Taylor Mac, Edwin Booth Award Ceremony, speech, Martin E. Segal Theatre Center, City University of New York, April 28, 2017, https://www.youtube.com/watch?v=dIkOH8gVyqU

3. Whitman's "Good Gray Poet" persona dates to the post–Civil War era, commencing with a pamphlet written in his defense, and possibly with his assistance. William Douglas O'Connor, *The Good Gray Poet* (New York: Bunce and Huntington, 1866),

https://whitmanarchive.org/criticism/disciples/tei/anc.00170.html. The epithet "Good Gay Poet" has been in circulation since the 1980s, at least. See, for example, Charley Shivley, ed., *Calamus Lovers: Walt Whitman's Working-Class Camerados* (San Francisco: Gay Sunshine Press, 1987).

4. Thomas Yingling, "Homosexuality and Utopian Discourse in American Poetry," introduction by Robyn Wiegman, in *Breaking Bounds: Whitman and American Cultural Studies*, eds. Betsy Erkkila and Jay Grossman (New York: Oxford University Press, 1996), 135–46. The *History*'s last line, sung by Mac and the audience, was this: "You can lie down or you can get up and play." Taylor Mac, "When All the Artists Leave or Die"; see Jennifer Schluesser, @jennyschluesser, Twitter post, video, October 9, 2016, https://twitter.com/jennyschuessler/status/785150559259074560

5. During *History* performances and in interviews, Mac has frequently described the show as formally inspired by his recognition that the 1987 AIDS Walk he attended in San Francisco as a teenager demonstrated to him how a community could "build itself up" even as it was "falling apart." Taylor Mac, Matt Ray, and Niegel Smith, "Sundance Theatre Lab: *A 24-Decade History of Popular Music*," September 16, 2016, https://www.youtube.com/watch?time_continue=235&v=hldiCsWXWf8&feature=emb_logo

6. "Worship the act of creation, not the creator; the making of art, not the artist." Taylor Mac, quoted by Angel Ysaguirre, @afraidoffun, Twitter post, photo, October 8, 2016, https://twitter.com/afraidoffun/status/784797149443813376. With editorial guidance, I use the pronoun "he" when referring to Mac as a creator of the *History* and other works, and "judy" (according to Mac's preference) when describing Mac's performance persona.

7. Betsy Erkkila, "Public Love: Whitman and Political Theory," in *Whitman East and West: New Contexts for Reading Walt Whitman*, ed. Ed Folsom (Iowa City: University of Iowa Press, 2002), 167.

8. José Esteban Muñoz, *Cruising Utopia: The Then and There of Queer Futurity* (New York: NYU Press, 2009), 118. Muñoz briefly touches on Whitman's practice and affirms his Brooklyn waterfront poems as utopian (189). Muñoz's work has been so widely engaged by performance scholars, including scholars who have written about Mac, that I will not rehearse his arguments here. See Sean F. Edgecomb, *Charles Ludlam Lives!* (Ann Arbor: University of Michigan Press, 2017), and Gaven D. Trinidad, "Queer Temporalities and Aesthetics in Taylor Mac's *The Lily's Revenge*" (MA thesis, University of Massachusetts–Amherst, 2018). Regarding the Brooklyn site, see also Hugh Ryan, *When Brooklyn Was Queer* (New York: St. Martin's Press, 2019). Of "Crossing Brooklyn Ferry," Ryan writes that the poem "contains perhaps the first description of cruising in American literature" (16).

9. Muñoz, *Cruising Utopia*, 189.

10. Mac has repeatedly described the show—and the rest of his work—as an effort to "remind" audiences of things they have "dismissed, forgotten, or buried." The phrase, spoken several times during the *History*, appears in Mac's "Manifesto" (2013), taylor-macnyc.com

11. Among commentators on Whitman, American critics were, as a group, late to affirm Whitman's homosexuality. In this they were aided by early biographers who took as evidence of heterosexuality Whitman's claim, in an 1890 letter to John Addington Symonds, that he had fathered "six illegitimate children" and declared accusations of

homosexuality "damnable." See, for example, Henry Bryan Binns, *Life of Walt Whitman* (London: Methuen, 1905). For an influential take on the Symonds letter, see Eve Kosofsky Sedgwick, *Between Men: English Literature and Male Homosocial Desire* (New York: Columbia University Press, 1985).

12. Whitman, *Leaves of Grass* (Brooklyn, NY: self pub., 1855), 29–30.

13. Whitman, *Leaves of Grass* (1855), 29, 55.

14. Across the ensuing editions, Whitman removed most passages directly referring to African American people. For studies that address Whitman's approach to race and center African American scholars' and writers' approach to his complex legacy, see Ivy G. Wilson, ed., *Whitman Noir: Black America and the Good Gray Poet* (Iowa City: University of Iowa Press, 2014). See also Ed Folsom, "'A Yet More Terrible and Deeply Connected Problem': Walt Whitman, Race, Reconstruction, and American Democracy," *American Literary History* 30, no. 3 (Fall 2018): 531–58.

15. See, for example, Dale Cockrell, who like some other scholars of blackface minstrelsy stresses the "transgressive ambiguity" and deep sentiment at the level of "musical understanding" in songs like "My Old Kentucky Home" (66). Cockrell, "Of Soundscapes and Blackface: From Fools to Foster," in *Burnt Cork: Traditions and Legacies of Blackface Minstrelsy*, ed. Stephen Johnson (Amherst: University of Massachusetts Press, 2012), 51–72. For a more critical approach to minstrelsy, see Eric Lott, who cites cultural historian Ann Douglas to argue that Foster's "emphasis on the departing and the departed . . . had the useful outcome of endowing Black people with human emotion, indeed the perpetual sorrow of life under slavery. That it is also one of minstrelsy's most insidious legacies—issuing today in, say, pious tributes to Martin Luther King, Jr., the hushed tears and whispers of greatness masking a lot of business as usual—should not allow us to overlook its Christian exaltation of the powerless in the nineteenth century." Lott, *Love and Theft: Blackface Minstrelsy and the American Working Class*, reissued ed. (New York: Oxford University Press, 2013), 195.

16. Saidiya V. Hartman argues that "the seeming transgression of the color line and the identification forged with the blackface mask though aversion and/or desire ultimately only served to reinforce mastery and servitude." Hartman, *Scenes of Subjection: Terror, Slavery, and Self-Making in Nineteenth Century America* (New York: Oxford University Press, 1997), esp. 25–50. See also Daphne Brooks, *Bodies in Dissent: Spectacular Performances of Race and Freedom, 1850–1910* (Durham: Duke University Press, 2006), esp. 25–29. On Foster and mass culture, see Karen L. Cox, *Dreaming of Dixie: How the South Was Created in American Popular Culture* (Chapel Hill: University of North Carolina Press, 2011), 11. Cox emphasizes that Foster and Dan Emmett ("Dixie") were—like their Tin Pan Alley followers—Northern white men whose biggest hits were sentimental songs about the antebellum South popular with Northerners and Southerners alike. Cox points out that lines like "still a-longin' for the old plantation" ("The Old Folks at Home") were used long after the Civil War to support the Lost Cause ideology, which promotes the lie that racial, gender, and economic relations in the antebellum South were beneficial to all.

17. In 1986, Kentucky House Rep. Carl R. Hines Sr. successfully introduced legislation (H.R. 159) to have the racist term replaced by "people" whenever "My Old Kentucky Home" is sung at state-sponsored events. Tom Elben, "Everyone Sings 'My Old Kentucky Home' at the Derby. Few know its controversial story," *Lexington Herald-*

Leader (April 27, 2018; updated May 9, 2018), https://www.kentucky.com/latest-news /article209975374.html. Catherine Herdman, "Interview with Carl R. Hines, Sr., June 28, 2006," Kentucky State Legislature Oral History Project, Louie B. Nunn Center for Oral History, University of Kentucky Libraries, https://kentuckyoralhistory.org/ark:/164 17/xt77wm13nn36

18. Ken Emerson, *Doo-dah! Stephen Foster and the Rise of American Popular Culture* (New York: Simon & Schuster, 1997), 187–90. Emerson writes that Foster "was among the first white boys to do what white boys (and the occasional girl) have been doing ever since—mimicking Black music, or what they think is Black music and Black style" (15).

19. See Joanna R. Smolko, "Southern-Fried Foster: Representing Race and Place through Music in Looney Tunes Cartoons," *American Music* 30, no. 3 (Fall 2012): 344–72.

20. Frederick Douglass, "The Anti-Slavery Movement, lecture delivered before the Rochester Ladies' Anti-Slavery Society," *The Life and Writings of Frederick Douglass*, ed. Philip S. Foner, vol. 2 (New York International Publishers, 1950), 356–57. Quoted in Emerson, *Doo-dah!*, 107.

21. Paul Robeson, "My Old Kentucky Home / Ol' Man River," 78 rpm recording (HMV, 1930). The song was itself incorporated into many of the innumerable stage adaptations of Stowe's novel (Emerson, *Doo-dah!*, 199–200). Both Robeson and Marian Anderson stopped performing Foster's song later in their careers. Emily Bingham points out that white and Black singers and audiences have used the song for very different—even opposite—purposes. Emily Bingham, *My Old Kentucky Home: The Astonishing Life and Reckoning of an Iconic American Song* (New York: Knopf, 2022).

22. Emerson, *Doo-dah!*, 234. My insistence that the "Home" is a plantation where the speaker is enslaved echoes the public statements of Frank X Walker, former poet laureate of Kentucky: "My issue [with the song] is that there was no good place to be a slave." "Churchill Downer: The Forgotten Racial History of Kentucky's State Song," *Morning Edition* (May 6, 2016), National Public Radio, https://www.npr.org/sections/co deswitch/2016/05/06/476890004/churchill-downer-the-forgotten-racial-history-of-ke ntuckys-state-song. See also Frank X Walker, "My Old Kentucky Home," *ACE Weekly* (November 21, 2002), https://www.aceweekly.com/2002/11/frank-x-walker-my-old-ke ntucky-home/

23. Mac and Ray may know that by turning "Massa's" minstrelsy against itself, they are extending the artistic practice of Foster's Black contemporaries William Wells Brown and Martin Delany, both of whom appropriated the song's paternalistic lyrics in 1850s novels to similarly excoriating effect. William Wells Brown, *Clotel, or, The President's Daughter* (1853), ed. Robert S. Levine (Boston: Bedford/St. Martin's Press, 2000); Martin R. Delany, *Blake, or, The Huts of America* (1859, 1861–62), ed. Jerome McGann (Cambridge, MA: Harvard University Press, 2017). On Wells and Foster, see Paul Gilmore, "'De Genewine Artekil': William Wells Brown, Blackface Minstrelsy, and Abolitionism," *American Literature* 69, no. 4 (December 1997): 758. On Delany, see also Emerson, *Doo-dah!*, 185. Mac describes "Camptown Races" as "insidious and obnoxious." "Taylor Mac on 20 Songs that Made the Cut for *A 24-Decade History of Popular Music*," *Vulture* (September 19, 2016), https://www.vulture.com/2016/09/taylor-mac-a-24-decade-histo ry-of-popular-music.html

24. Whitman, *Leaves of Grass* (1855), 29.

25. So total did Whitman's triumph seem to me during the performance that I had forgotten the fact that Mac allowed Foster to keep the paternal epithet. See Jennifer Krasinski, "'Everything You're Feeling Is Appropriate,'" *Theater* 47, no. 3 (2017): 8.

26. Whitman, *Leaves of Grass* (1855), 29.

27. Taylor Mac, *The Dying Sentimentalist*; the monologue premiered as part of the series *Our War*, dir. Anita Maynard-Losh, dramaturg Jocelyn Clarke, Arena Stage, October 21–November 9, 2014. I attended the twenty-four-hour *History* show and also a stand-alone performance of *Whitman vs. Foster* at the University of Iowa's Hancher Auditorium (November 5, 2015). At both shows, Mac performed *The Dying Sentimentalist* after Foster's "Beautiful Dreamer," though I cannot confirm that judy did so during every performance of that decade.

28. Horace Traubel, *With Walt Whitman in Camden*, vol. 6, eds. Gertrude Traubel and William White (Carbondale: Southern Illinois University Press, 1982), https://whitmanarchive.org/criticism/disciples/traubel/WWWiC/6/whole.html. In this biographical account of the conversations Traubel had with Whitman from the late 1880s until the poet's death in 1892, Whitman describes "The Old Folks at Home" and "Old Black Joe" as "superb . . . exquisite specimens, some of them, out of the heart of nature . . . [America's] best work so far" (120). He does not name Foster. In contrast to Mac's *History*, the lyric baritone Thomas Hampson's *Beyond Liberty: Songs of America* project includes both Foster songs and Whitman settings without placing the two in stark opposition to one another.

29. The 1855 frontispiece engraving of Whitman dressed in the clothes of a laborer, based on Gabriel Harrison's 1854 daguerreotype, was replaced in the 1860 edition with a portrait of the poet's hatless head and chest. See Whitman, *Leaves of Grass* (1860), https://whitmanarchive.org/published/LG/figures/ppp.01500.008.jpg. See also Ed Folsom, *Whitman Making Books/Books Making Whitman: A Catalogue and a Commentary* (Iowa City: Obermann Center for Advanced Studies, University of Iowa, 2005), https://whitmanarchive.org/criticism/current/anc.00150.html. Discussions of the portrait's homoeroticism are long-running, as are debates on Whitman's gendering of the poet-speaker, who is "maternal as well as paternal" (*Leaves* 1855, 23) and who occasionally takes up the point of view of female characters (19). Regarding the images of nude male models in Mac's costume: on at least one tour stop, Machine Dazzle was required to cover the exposed genitals of the male models whose images adorn the magazine sheets on the skirt. He did so by adding stars, which delightfully drew attention to what they were supposed to be covering. Kim Marra, email correspondence with the author, June 25, 2020.

30. Whitman, *Leaves of Grass* (1855), 29.

31. Whitman's speaking not just *for* but *as* the oppressed, without acknowledging his own difference, has generated strong debate. Peter Coviello points out that D. H. Lawrence, who accused Whitman of "'false sympathy,'" was by no means the only reader to have rejected Whitman's all-encompassing persona. Coviello, *Intimacy in America: Dreams of Affiliation in Antebellum Literature* (Minneapolis: University of Minnesota Press, 2005), 134.

32. Quoted by St. Ann's Warehouse, @stannswarehouse, Twitter post, October 8, 2016, 12:01 p.m., https://twitter.com/stannswarehouse/status/784800998619508740. Because recordings of the show have not been released, I cannot confirm that my rendering of spoken lines is correct. I cite other forms of documentation when possible.

33. Steve Turner, *Amazing Grace: The Story of America's Most Beloved Song* (New York: Ecco, 1992). Shape-note advocate William Walker set Newton's lyrics to the soaring "New Britain" (G major) in around 1835.

34. A clip of the St. Ann's Warehouse audio recording of "Amazing Grace" accompanies a video trailer created for 2017 performances of the *History* at San Francisco's Curran Theatre, https://www.youtube.com/watch?v=JHSaoMVqta4. A 2012 Joe's Pub workshop performance of "Amazing Grace," also in E minor but arranged slightly differently, can be heard on Taylor Mac's Vimeo channel, https://vimeo.com/41516001. "House of the Rising Sun," which dates back well over a century, has been recorded dozens of times since the 1930s by artists ranging from the Appalachian singer Georgia Turner to Nina Simone; Dave Van Ronk's arrangement in A minor, recorded by Bob Dylan and then the Animals, remains the best known. On Ray's re-setting of the lyrics to the tune of "Sun," see an interview with Carl Wilson, "Songs for the Fallen," the Curran blog, September 14, 2017, https://sfcurran.com/the-currant/articles/songs-for-the-fallen/. On Whitman's own brief but galvanizing visit to New Orleans, see Matt Sandler, "Kindred Darkness: Whitman in New Orleans," in *Whitman Noir*, ed. Wilson (54–80); and Folsom, "'Yet More Terrible,'" esp. 534–37.

35. Timothy White Eagle also serves as artistic director of the Dandy Minions, the *History*'s ensemble. On White Eagle's background and performance practice, see "About," Timothy White Eagle, http://www.whiteeagle.me/about

36. Whitman, *Leaves of Grass* (1855), 22.

37. Whitman, *Leaves of Grass* (1855), 25.

38. Whitman, *Leaves of Grass* (1855), 39.

39. In his preparatory notebooks (c. 1847) Whitman writes, "I am the poet of slaves, / and of the masters of slaves . . . I go with the slaves of the earth equally with the / masters . . . Entering into both, / so that both shall understand / me alike." Whitman, Talbot Wilson (Notebook LC #80), 35 verso, https://whitmanarchive.org/manuscripts/notebooks/transcriptions/loc.00141.html

40. As the *History* has toured, Mac has been speaking in Whitmanesque terms about his performance persona as a "bridge between the normative and the insane, between male and female, between the queers and the straights, and the West Coast thing and the East Coast thing." Jessica Gelt, "Taylor Mac Brings 24 Decades of Delirium to Los Angeles," *Los Angeles Times* (June 20, 2017), https://www.latimes.com/entertainment/arts/la-et-cm-taylor-mac-20170620-story.html

41. Coviello, *Intimacy in America*, 127.

42. Yingling, "Homosexuality and Utopian Discourse in American Poetry," 141, 146.

43. Whitman, *Leaves of Grass* (New York: self-pub., 1867), 191.

44. Quoted in Rob Onorato, "One Queen's Highly Personal/Subjective Reaction to Taylor Mac's *A 24-Decade History of Popular Music*," HowlRound Theatre Commons (December 15, 2016), https://howlround.com/one-queens-highly-personalsubjective-reaction-taylor-macs-24-decade-history-popular-music

45. On *The Lily's Revenge* (2009) as a rejection of LGBTQ+ political activities focused on same-sex marriage, see Trinidad, "Queer Temporality and Aesthetics." See also Jason Fitzgerald, review of *The Lily's Revenge*, *Theatre Journal* 62, no. 3 (October 2010): 457–58. Fitzgerald describes the play as "a parable of utopian revolution" (458).

46. Muñoz performs a reading of John Giorno's chapter in *You Got to Burn to Shine* on "Great Anonymous Sex," set in the Prince Street public toilets. He claims that "our

remembrances and their ritualized tellings . . . help us carve out a space for actual, living sexual citizenship." Muñoz, *Cruising Utopia*, 35.

47. Onorato, "One Queen."

48. Taylor Mac, "Comparison Is Violence, or, the Ziggy Stardust Meets Tiny Tim Songbook," June 10–11, 2010, the Arches, Glasgow.

49. Taylor Mac, "Fear Itself," *The Face of Liberalism* (2003). On Mac's "antipatriotic" makeup design for that show, see Edgecomb, *Charles Ludlam Lives!*, 149. For a recording of the song accompanying a stand-alone short film, see Taylor Mac, "Walk" (dir. Matthew Snead), 2007, https://www.youtube.com/watch?v=cu_1WeDEGTA

50. Edgecomb, *Charles Ludlam Lives!*, 151.

51. On Pfaff's Saloon at 647 Broadway, where Whitman frequently drank, talked, listened, and cruised, see Stephanie M. Blalock, *"GO TO PFAFF'S!": The History of a Restaurant and Lager Beer Saloon* (Bethlehem, PA: Lehigh University Press, 2014); and Justin Martin, *Rebel Souls: Walt Whitman and America's First Bohemians* (Philadelphia: Da Capo, 2014).

52. Whitman, *Leaves of Grass* (1855), xvi.

53. Edgecomb, *Charles Ludlam Lives!*, 126. Here Edgecomb is drawing on David Román's work on queer temporalities, and specifically on Román's concept of "archival drag." See Román, *Performance in America: Contemporary US Culture and the Performing Arts* (Durham: Duke University Press, 2005), esp. 139–78. Edgecomb also engages with Elizabeth Freeman's cognate theory of "temporal drag," which she has most recently defined as "the historicist aspect of camp sensibility." Freeman, *Beside You in Time: Sense Methods and Queer Sociabilities in the American 19th Century* (Durham: Duke University Press, 2019).

54. David Bowie, vocalist, "Heroes," by David Bowie and Brian Eno, produced by Tony Visconti, track 3 on *Heroes*, RCA Victor PL-12522, 1977.

55. Jill Dolan, *Utopia in Performance: Finding Hope at the Theater* (Ann Arbor: University of Michigan Press), 2005; on Dolan's own uptake of Bloch, see 8, 13, 97–98, 141–42. See also Muñoz, *Cruising Utopia*, 17. Duška Radosavljević refers to Dolan's thinking when she suggests briefly, in her review of a 2018 *History* performance, that "the notion of theatre as a utopia . . . suggests itself here anew." Radosavljević, "Taylor Mac—A 24-Decade History of Popular Music: The First Act at the Barbican," *Exeunt Magazine* (July 2, 2018), http://exeuntmagazine.com/reviews/review-taylor-mac-24-decade-history-popular-music-first-act-barbican/

56. Dolan, *Utopia in Performance*, 6–7.

57. Gelt, "Taylor Mac Brings 24 Decades of Delirium to Los Angeles."

58. Ari Shapiro, "Taylor Mac on Making a Better World in 24 Hours," *All Things Considered*, National Public Radio (December 28, 2016), https://www.npr.org/2016/12/28/507267783/taylor-mac-on-making-a-better-world-in-24-hours

59. Coviello, *Intimacy in America*, 155.

60. Coviello, *Intimacy in America*, 155. Coviello is here drawing on Michael Warner, "Whitman Drunk," in *Breaking Bounds*, eds. Erkkila and Grossman, 30–43.

61. Gelt, "Taylor Mac Brings 24 Decades of Delirium to Los Angeles."

62. Elizabeth Freeman, *Time Binds: Queer Temporalities, Queer Histories* (Durham: Duke University Press, 2010). On durational performance as a challenge to dominant temporal regimes, see Adrian Heathfield, "Impress of Time," in *Out of Now: The Life-*

works of Tehching Hsieh, by Adrian Heathfield and Tehching Hsieh (Cambridge, MA: MIT Press, 2009); Jonathan Kalb, *Great Lengths: Seven Works of Marathon Theater* (Ann Arbor: University of Michigan Press, 2011); and Lawrence Switzky, "Marathon Theatre as Affective Labour: Productive Exhaustion in *The Godot Cycle* and *Life and Times*," *Canadian Theatre Review* 162 (Spring 2015): 26–30.

63. Gelt, "Taylor Mac Brings 24 Decades of Delirium to Los Angeles."

64. Bertolt Brecht, *Brecht on Theatre: The Development of an Aesthetic*, ed. and trans. John Willett (New York: Hill and Wang, 1977).

65. Fitzgerald, review of *The Lily's Revenge*, 458.

66. Edgecomb, *Charles Ludlam Lives!*, 9–16.

67. Whitman, *Leaves of Grass* (1867), 77.

68. James Perrin Warren, "Style," *A Companion to Walt Whitman*, 383.

69. Mac, Ray, and Smith, "Sundance Theatre Lab."

70. Mac, Ray, and Smith, "Sundance Theatre Lab."

71. Whitman, *Leaves of Grass* (1855), vi.

72. Whitman, *Leaves of Grass* (1867), 379.

73. Whitman, *Leaves of Grass* (1867), 258.

74. Whitman, *Leaves of Grass* (1867), 186.

75. Whitman, *Leaves of Grass* (1867), 122. See Warner, "Whitman Drunk," on how poems like "Whoever You Are . . ." and "To a Stranger" "mim[e] the phenomenology of cruising" (41).

76. R. Justin Hunt, "Queer Debts and Bad Documents: Taylor Mac's *Young Ladies Of . . .*," in *Queer Dramaturgies: International Perspectives on Where Performance Leads Queer*, eds. Alyson Campbell and Stephen Farrier (London: Palgrave, 2016), 210–222.

77. Kalle Westerling, review of *A 24-Decade History of Popular Music*, by Taylor Mac, directed by Niegel Smith, St. Ann's Warehouse, *Theatre Journal* 69, no. 3 (September 2017): 408–9.

78. Whitman, *Leaves of Grass* (1867), 192.

SEVEN

Circles and Lines

Community and Legacy in Taylor Mac's Gary: A Sequel to "Titus Andronicus"

Erika T. Lin

Taylor Mac's first Broadway play, *Gary: A Sequel to "Titus Andronicus,"* is the most commercial theatrical venture in his artistic trajectory. The institutional conditions of its production thus sit uneasily with the view, both in this play and in his earlier work, of capitalist political economy as antithetical to affective community. In this essay, I therefore focus on the script of *Gary* to get at important dimensions of Mac's vision, whether or not they were fully realized onstage in the 2019 production. Imagined as taking place immediately after Shakespeare's bloodiest tragedy ends with a giant pile of corpses, *Gary* raises crucial questions about not only who is forced to clean up the mess but also how one goes about doing so. As in its sixteenth-century antecedent, the play uses the literal to figure the metaphorical. What does it mean to inherit a patriarchal history where "civilization" is founded on death and sexual violence? If our present state of affairs is like a revenge tragedy—a genre defined by the circularity of its horrors, with cruelty and brutality begetting more of the same—is it possible to break the cycle, transforming tragedy into comedy? How do we fashion a new legacy for the future, turning death into life? What kind of work must we do to build a better world out of the rubble of the past? This essay examines Mac's exploration of these questions by looking at the artistic vision laid out in the Prologue and its realization in the play-within-the-play known as the Fooling. I center my analysis on the play's attitudes toward two key issues: (1) narrative, a linear form laden with the legacy of what came before, and (2) affective experience, generated through performance and encircling the audience. The dynamic interrelation between these two, I argue, constitutes a tentative response to how we create new forms of community through art, making meaning amid the mess of material reality.

Gary follows the story of a clown with a minor role in the original play, who in Mac's sequel takes a job cleaning up the giant mound of corpses that remains at the end of *Titus Andronicus*. Gary is helplessly inept at this work, constantly lost in daydreams about becoming a court jester, or Fool. He is schooled in his tasks by the more experienced maid Janice, who labors without complaint at "process[ing]"[1] the bodies. At key moments, the two are joined as well by the midwife Carol, a character based on the Nurse in Shakespeare's drama who delivers Tamora's baby and is therefore killed to prevent disclosure of the queen's affair with Aaron the Moor. That child appears at the end of *Gary*, represented by a "real baby" (4, 50) who is "visibly dark-skinned" (4).

The overall narrative thus follows a clear linear arc: the end of Shakespeare's tragedy leads straight into the beginning of Mac's play. The Prologue itself highlights the issue of narrative form from its very first lines, delivered by Carol, who is bleeding from her neck:

> Like God, a sequel hides inside an ending:
> When time is up you pray that it's extending.
> For life, to cultured, and to the philistine
> Once felt, is craved 'til thrills become routine.
> But once routine the thrills, to thrill, must grow.
> And if they don't, an outrage starts to show.
> So double up on savagery and war:
> To satisfy you multiply the gore. (7)

If novelty, the play seems to ask, necessarily becomes routine over time, then spectacle must be ratcheted up to feed the craving for sensation that may be initially desired but is also, through the process, amplified. The need to "multiply the gore" then drives the story to require ever-greater "savagery and war." In this pattern, the "sequel" is the built-in circularity inherent in all linear narrative, where the seeming "ending" is actually "extending." The repetition itself over time forces further outrages, so that violence seems to be a never-ending cycle that cannot be broken.

From the outset, then, *Gary* not only invokes its sixteenth-century antecedent but also recursively reflects on that play's structure. *Titus Andronicus* is notable for being one of Shakespeare's earliest revenge tragedies, deploying a variety of dramatic conventions that are also exhibited later on in *Hamlet*.[2] One pervasive strategy was the use of the literal to figure the metaphorical, a technique that is also central to Mac's play and that bears on the relation between linear and circular narrative forms. In revenge tragedy, when heads of state are brought low, figurative decapitation leads to actual beheading. When the military turns against its leaders, the hands that bear arms are literally cut off. The fracturing of the body politic is concretized in the dismemberment of the physical body, a logic that integrates narrative structure with stage action. Such generic conventions grow out of early modern understandings of the sacred and the profane as intimately—and materially—connected. Human actions were believed to have very real spiritual consequences, and the heavenly truth was thought to manifest in palpable ways on earth. Macrocosm and microcosm were directly linked, it was widely held, so the overturning of social hierarchies necessarily led to chaos and ruin. This was not merely a metaphor; that is, the inversion of worldly degree was not simply *styled* as destructive to proscribe it as immoral. Rather, failure to mirror divine order was understood to result in disaster because the supernatural was literally incarnated in the mortal.[3] This mode of thinking is analogic and metonymic. And these same interpretive tendencies help explain early modern revenge tragedy's interweaving of linearity and circularity in its narrative forms: violence begets more violence when humans are left to themselves because of original sin, but all-seeing God can discern true from false, so as the popular saying went, "murder will out," and justice will be restored in the end. The trajectory of providential history is a linear one, teleologically headed toward its preordained end; it is only poor, limited mortals who get stuck in an endless cycle of suffering.

These themes, conventions, and forms are reappropriated and reimagined in Taylor Mac's play. In *Gary*, the linear is the unending path toward increasing sensationalism that results from a recursive process that numbs the senses and eventuates in wholesale destruction. Mac underscores the process of repetition in his own verbal form when Carol says "once routine the thrills, to thrill, must grow." The line echoes Shakespeare's own metrical rhythms and wordplay, as for example in Sonnet 83 when he writes "Speaking of worth, what worth in you doth grow," or in *Love's Labor's Lost* when Berowne says "Study knows that which yet it doth not know."[4] Moreover, the content of Carol's line describes the actual historical trajectory of revenge tragedy. As early modern audiences became accustomed to its conventions, the mechanisms through which killing took place became ever more elaborate, as if playwrights sought to outdo each other with their ingenuity. At the genre's height in the early seventeenth century, plays depicted murder via, for instance, poisoned incense used as special effect in a play-within-a-play (Thomas Middleton's *Women Beware Women*), snapping a man's neck while inverted over a vaulting horse (John Webster's *The White Devil*), and dressing an exhumed corpse in a wedding gown and painting its lips with poison to kill the groom at the very moment he kisses the "bride" (Thomas Middleton and/or Cyril Tourneur's *The Revenger's Tragedy*).

The increasing sensationalism of Jacobean revenge tragedy reflects precisely the sentiment in *Gary* that "once routine the thrills, to thrill, must grow," and thus "To satisfy you multiply the gore." Presenting "A scene so monstrous it sends up the savage" (7) may be for laudable ends—"Presumably to snuff what makes us ravage" (7), curing blood lust by "feasting on the gore 'til you are ill; / . . . / Until you vomit what did once fulfill" (7).[5] But in the "centuries of applause" generated by such violence (8), there are also potentially negative real-world consequences—and *Gary* seems to imply that those consequences are specifically mobilized through audience affect. As the stage direction notes, it is at just this point in the action that the performer playing Carol "takes her hand away from the wound. Blood runs down her for the rest of the prologue. What was funny is now disturbing" (8). How, then, *can* theater work against violence? What narratives will be most effective? And how to enlist the cooperation of the audience to help build a better world? These are the questions laid out in the Prologue—and the rest of the play constitutes a sort of response, if not answer, to these ethical dilemmas. That response involves tracing the complex workings of two interlocking aspects of theater: narrative content and presentational experience. The former is linear: narrative must grapple with before and after, with whether to "surpass the past or be its equal" (8), whether to "affirm or break the bloody sequel" (8). The latter is circular: presentational experience encompasses the audience, both elicits and depends on their reactions, whether "feasting on the gore 'til you are ill" (7) or "applauding because her throat is slit" (7).

The dynamic interplay between these two modes is established at the end of the Prologue when Gary enters. The question of who must "clean up" (8) the mess of history is narrativized in the play by literally centering the story on maids. At this crucial juncture in the Prologue, it is also enacted experientially by tying the presentational action onstage directly to audience response. Carol says "Enter the maid" (8)—and Gary appears. In a classic invocation of the *theatrum mundi* trope, Carol's line collapses the distance between dramatic fiction and presentational action. The dialogue *is* a stage direction. It is a speech act, conjuring the clown. When "Gary enters, pulling a mop and bucket with him," the stage direction notes that "We hear entrance applause. Gary, who doesn't notice Carol, looks into the audience" (8); he says "A maid just enters and he gets applause? Best first day on the job that ever was" (8). The joke, of course, is that Broadway audiences tend to applaud at the first entrance of any celebrity, a sign of their enthusiasm for the actor, not the character. The applause is thus for performance achievements, not narrative content, for Nathan Lane, not for "A maid [who] just enters." The "job" that spectators value is the actor's, not the cleaner's.[6] Artistic achievement is lauded, whereas manual labor is ignored.

On one level—the more cognitive level—the play invites audiences to reflect on that disjunction, to ask whose work is more valued. On another level, though, a more affective level—the moment provokes laughter, the desired response for a lauded comedian. Aside from the especially cerebral types, who might reflect on their own experiences while having them (and it is downtown theater, not Broadway, that explicitly espouses self-reflexivity as a virtue), the line does not seem structured to make spectators particularly uncomfortable. This laughter, in other words, is not the kind that forces audiences to react, reflect, and then feel horrified at their own reactions. In *A 24-Decade History of Popular Music*, when Mac performs comfortingly familiar songs by Stephen Foster that cause listeners to sway or nod along in enjoyment, and then immediately informs them of Foster's virulent racism, he forces them to confront the implications of their own unthinking response. This opening moment in *Gary*, by contrast, produces an affective response that lands less as indictment than as question: Why *do* we applaud at art? How does art relate to other forms of labor? How can we leverage audience response, specifically laughter, to transform tragedy into comedy, to break a cycle of violence that has led—seemingly inexorably—to the current apocalyptic moment?

The part of Mac's play that explores these questions most fully is the lead-up to and performance of the inset show known as the Fooling, a ridiculously over-the-top display replete with explosions and animated corpses created by Gary and involving Janice and Carol. As the author's headnote describes, "It is one of the more spectacular moments ever to be seen in the history of theater" (5). The incorporation of such an elaborate entertainment into the plot of *Gary* follows in the early modern revenge tragedy tradition, which often featured inset masques, dumbshows, or other spectacles in which characters from the main story performed. Such moments call attention to the viewing practices of actual spectators by self-consciously doubling them through plays-within-plays. In doing so, both early modern revenge tragedies and Mac's play raise questions about the ethics of artistic creation and audience complicity.

Indeed, early modern genre theory is a complex field that weaves together audience affect and narrative form. Drawing on Aristotle, Renaissance humanists viewed tragic *catharsis* as beneficial purgation necessary for the proper working of the *polis*.[7] The connection between social order and genre theory also extended beyond learned writers, with numerous anecdotes circulating in popular literature about tyrants, murderers, and adulterous women moved to confess their crimes after watching a play. Such discourses were integrated outright into early modern revenge tragedy through the use of inset entertainments. The most famous example is, of course, *Hamlet*, in which "the play's the thing / Wherein I'll catch the conscience of the King" (2.2.604–5). But in *Titus Andronicus* as well, the banquet scene that caps the play is where the title character, dressed "like a cook" (5.3.25.s.d.), sets up the unwitting participation of his antagonists—who are tyrannous, murderous, and adulterous—in a spectacle of cannibalism that leads to the revelation of their crimes and ultimate slaughter. In revenge tragedy, such plays-within-plays and spectacular displays were often the climax of the story, where the events set in motion at the beginning of the narrative come to a head.

Unlike in early modern genre theory, for Mac comedy and tragedy serve as indexical signifiers pointing to positive and negative social outcomes respectively, but both still involve moving the audience emotionally. The play makes this connection evident when it describes the planning for the Fooling in explicitly political terms. When Janice reminds Gary of "the inauguration banquet happening in the morning" (28) and demands "help me clean the goddamn coup" (28), her statement prompts Gary to shout "THAT'S IT. WE'RE GONNA STAGE A COUP!" (29):

GARY. We're gonna make a spectacle that is its own kind of coup.
JANICE. We ain't got coup enough?
GARY. Not a violent coup. An artistic one. A sort of theatrical revenge on the Andronicus revenge. A comedy revenge to end all revenge.

Well not just a comedy. A sorta folly. No a spectacle. Or a comedy folly that is a spectacle. Sorta a machination. (29)[8]

The speech calls to mind Polonius's famous description of those who per-form the play-within-the-play in *Hamlet* as the "best actors in the world, either for tragedy, comedy, history, pastoral, pastoral-comical, historical-pastoral, [tragical-historical, tragical-comical-historical-pastoral,] scene individable, or poem unlimited" (2.2.396–400). This echo of Shakespeare resonates with Gary's subsequent remark that the show must have "all the history in it. All the conflicts" (29). Whether intentional or not, this tacit nod to Mac's literary antecedents gestures toward the weight of dramatic history. In calling attention to questions of genre, the play implicitly asks how to break from revenge tragedy's conventions and thus from the legacy of this cycle of violence that the genre represents.

Moreover, the question here, as in the Prologue, is how a transforma-tion of violence into a comic entertainment affects the audience. Does "put[ting] all the murder and mayhem in one place" enable them to "see what's what" (29)? How can and should artists leverage audience affect toward positive social ends? Such issues are especially pertinent when dealing with spectacle, which numerous theorists have described as pro-ducing a politically passive, vacuous spectator who treats art as commod-ity.[9] Certainly, that charge might be levied against Broadway playgoers, for whom theater is a tourist destination and a site for capitalist consump-tion. Indeed, the inset entertainment's most memorable feature in the 2019 production was the reanimation of the dead bodies and their forma-tion into a kind of puppet kick line that danced across the stage with the corpses' penises moving in synchrony. The stage direction in Mac's play does include this detail, but in reading the script it seems more a culmina-tion of the extensive mayhem that preceded it than the main feature of the Fooling as it was on Broadway.

Such sensationalism is explicitly politicized in Mac's script through topical references to US electoral affairs. As Gary puts it, the "artistic" coup that becomes the Fooling must "theatricalize the sequels after the sequel after the sequels. And all the orgies of hyperbole, the grabbing of privacy and privates, takeovers, tantrums, endless campaigns, pillaged elections, apocalyptic-weather-spewing-forth-shark-attack-family-feuds!" (29). In alluding to the Access Hollywood tapes, in which then-presidential can-didate Donald Trump bragged about grabbing women's genitals, and his baseless claims of voter fraud, the line considers how stage violence is related to state violence—here, the 2016 US presidential election, though also, in a prophetic turn, the 2020 election and subsequent coup attempt on January 6, 2021. The remedy Gary proposes is akin to what Judith Butler has referred to as "hyperbolic citation," whereby an act is exaggerated in precisely the way necessary to expose—and thus undermine and reverse—the (otherwise mystified and naturalized) discourses and ideologies that subtend it.[10] The Fooling's outrageousness is to amplify the spectacle "to such a ridiculous degree ya can't see anything but its ridiculousness" (29). When the entertainment is realized, this hyperbolic quality is explicitly extended to the theater event itself. As the stage direction puts it, "the Rube Goldberg machine should be a theatrical faking of one, that gives the appearance of moments propelled into other moments, but which becomes fantastic—perhaps wonderfully obvious—in its faking" (49). The Fooling's "wonderful obvious[ness]," in other words, reveals the artifice of theater, unabashedly showcases the fakery that makes theater work. It lays bare, both literally and figuratively, the elaborate machinery that is normally hidden.

In this sense, the play seems to espouse a decidedly queer aesthetic in which the appropriate is overthrown by the ridiculous, in which that deemed shameful by straight culture is unapologetically displayed and celebrated. Where *Gary* supersedes this model, however, is in its ambition to reach beyond queer subculture by fostering positive communal affect among a broader general audience. The Fooling, as Gary envisions it, aims to force spectators to greater self-awareness:

> [W]hen the court sees it, they'll be a little taken aback at first. They'll [*sic*] be a moment of silence, don't kid yourself. But then, in the distance, one soul will feel a bubbling finding its way to their hands. "What am I doing," they'll wonder. "Why am I clapping?" And they'll realize. They're clapping for hope. (29–30)

The series of questions the imagined spectators ask themselves grows out of the seemingly unmotivated nature of their actions. Their bodies respond first; their minds then follow. That process leads them to "realize" and name the feeling they have as "hope." The "court" here serves as the onstage representative of the real-life audience, a comparison driven home in dialogue after the inset show (and attendees of the 2019 Broadway production did indeed applaud a great deal at the Fooling). The court is presumptively straight (and white and elite). It is, at first, taken aback. But the power of theater to produce overt expressions of feeling is central to this vision.

In this view, self-awareness is not so much the Brechtian sharpening of critical insight or building of proletarian solidarity but rather affect as a spontaneous communal group experience:

> And soon it spreads. Not just one court member but two. Then more. Row after row, gaining speed, soon all the court, the clapping turns to cheering, then standing on their feet, on chairs, reaching ever higher to touch the ingenuity that could be theirs as well. If two maids could turn the hopelessness of a massacre into a coup of beauty, they too can imagine a better world. New ways of government will spring forth, new mechanisms of distribution. (30)

This utopian vision springs from theater's ability to encourage audience identification with onstage characters. If two (lowly) maids can transform "massacre" into "beauty," then playgoers will believe that "the ingenuity . . . could be theirs as well" to "imagine a better world." This "ingenuity" is, for Mac, clearly wrapped up with artistic creation. The word appears throughout the play. It is used when Gary describes escaping the hangman's noose as "me first ingenuity" (14) and then tied to the aspiring Fool's poetic pretensions: "Never rhymed before. Ooo, me ingenuity is picking up the speed" (14). Later, when accused of spouting blank verse, Gary again claims he is "Using me ingenuity" (21). In this vein, theater can inspire others and help to create "a better world."

It is hard to avoid the play's insistence, however, on the gendered nature of artistic work. Men, it seems to imply, get to go off on these self-indulgent flights of fancy, while women do all the (invisible) labor. Janice, for instance, repudiates Gary's "ingenuity" as mere "plopping about" (16). Poetry and clowning, she insists, do not count as real work. Gary suggests presenting the corpses "all in a line kicking in the same direction" to "symbolize a revolt from tragedy" (43). To Janice, this is "Just more plopping about" and "Just more shuffling. Making a mess ya can confuse with a purpose. Plopping and shuffling. Revolt after revolt. Never thinking a revolt could be to clean" (43). In "refus[ing] to pick up a mess so people see the error of their ways" (43), she says, Gary will "make an even bigger massacre" (44), eventually "causing more death, and so on until the entire world looks just like this room. So, yes, you're ingenious but unless ya want to be responsible for the fall of the Roman Empire, BEST GET

CLEANING!" (44). Her frustration at Gary's artistic airs leads her to accidentally "suck . . . the wrong tube" (44), physically enacting the metaphor of women having to swallow men's shit. After she vomits and "get[s] all the clown out of ya" (45), Janice finally "pulls the curtain closed" (45)—and then proceeds to speak in rhyming verse herself, which she later refers to as "using me ingenuity" (47).

It is at this crucial moment that the actual playhouse audience is integrated into the action. In the middle of her long monologue, Janice asks "Does anyone have a mint?" (45). The brief stage direction in earlier versions of the play ("after she gets it")[11] is considerably expanded in the Dramatists Acting Edition:

> If an audience member doesn't volunteer a mint, Janice says things like: "No really, I'm actually asking. Does anyone?" If they still don't offer one, she could say, "It's alright, I'll wait. Anyone?" If they still don't, she can ask sincerely, "Really?" If they still don't: She shrugs and continues on with the scene. If they do have one she can say, "Appreciate it." Or, if nobody in the orchestra has one and there's a balcony in the theater, "Feel free to throw one down from the balcony . . . I'll wait." If someone does she can say, "Oh there ya go . . . you can just sort of pass that up to me . . . or . . . oh never mind . . . getting a little too elaborate." (45–46)

This significant revision does not just elaborate on the stage business; it integrates into the script precisely the sort of improvisatory, cabaret-style banter with the audience that Taylor Mac himself might engage in. Coming as it does at the halfway point of an extended soliloquy in iambic pentameter, this audience interaction might seem incongruent. But that, I would argue, is precisely the point. Art, the play seems to imply, *requires* the audience. It has no meaning without them. Dramatic form, no matter how ornate, comes down to interpersonal exchange between performers and spectators—a figurative, affective exchange that is here literalized in the exchange of an actual object to be consumed. That this object is a mint is used to turn the gaze back on the audience. As the stage direction instructs, Janice "unwraps the mint as noisily as possible, while looking at an audience member who, earlier, was unwrapping theirs" (46).

Soon thereafter Janice "pulls the curtain open, revealing Carol," whom she and Gary then try to cheer up. "Look at the clown. I can do tricks. Woooo!" (48), Janice says, then "does a pratfall" (48). Gary "tries to juggle and drops things" (48), leading Carol to "throw . . . poo" (48) at him. They both then try to tell a joke about "The maid, the clown and the midwife who walked into a . . ." (48), when they are interrupted by the Fooling:

> Gary unties a leg that is above a teeter-totter-like catapult. The leg drops and catapults a severed head across the room where it knocks over an arm that smacks a butt on a corpse that leaps forward and starts a domino of corpses. (48)

This "Rube Goldberg machine" (48) leads to increasingly frenetic and wild spectacles, with "miniature bombings, infernos and floods" (48), a flying "dead rat with pigeon–pheasant wings glued on it" (49), and "sparks of smoke [that] explode and crescendo into an explosion of an explosion" (49). The entire extravaganza culminates in a wedding ceremony with

> Janice, as Emperor–Maid officiate, and Gary and the handsome corpse as grooms . . . while cannons explode and white and red rose petals fall from the ceiling. At this moment all the corpses lose their clothes and all their penises, at the same time, move from right to left [yes really]. (49)

As in its generic precursors, the Fooling in *Gary* also functions as its culminating episode, but whereas inset entertainments in early modern revenge tragedy often led to their violent finales, Mac's "machine made from the slaughter" (5) aims to transform tragedy into comedy.[12] Following after the (unsuccessful) clowning for Carol, the inset show takes the detritus of destruction and turns it into the pinnacle of theatrical spectacle.

Moreover, the Fooling not only animates the dead, quite literally, but culminates in marriage, the proverbial conclusion to a Shakespearean comedy. For the "wedding canopy" (49), Gary appropriates "Lavinia's branches" (49)—which she "used . . . for arms when they chomped [*sic*] them off her . . . . After raping her and cutting out her tongue. Being more cruel to her than anyone in the world for the entertainment of it. For the ridiculousness. For someone's fooling" (32). This comparison originates in Shakespeare's reference to those assaulting Lavinia having "lopp'd and hew'd, and made thy body bare / Of her two branches" (*Titus Andronicus*, 2.4.17–18), but has its most potent recent illustration in Julie Taymor's 1999 film *Titus*, which literalizes the metaphor by showing Lavinia's amputated arms intentionally impaled with tree branches. Such horrific images are but one example of the violence that Mac is trying to work against by using art to transform death into life, tragedy into comedy.

The postshow denouement picks up on this misogyny by making explicit that artistic redemption is not equally available to all. Incorporating the audience into the show through spectacle may produce a circle of hope, a marriage instead of a slaughter, but that narrative is predicated on the subjugation of women in heteropatriarchy. Lavinia's branches bless the marriage of two men. The play here calls attention to the real-life audience's response to the Fooling:

> JANICE. (*Gesturing to the audience.*) Well some of the court seemed to like it.
> GARY. What ya saying, the court's been here from the top?
> JANICE. Gotta arrive early to get a good seat for an inauguration. Who'd ya think they were?
> GARY. Me imaginary friends.
> JANICE. No, that's the court. (49)

Interpellating actual theatergoers into the action by hailing them as the Roman court, Mac implies they are passive spectators, politically bankrupt supporters of the existing status quo and consumers of the spectacle. (One typescript even alludes directly to the cost of commercial theater, with Janice saying "Ya know how much these tickets are? That's the court right there."[13]) Artists, in other words, are in a bind, since audiences dictate what gets put onstage and how it is interpreted. But even amid this deflating scenario, Mac offers a possible vision for how art might yet "save the world" (50): Janice imagines a spectacle with "a line of *LIVING* women kicking all in one direction, symbolizing a revolt, and taking over the world" (50). That feminist fantasy does not come to fruition in this play. *Gary*, that is, remains a tragedy because no one listens to Janice—but, the play implies, if spectators heeded Cassandra, what a better world it would be!

This hopeful view, of how art might leverage spectacle to overthrow a patriarchal regime, culminates in the play's final image of the "darkskinned baby" (4). In Shakespeare's drama, Tamora (unlike Lavinia) is not raped; she actively chooses Aaron the Moor for her lover. Their child is thus a reminder of women's sexual agency and ability to interrupt patrilineage.[14] In Mac's sequel, that agency is transferred to the infant boy, for as Gary instructs, "when all the men's penises go from right to left, at the same time, that's your cue, you're gonna enter crawling across the hall with a look on your face like a munching shark who's gonna eat the tragedy of the world" (52). On the one hand, this is dispiriting: how likely is it really that a single artist, vulnerable as this child, could end the eternal tragedy of the world?

On the other hand, there is theatrical power—and narrative weight—in the irony of the moment. Gary tells the baby what to do—but of course no one can control a baby. An infant in a "shark onesie" (51) will decide how the story ends. The baby's agency, and by extension the potential for new beginnings, is underscored in an expansion of a stage direction across script revisions. Where in an earlier draft there is the brief reference "Carol suddenly enters with a pram,"[15] later versions involve much more elaborate stage business:

> Carol enters with a real baby. No matter how the baby responds [sleeps, cries, poops, laughs] the actors play the remaining scene and incorporate the baby into it. This means the end of the play will be played differently every night depending on how the baby responds. Some nights the actors will need to shout over crying. Others [sic] times they'll try to comfort it. Sometimes they'll be more quiet to not wake it up. Maybe one night Gary changes it onstage. (50)[16]

The baby is the one who "upstages all" and "steals the show" (51). In a twist on the old adage never to go onstage after animals and children, Gary incorporates both, noting that "The sensible theatrical advice / That's passed through all the genres and the ages / Is never work with babies dressed as fish" (51). The power of theater, in other words, lies in how it captivates spectators, whether through large spectacles (like the Fooling) or small ones (like the child). The Prologue and Epilogue that bookend the play thus pointedly reverse beginning and end, entrance and exit, birth and death. If the past is tragedy, Mac asks, can the future be comedy? Can sorrow be transformed to joy? Perhaps the best contemporary "sequel" to "classic" tragedy is the one that artists and audiences create together in community, turning the legacy of violence into the promise of new life, processing corpses into babies. As Gary says to the child in his last line, "Ya know what I mean?" (52). And as Mac says to us in his, "The end?" (52).

Notes

Many thanks to Viva DeConcini and Jennie Youssef for their generous feedback on earlier versions of this essay.

1. Taylor Mac, *Gary: A Sequel to "Titus Andronicus,"* Acting Edition (New York: Dramatists Play Service, 2020), 4. Subsequent citations will be in the body of the text. Unless otherwise noted, all quotations from *Gary* are from this edition and have been cross-checked against the following for any substantive differences: Taylor Mac, "Gary: A Sequel to Titus Andronicus," August 7, 2019 typescript, courtesy of the author; Taylor Mac, *Gary: A Sequel to Titus Andronicus*, directed by George C. Wolfe, June 14, 2019 videorecording (New York: Theatre on Film and Tape Archive, 2019), DVD, New York Public Library for the Performing Arts, Billy Rose Theatre Division, Theatre on Film and Tape Archive, NCOV 4269; and Taylor Mac, "Gary: A Sequel to Titus Andronicus," June 5, 2019 typescript, New York Public Library for the Performing Arts, Billy Rose Theatre Division, NCOF+ 17–4390. Quotations from the dramatis personae and other prefatory material have been cross-checked against the August 7, 2019 typescript only, as the June 5, 2019 typescript begins directly with the Prologue, corresponding to p. 7 of the Dramatists Acting Edition. Unfortunately Taylor Mac, *Gary: A Sequel to "Titus Andronicus"* (New York: Theatre Communications Group, 2021) appeared after this volume was already in press and could not be taken fully into account.

2. On revenge tragedy, see especially Tanya Pollard, "Tragedy and Revenge," in *The Cambridge Companion to English Renaissance Tragedy*, eds. Emma Smith and Garrett A. Sullivan Jr. (New York: Cambridge University Press, 2010), 58–72; and Marissa Greenberg, *Metropolitan Tragedy: Genre, Justice, and the City in Early Modern England* (Toronto: University of Toronto Press, 2015), 47–75.

3. For a fuller account of the theatrical implications of these beliefs, see my discussion of allegory and mimesis in *The Spanish Tragedy*, another early example of revenge tragedy, in Erika T. Lin, *Shakespeare and the Materiality of Performance* (New York: Palgrave Macmillan, 2012), 71–104.

4. G. Blakemore Evans et al., eds., *The Riverside Shakespeare*, 2nd ed. (Boston: Houghton Mifflin, 1997), 83.8, 1.1.68. Subsequent citations will be in the body of the text. Unless otherwise noted, all quotations from Shakespeare are from this edition and have been cross-checked against the following for any substantive differences: Jonathan Bate, ed., *Titus Andronicus*, rev. ed., Arden Shakespeare, Third Series (London: Bloomsbury Arden Shakespeare, 2018); Stephen Greenblatt et al., eds., *The Norton Shakespeare* (New York: Norton, 1997); Charlton Hinman, ed., *The First Folio of Shakespeare* (New York: Norton, 1968); and Stephen Booth, *Shakespeare's Sonnets* (New Haven: Yale University Press, 1977).

5. The sentiment echoes the beginning of *Twelfth Night*, when Orsino opines "Give me excess of it; that surfeiting, / the appetite may sicken, and so die" (1.1.2–3). But Shakespeare refers not to violence but to lovesickness; his preceding line is "If music be the food of love, play on" (1.1.1). Music, too, is Mac's cure: although he uses it less in this play than in his other work, especially *A 24-Decade History of Popular Music*, sound encircles the audience, resonates through their bodies.

6. Indeed, the issue of labor is emphasized in the author's revisions: Gary's line "Best

day ever!" (2) in the June 5, 2019 typescript is replaced in the August 7, 2019 typescript and the Dramatists Acting Edition with "Best first day on the job that ever was" (8).

7. For a more nuanced account of differences between English and Continental understandings of *catharsis*, see Greenberg, *Metropolitan Tragedy*, 76–107.

8. The June 5, 2019 typescript interpolates a few additional lines, which were cut in subsequent versions, including a mention of the "artistic" coup as "a transformation of the calamity we got here" (32). This reference calls to mind Mac's frequent advice that, when live performers are faced with unexpected audience disruptions, the best strategy is "incorporating the calamity." Sasha Weiss, "Taylor Mac Wants Theater to Make You Uncomfortable," *New York Times Magazine*, April 2, 2019, https://www.nytimes.com/2019/04/02/magazine/taylor-mac-gary-broadway.html. Such resonances, in this context, envision the reparation of tragic outcomes through virtuosic (comedic) improvisation, underscoring performance's political potential.

9. See Bertolt Brecht, *Brecht on Theatre: The Development of an Aesthetic*, ed. and trans. John Willett (New York: Hill and Wang, 1964); Guy Debord, *The Society of the Spectacle* (1967; repr., New York: Zone Books, 1994); Jean Baudrillard, *Simulations*, trans. Paul Foss, Paul Patton, and Philip Beitchman (New York: Semiotext(e), 1983); and Jean Baudrillard, *Simulacra and Simulation*, trans. Sheila Faria Glaser (Ann Arbor: University of Michigan Press, 1994). For an important attempt to recuperate the spectator, see Jacques Rancière, *The Emancipated Spectator*, trans. Gregory Elliott (London: Verso, 2009).

10. Judith Butler, *Bodies That Matter: On the Discursive Limits of "Sex"* (New York: Routledge, 1993), 232.

11. Mac, "Gary," June 5, 2019 typescript; Mac, *Gary*, June 14, 2019 videorecording; and Mac, "Gary," August 7, 2019 typescript.

12. This is not to say that early modern revenge tragedy did not involve comic elements. On the pleasures of theatrical dismemberment and their relation to festive sport, in a variety of early modern plays including *Titus Andronicus*, see Lin, *Shakespeare and the Materiality of Performance*, 135–65.

13. Mac, "Gary," August 7, 2019 typescript, 58. None of the other versions include this reference to the cost of admission.

14. On female sexual desire subverting patrilineal inheritance, see Phyllis Rackin, *Stages of History: Shakespeare's English Chronicles* (Ithaca, NY: Cornell University Press, 1990), 146–200. On Tamora's sexual desire in relation to white patriarchy, see Francesca T. Royster, "White-limed Walls: Whiteness and Gothic Extremism in Shakespeare's *Titus Andronicus*," *Shakespeare Quarterly* 51 (2000): 432–55. In *Gary*, although the baby's skin color is noted, issues of race remain largely unaddressed.

15. Mac, "Gary," June 5, 2019 typescript, 62.

16. And the list continues. The quoted selection comprises only about half of the expanded stage direction. See also Mac, "Gary," August 7, 2019 typescript, 60.

EIGHT

Designturgy, Being Queer
Taylor Mac Wears Machine Dazzle in 24 Decades

Sissi Liu

For the viewer-participants of Taylor Mac's now legendary work *A 24-Decade History of Popular Music* (hereafter *24DH*), the scenic set-like and sculptural costumes designed by Machine Dazzle constitute the most provocative visual spectacle of the twenty-four-hour adventure. From wigs made of 3D glasses or champagne corks, to an antebellum freedom-river necklace, to four-foot-tall, six-foot-wide light-up butterfly wings in the shape of double vulva inspired by lesbians, to an AIDS shroud consisting of hundreds of cassettes, to a phosphorescent hooded centerpiece with ping-pong-ball eyelets on Mars, Machine Dazzle arouses the wildest and queerest imaginations in those who experience the performances. His designs are not merely costumes; they amount to living sets that challenge chrono-normative ways of being and offer queer modes of unpacking and reenacting history. Without underestimating Mac's role as writer, codirector, and performer, I argue that much of the show's affective and transgressive efficacy flows from the designs. In this essay, I propose *designturgy* as a productive method for conceptualizing designs like those of Machine Dazzle that place design at the heart of a production. By analyzing Machine Dazzle's method and practice in *24DH*, I highlight what designturgy—especially a queer one—looks like and how it functions in performance.

Designturgy and Queerness

I coin the term *designturgy*—short for "design dramaturgy"—to emphasize
the connection between *design* (herein costume design) and *dramaturgy*,
and to highlight the dramaturgical nature of design. Design is the process of
conceiving and giving form and/or content to artifacts and experiences, for
the purpose of solving problems and making connections among people,
communities, times, and spaces. A designer's work in many ways parallels
a dramaturg's task. Broadly defined, dramaturgy is a comprehensive theory
of "play-making." In the Brechtian sense, dramaturgy "comprises the entire
conceptual preparation from its inception to its realization."[1] In contemporary theater-making, dramaturgy has increasingly become an important
skill that is, as Magda Romanska notes, "detached from the specific theatrical function" and necessary for the entire creative team to "employ in the
process of development and audience outreach"; it also comprises tools to
"cross artistic boundaries and gain applicability in a world outside of theatre."[2] Like a dramaturg, at the beginning stage of a production the designer
conducts research on sociohistorical and vernacular contexts of the performance. Like a dramaturg, based on research the designer develops a holistic overall concept for all the items in a performance. Like a dramaturg, the
designer then thinks compositionally and structurally throughout the rest
of the phases of the design work, building interconnections between the
visual outcome and the messages of the performance.

    Why do we need this special frame—designturgy—if designers do dra-
maturgical work already? Designturgy is a concept, both dramatic and
postdramatic, that highlights the central role of design in stage productions and other performative activities, including performance art, concerts, fashion runway shows, gaming, and mixed reality experiences.[3]
From a practicum perspective, designturgy refers to a particular kind of
design process/product, and from a theoretical one, to a particular critical
lens for analyzing designturgical results. As a design process, designturgy
generates an overarching design philosophy that not only ties together a
performance conceptually but extends beyond a specific performance. In
a stage production, a designer supports and realizes the director's visions;
a designturg goes beyond the director's artistic expectations. Designturgs
may work with directors, but their vision operates as a distinct element
in conversation with a director's vision rather than being subordinate to
it. Designturgy encompasses design but goes further than the normal
requirements of design. As a theoretical method, designturgy demands a

new mode of analysis for the theater/performance critic, historian, theorist, and common viewer. A designturgical analysis explores both standard design questions and the extra ones that turn design into designturgy. Some standard questions include: How does the design represent
the where, when, and who (the race, class, gender, and sexuality of the
"who")? Are there metaphoric messages in the opening and ending of a
performance? Does the design surprise and startle? Is there historicity in
the design? Is there activism in the design? Some extra-layer questions
include: Does the design develop a holistic overall concept for the performance? What are the semiotic interpretations of different layers and
levels of the design—and how do they interact with one another? How
is the design performed over time? Does the design compress, suspend,
or elongate time? How does design convey affective experiences visually?
How does design provide transgressive power to a performance? How
does design hold the entire performance together?

Designturgy proves especially amenable to queer performance. Designturgy as a practice, although not always queer, can often be approached
from a queer lens. A good example would be *Scenario* (1997), a dance piece
choreographed by Merce Cunningham, sometimes dubbed the "lumps
and bumps" show—with gingham outfits featuring down padding that
form irregular bumps on dancers' shoulders, chests, backs, and hips. Rei
Kawakubo had free reign to create her distinct costume and stage designturgy to explore the balance of distorted bodies, twisted spatial relations,
and radical movement. Designturgy as a theoretical method also parallels
with queer critique. In the chapter "Critically Queer" from *Bodies That
Matter*, Judith Butler writes that "[i]t's necessary to affirm the contingency
of the term, . . . to let it take on meanings that cannot now be anticipated
by a younger generation whose political vocabulary may well carry a very
different set of investments."[4] The term *queer*, contingent and constantly
shifting, resists a static notion of its potential subjects, audience, and participants. Queer theory, in its first and second waves since its rise after
1990, has generated key concepts and methods with a wide critical reach.
The first wave spawned concepts of, among others, sexual politics, homo-
sociality, camp, queer nation, and queer performativity; the second wave
encompasses temporality, futurity, historiography, utopia, gaiety, and so
on. Posing deep challenges to the normative frameworks of knowledge
and world-making, queer resists confining aspects of identity in favor of
creative and playful flux. Queer as method rethinks relationships between
intersectionality and normalization. In a similar vein, designturgy con-

templates the historical variety and complexity of the other ways of being in the world, moves across subjectivities, forms, spaces, and cultures, and insists on considerations of oppression and activism.

Taylor Mac's and Machine Dazzle's work is an outstanding example of how the method of designturgy can advance a queer critique. It offers ample ground for exploring concepts of archival drag (Román),[5] queer temporalities (Freeman),[6] gaiety as embodied thought (Warner),[7] and the queer legacy of the Ridiculous Theater (Edgecomb).[8] In *24DH*, observe Román et al., "the community [is] actively rebuilding itself," as the audience "take[s] seriously the power of queer intimacy" and participates in a "'radical faerie realness ritual' meant to honor the past, deconstruct the present, and move the culture forward by creating something out of this process."[9] Designturgy in this work propels the building and rebuilding of community through a strong queer sensibility.

As one of Taylor Mac's closest collaborators, Machine Dazzle is no ordinary "costume designer." He calls himself a "disguise" designer who makes things that imitate costumes.[10] Among the many things he designs are clothing, accessories, wall art, and household deco. An autodidact, he never went to design school, admits to having no tailoring skills, and creates art based on instinct rather than training. One unique aspect of his design process is the constant and incremental changes he makes to his works, which put his design in a permanent living state. It is therefore impossible to give any of his *24DH* costumes a solid or complete description, as they change from one performance to another and, like human beings, gain or lose a few pounds and switch to a different hair color on occasion. This also reflects Machine's queer designturgy of always surprising the audience and "keeping them guessing."[11] An extraordinary aspect of Machine as the *24DH* designer is his stage appearances alongside Taylor Mac. On the stage, he is not only Taylor's dresser, but caretaker, lover, midwife, alter ego, and comrade. His stage roles in the performance other than his role as the designer offer additional layers to his queer designturgy in *24DH*. I now turn to a thick description/analysis of Machine Dazzle's designturgy as it plays out in the twenty-four decades of Mac's production.

Wearable Sets

At the start of the show, the stage space is populated with twenty-four backup musicians (including Mac) and knitters, who are seated stage left and right under unostentatious lighting. The set consists of twenty-four strings of lights, indistinctly asymmetrical on the back wall, resembling twenty-four roads that lead to a distant horizon. The set designer, Mimi Lien, strategically made a minimalist set that befits a twenty-four-hour concert covering twenty-four decades of the historical period. The string lights are selectively lit throughout the twenty-four hours, giving the concert minimum scenic support. Taylor Mac's larger-than-life attire therefore stepped in to become more than costume sets and props, which turned out to be the visual center of the stage. Machine Dazzle thereby plays the role of the scene-setter who magically turns anything into a wearable set, whether it be fireworks, a barrel, a river, a picket fence, ice cream, the AIDS epidemic, or a vulva.

Designturgically, I propose, the opening and ending attire of the twenty-four decades form a full circle from birth to rebirth. Both ensembles are highly representative of Machine Dazzle's designturgy of surprises. The opening costume (the first decade, 1776–85) signifies the birth of US nationhood and heated celebration. For the beginning decade of US nationhood, one would naturally expect to see some reference to the "Star-Spangled Banner." The designer, however, cleverly shunned the national flag, and instead employed pennants and Mylar ribbons of vibrant colors other than white, red, and Old Glory blue. The pennants were hooped together to form four pannier-like layers that increased in size as they went down the waistline. Machine Dazzle piles up the Mylar ribbons to create a tall headdress with long celebratory strips falling down from the top. Mylar, a heat-resistant material, is used here effectively to symbolize massive energy, festivity, and explosive enthusiasm. The crowning characteristic of this look is the exploding fireworks constructed with long sticks extending from Taylor Mac's lower back and Mylar blossoms as firework tips. The bodice features a large number 13 in glistening purplish-blue Mylar, indicating the thirteen colonies that declared independence.

The ending decade (the twenty-fourth decade, 2006–16), in contrast with the heat and fireworks celebrating the birth of the nation, encapsulates a different kind of birth—the unflashy and lonesome rebirth of the self. After each hour of the performance, a backup musician is sent off the stage, resembling how AIDS took away lives one by one. At the beginning of the last decade, all the other twenty-three musicians are gone, leaving Taylor Mac as the sole performer on an empty stage. The decade begins with a giant pink cloth in the shape of a vulva descending from the ceiling. An almost naked Taylor Mac pokes his cleanly shaven head through the labia, and—again surprising the audience—the vulva cloth niftily falls onto him and turns into a dress (fig. 22). It epitomizes the tactically designed and surprising transformation of props and set into attire. Wearing nothing but the vulva (dress) and holding a ukulele, Taylor, like a baby in the liminal space between the mother's womb and the outside world, croons original songs and poems about what the world in 2016 was like—the Orlando nightclub shooting and corpses being washed up on the Mexican shore. A refrain that Taylor invites the audience to sing along with—"I'm looking for world peace, or who / Who in the room to screw"—bares to the core one's rebirth through a new world of peace and/or libidinal and psychosomatic contentment.

These wearable sets are structured in levels and layers. Vertically, the ensemble comprises the headdress, the main attire, and the footwear. The item at the highest visual point—either the headdress or the back item—is usually the highlight of the ensemble. Hand-decorated stilettos tend to complement the ensemble with coordinating colors and glitter. The main attire constitutes a key designturgical site where the designer provokes the spectators with the magic of concealing and revealing. The main attire could be one piece, or one piece plus a back item, or multiple layers of garments. For instance, the vulva dress of the last decade, in accordance with the diminishing dramaturgy of the twenty-four-hour piece, is the only example of a one-piece ensemble—the barest of all. The opening attire exemplifies one piece plus a back item, consisting of the pennant dress with a "13" bodice and a fireworks sculpture with shoulder straps worn like a backpack.

Machine Dazzle sketches two important designturgical gestures, I observe, over the decades: adding-up, and stripping-down. The adding-up is best seen in the Great Depression decade (the sixteenth decade, 1926–35). Featuring songs such as "All of Me" and "It Won't Kill Me," this decade leads us to think of the worst times in life with minimal material possessions, when a bowl of soup (during this hour each audience member indeed receives a paper bowl of hot soup) could save one from dying of starvation. The attire begins with a layer of 1930s-style black sequin–dotted bathing suit covering only the trunk of Taylor's body. To complement it, Taylor also wears a headdress of large cloth-textured candies and candy wrappers whose colors match those of the sequins. Then Machine, also dressed in black, comes onstage with a large cart, takes an ice cream cone–colored skirt from the cart to put on Taylor, and then a vanilla and chocolate-brown top, and then a head cloth with a large cherry on top.

Machine thereby turns Taylor into a big chocolate-vanilla ice cream with a cherry topping. This visual adding up throws into sharp relief the historical stripping-down of food and consumables during the Great Depression. The simple pleasures and comfort provided by candies and ice cream are highlighted as glamorous luxuries despite the material dearth.

Each decade ends in a strip-down, with Machine stripping Taylor of the previous decade's wearable set and dressing him for the new decade either in front of the audience or behind a shadow screen to maximize the surprise. Stripping down as designturgy takes place during several other decades' performances as well. A good example is the post–World War II white-suburban America decade (the eighteenth decade, 1946–55). At the beginning of the decade Taylor Mac is fully dressed. Visually, all we can see is a wig made of 3D glasses—an invention at the time—and a shawl made of foam to resemble a picket fence, which concealed everything underneath. A symbol of white American suburban middle-class property and comfort, the shawl fence is soon taken off to parallel Taylor's orchestration of "white flight": no white shawl, no seated white people at the center. As the shawl is lifted, all the white audience members sitting in the middle sections of the orchestra and mezzanine are asked to leave their seats, and audience members of color are invited to take these seats for as long as they like. White audience members are specifically instructed not to bother the people of color who have taken their seats, and therefore must either look for empty seats in the side sections—the "suburbs"—of the theater or simply stand up. Underneath the shawl is a blue starry sky top, a light blue skirt with white clouds and fishes on it, and a big, white belt made of large zip ties with single-family houses glued onto it hanging down three feet (see the background center of fig. 27). After white people's seats are taken by people of color, Taylor takes off another white item, the zip-ties belt, leaving on only the blue starry sky, clouds, and ponds of fish—public "properties" that whites share with racial minorities after being deprived of the comfortable seats for which they have paid a handsome amount.

Taking off a set-like garment is not always a subtractive gesture. Designturgically, this gesture can accrue meaning through the new positioning of the stripped garment and bring surprises through unveiling. Such additive stripping is seen in the attire for the underground-railroad decade (the eighth decade, 1846–55). Underground-railroad stories about guiding the slaves to safety and freedom gave hope to millions of slaves, although, as Taylor emphasizes, only 100,000 out of four million slaves successfully escaped and attained freedom during the antebellum era. This decade is a great challenge to the designer not only because it is a white artist that Machine has to dress, but because his design has to visually convey affects of longing, sense of direction, waiting, and transformation. Machine's designturgy achieves this through a thoughtfully unfolded set that incorporates a river, weathervane, timepiece, and monarch butterflies. At the beginning of the decade, Taylor is visibly dressed in a golden weathervane headdress in the form of a rooster and arrow, along with a blue chiffon river decorated with grayish stones (stuffed with scraps) and green gauze grass. The river bears histories, tells stories, and leads to unknowable spacetime. The river wearable set reflects endless longings about emancipation and a utopian world in which racial oppression comes to an end. While singing the Hutchinson Family Singers' antislavery songs, Taylor strips down the river and places it on the floor, revealing a dress of a thousand monarch butterflies—a symbol of massive transformation, on top of which is a large golden clock-dial necklace, indicating the unmeasurable waiting time before attaining emancipation. The gesture of unveiling the butterflies materializes the transition from longing to a state of utopia. The same gesture of putting the river down restores the river to its original positioning, suggesting that the utopia of equity is the world order as it always should have been.

Queering History, Queer Time

Queer temporalities offer us ways to queer the relationship among the past, present, and future. They challenge heteronormative conceptions of time, or "chrononormativity."[12] In *Time Binds: Queer Temporalities, Queer Histories*, Elizabeth Freeman posits that the body performs an encounter between past and present, which leads to "affective history," or erotohistoriography, which "sees the body as method, and historical consciousness as something intimately involved with corporeal sensations."[13] The body therefore queers history and generates queer time through resisting a continuous timeline of history and reimagining connections between past and present. In Machine Dazzle's designturgy, I argue, the body as an agent of queer time constantly intervenes, refuses, and challenges chrononormative expectations and suggests new modes of reenacting history.

The seventh decade (1836–45) takes place in a boxing ring, and two audience members invited onstage to impersonate Stephen Foster and

Fig. 22. The ending ensemble, the 24th decade, 2006–16. Photo: Sarah Walker.

Walt Whitman perform an "epic smackdown" for the title of "father of American song," while Taylor performs as the MC.[14] Commonly regarded as "the father of American music," Foster wrote numerous blackface minstrel songs; "My Old Kentucky Home"—the official Kentucky state song, as Taylor points out—is a minstrel song by Foster. Whitman, a great American queer poet who never openly came out, wrote "Song of Myself," among other poems, that explicitly depicted gay sexuality. As the two represent systematic racial insensitivity and clairvoyant sexual liberation, respectively, Whitman easily wins four rounds but ultimately gives up, because he is, according to Taylor, "not interested in winning"—thus queering the contest and queering heteronormative historiography. Taylor's bodice is a large cloth of a black-and-white checkered chessboard with chess pieces glued on, indicating competition. A grass-green hat with flower strings hanging down evokes Whitman's *Leaves of Grass*. The key item of this decade is a potato chip–bag skirt (potato chips were invented during this decade); each potato chip bag is decorated with a nude male body cutout, most of them with erections. The male nude erotica is not only a symbol of gay (W)alt Whitman, but erotohistoriography that linked sexual dissonance with temporal discordance, or queer time.

Fig. 23. Shining breast headlamps in the Stonewall Riots ensemble, the 20th decade, 1966–75. Photo: Sarah Walker.

Fig. 24. The AIDS ensemble, the 22nd decade, 1986–95. Photo: Sarah Walker.

Fig. 25. The lesbian ensemble, the 23rd decade, 1996–2005. Photo: Sarah Walker.

Fig. 26. The "Marskado" ensemble, with Taylor and a random spectator/participant on judy's left, the 11th decade, 1876–95. Photo: Sarah Walker.

Fig. 27. Machine Dazzle poses in front of his designs. Photo: Willa Folmar.

Taylor and Machine transform even wartime into high queer time. For the World War I decade (the fourteenth decade, 1906–15), the attire effectively weaves together historical accuracy and erotohistoriography. The vintage burgundy curtain dress has a backdrop of black and white dazzle camouflage, a military invention of the time. Another military invention, the gas mask, is worn beneath the feathery hat as the inner-layer headdress. Other civil inventions of the time, such as zippers, and fortune cookies (here made of nude-color bras) are placed, with a wink, at the inner rim of the hat and the rear part of the curtain dress. Right above the rear end hangs a pair of breasts made of a bra with white Life Savers candies glued to it, which turn out later to be a tribute to gay sex and lesbian fisting sessions under the moonlight before the war. Per Taylor's request, audience members and the designer himself come to the stage during Taylor's rendition of "Shine on, Harvest Moon" (a 1908 Ziegfeld Follies song) and flash their bare buttocks each time Taylor sings the word "moon." For the World War II decade (the seventeenth decade, 1936–45), the focus of the designturgy shifts to historical commentary and intervention, most clearly seen in the headdress, for which Machine uses a Slinky—a historical invention then—and inserts yellow smileys to create an entrapment metaphor for the Japanese internment camp during the war (see the far left of fig. 27). This detail is contrasted with the dark green tone dress employing historical images from bomber planes and military duffle bags (see also the left center of fig. 27).

The designturgy for the post–civil rights movement decades displays profound affective efficacy. The four decades following the civil rights movement suspend or elongate time. The Stonewall riots decade (the twentieth decade, 1966–75) parallels the riots after the death of Judy Garland, a gay icon whose name Taylor takes as their/judy's gender pronoun. The attire reflects the late 1960s and early '70s explosion of styles: big Afro and bouffant hair, boho lightweight dress, bright colors, and bold prints. The most visceral item employed during this decade is a pair of halogen headlamps (a historical invention of the time) that function as breasts shining like headlights.[15] As the houselights turn off, the breast headlamps, like two time tunnels in complete darkness, shine on audience members' faces and transport them in history to a reimagined time and place, a liminal space where all boundaries are blurred, a safe haven that allows for moments of indulged emotions and reflection (fig. 23, see also fig. 27 for the back of the attire). The ensemble for the backroom sex-party decade (the twenty-first decade, 1976–85) has different shades of purple in honor of gay icon Prince, referencing David Bowie's glam-rock style (see the far right of fig. 27). The most explicitly sexual decade of the whole show, this hour starts with Machine coming to the stage seductively dressed with a bullwhip butt plug.[16] Machine dresses Taylor in front of the audience, transferring his top and Mohawk headpiece onto Taylor, and once Taylor is fully dressed, the two make out for about half a minute, stopping normative time.

The AIDS decade (the twenty-second decade, 1986–95) is an especially personal decade for Mac, who describes 24DH as a metaphorical repre-sentation of and homage to the AIDS walk in San Francisco in 1987—an event that inspired the fourteen-year-old Mac to make theater. During both events—the AIDS walk and the 24DH, everyone falls apart—disin-tegrated by either the lengthiness of the show or by the AIDS virus thirty years ago—while a community is being built up.[17] The designturgy here reflects such "falling apart": on judy's shoulders Taylor carries a large gate-like frame that holds up three huge skulls symbolizing the aftermath of AIDS that hovers over Taylor, lending temporal precarity and urgency. Beneath the skulls, Taylor is covered with a shroud made of innumerable cassettes—an indication of countless AIDS victims as well as a temporal prolongation and perpetuation of AIDS victims' voices after their deaths (fig. 24). The penultimate decade is the lesbian decade (1996–2005), dur-ing which Taylor invites all the lesbians in the theater to the stage to per-form themselves and to rally. Taylor wears a nude bodysuit decorated with "goddess," "mother," and "sister" tattoos, fake breasts, a pair of denim shorts, and pink tassels concealing Taylor's calves. Taylor's final transfor-mation in this decade is completed with four-foot-tall, six-foot-wide but-terfly wings in the shape of a double vulva, as judy becomes a member of the lesbian avengers holding an ancient lesbian scroll, ready to join a dyke march and lead humanity to prolonged liberty (fig. 25).

Queer time is also largely compressed time that provokes affective des-titution in Machine and Mac's designturgy. The ensemble that Machine intends to be, and regards as, "the most beautiful" is the attire for the much-truncated blindfold/dandy decade (the fifth decade, 1816–25). Dur-ing most of this decade, audience members are instructed to blindfold themselves (and "no peeking"). For the first half of the decade, audience members listen to an almost naked Taylor sing in a dimmed theater with no houselights (yes, I peeked!). During the second half, Dandy Minions are instructed to hand out flowers to blindfolded audience members to first feel the flower and then pass it along to the next person. They then hand out fruits (in my case, grapes), and ask each audience member, still with blindfold on, to first feel the piece of fruit and then tease a neighbor on the face and neck with that piece, and then after much teasing and screaming and surprised laughter feed the fruit into the mouth of that neighbor. Then the roles reverse. After all that playing and some self-touching instructed by Taylor, we are finally allowed to remove our blindfolds, only to see Taylor in the dandiest ensemble for less than two minutes—the most beautiful costume for the shortest period. The ensemble features a hat, a coat atop a dress, and a long, full-body-length necklace. At least seven colors, symbolizing the rainbow, and three kinds of fabrics are used, but their combination is well-balanced and refreshing. Lightweight materials such as chiffon and rayon provide counterpoint to the heavy embroidery and metallic pink ruffles. Presenting the dandy dress in queer time during the dandy decade reimagines the relationship of the past, present, and future, and points to an affective historical consciousness that closely intertwines with corporeal sensations.

DIY Fashion Activism

I submit that at the center of Machine Dazzle's design philosophy is DIY (do-it-yourself) fashion activism at the grassroots level. His designturgy inspires DIY design endeavors of making one's own fashion, for everyday wear, protests, and performances both onstage and off. Without any training in design, Machine himself started out at the grassroots level, as a DIY costume designer for himself and his subcultural performers from the Dazzle Dancers. The term DIY came to be associated with the counterculture of the late 1960s, when fashion activism at the grassroots level quickly went mainstream, breaking down the boundaries between art and protest. DIY activism has in many ways contributed to fashion history. Since the 1990s, scholars such as John Hartley, Elizabeth Jacka, and Matt Ratto and Megan Boler have written about what they call "DIY citizenship" to indicate "a choice people can make for themselves [so as to] change a given identity, or move into or out of a repertoire of identities,"[18] and "a twenty-first-century amalgamation of politics, culture, arts, and technology that in turn constitutes identities rooted in diverse making practices."[19] Queer DIY fashion activism disrupts the status quo and normative world-making while building sociopolitically engaging communities through making, displaying, distributing, and spectating items of idiosyncratic nature. Machine Dazzle's fashion activism deploys accessible and eco-conscious materials such as found objects; it insists on historical research, and emphasizes surprises and twists, constant experiments, additive philosophy, and a keen queer sensibility.

Found materials are key to Machine Dazzle's designturgy. These everyday life objects are cheap and accessible—easily found in inexpensive stores and trash cans. Echoing Mac's mantra in *24DH*, "perfection is for assholes," Machine almost never uses designer fabric and does not pursue high tailoring or perfect execution. His design process centers on looking for trashy items lying around and giving them life by turning them into something gorgeous and irresistible. He infuses design into trashy objects, and his finished looks materially carry out those designs. In *24DH*, some of the most memorable items are made of trashy objects. One is a rope dress for the Stonewall-riots decade made from hardware-store ropes tied into knots and painted with rainbow colors. Another one is a series of severed human heads hanging from the waist in the attire for the second decade (1786–95), which illustrates the outcome of revolutions as well as slave-trade victims crossing the Atlantic. These heads are made from foam, which is shaped, burned, and colored in pink and dark brown to symbolize decomposition.

Foam of a different kind is used in the "Marskado" decade (the eleventh decade, 1876–95). This decade mocks a "new kind of blackface minstrelsy": one of the most popular comic operas traditionally performed in yellowface, *The Mikado* by Gilbert and Sullivan. Instead of setting the decade in a purely imagined Japan, it is set on Mars (hence "Marskado") and takes place entirely in blacklight. The setting and mode of this decade enable the designer to use found materials such as thin foam and ramie; he coats them with phosphorescent paint to create Taylor's centerpiece, a beak-shaped hood. The reference to the kimono (and the pagoda, seen in a hat designed for an audience volunteer) might be a bit too literal, but it is a historically accurate representation of Europeans wearing kimono-like costumes. The most creative found objects used in this decade's attire are ping-pong balls painted as eyelets that decorate the hood (fig. 26). Ping-pong balls, crucial props that bring the whole show together, are handed out to each audience member in paper bags to reenact wars, to hit the performers onstage or hit one another with, or to place in one's mouth only to transfer it to a neighbor's open mouth and thus build community together.

For the Temperance decade (the third decade, 1796–1805), Taylor plays the role of dipsomaniac Crazy Jane, and her attire uses found objects to

Historically Accurate Items that Machine Dazzle Uses in His Designs

Decade number in *A 24-Decade History of Popular Music*	Decade	Historical inventions/items at the time
Second decade	1786–95	Steam engine and steam pipes
Seventh decade	1836–45	Potato chips
Ninth decade	1856–65	Hot dogs, barbed wire
Tenth decade	1866–75	Dynamite, typewriter
Fourteenth decade	1906–15	Gas mask, zipper, black-and-white dazzle camouflage
Sixteenth decade	1926–35	Ice cream cone
Seventeenth decade	1936–45	Slinky, historical images from bomber planes, military duffle bags
Eighteenth decade	1946–55	Large zip ties
Nineteenth decade	1956–65	Barbie dolls, Andy Warhol's Campbell soup can paintings

reflect the hedonic pleasures of drinking and its aftermaths. The wild wig is made of used champagne corks, forming two large braids, and more corks bounce on wires that stick out from the sides of the head. Crazy Jane lives in a big wine barrel, which she wears like a huge suspender skirt. On the barrel skirt, two shades of pink padded cloth covered with sequins are shaped into tongues sticking out of mouths. Snakes, which stand for alcohol, are made from padded cloth and sequins in green, the color of poison. Under the big wine barrel, Crazy Jane has all her daily-life supplies, such as toiletries and bedroom items worn on a one-piece white lingerie. Found items such as a used bath sponge and pill cases become part of a dramatic story.

After hours of interviews and close observation of Machine Dazzle's working process, I here attempt to enunciate his designturgy in *24DH*. I argue that Machine's designturgy is articulated temporally, weaving together historical accuracy and chaotic temporality, effectively transforming social activism into theatrical affect. Not always informed about the content of the performance or the songs, Machine relies heavily on historical research, which revolves around the inventions and fashion styles of each of the twenty-four decades. He is always inspired by historical inventions at the time and looks for creative ways to employ them in the costumes. This table lists the notable historically accurate items that Machine Dazzle makes use of in his designs.

In our interviews, Machine tells me that his creative process starts with looking for materials, not sketching; his design process involves little or no sketching. His penchant for found objects originates from a belief that the universe provides signs at any given time. Machine experiments and designs as he makes. Unlike other established designers, he does not have a studio, and space is so limited in his shared apartment in Brooklyn that he usually works on the floor, in his bed, or in his back garden of well-tended plants and flowers. He does not own a computer and chooses not to follow the news or stay informed. He is constantly inspired by nature, music, and human emotions.

Machine is a maximalist. His designturgy is one of continuous additions, changes, and twists; he believes that "more is more."[20] He usually starts with small concrete ideas rather than large abstract concepts. He builds up from the small and stays detail-oriented, constantly making changes as he experiments with ideas. Machine likes to imitate historically popular items, but always gives them a twist to whet people's curiosity. A good example, I observe, is the ensemble for the nineteenth decade (1956–65), which is an imitation of Jacqueline Kennedy's pink bouclé suit. Machine's rendition employs large red-and-white stripes—a part of the Star Spangled Banner (the star part is on the back of the suit); he hand-paints large pink polka dots onto the striped suit to make it pink with gradation (fig. 27). The polka dots might well be a tribute to Roy Lichtenstein's comic strip–inspired pop art of the early 1960s and Yayoi Kusama's staged happenings and body-painting festivals throughout the '60s in support of the antiwar movement and sexual liberation.

In 24DH's promotional materials and during the concerts, audience members are reminded to put on their most outrageous outfits to attend the performances, thus putting on performances of their own and making political statements as they would in protests, rallies, and queer parties. As I recall, many of us who went to see the show hand-made or designed our own ensembles specifically for the occasion in support of our queer idols and in protest of gun violence, white supremacy, homophobia, heteronormative patriarchy, cisnormativity, systematic oppression, xenophobia, nationalism, jingoism, imperialism, and so on. As we dressed ourselves in historically relevant styles, glitters, stilettos, and vagina onesies we became a crucial part of the meaning-making process, and we played roles in a queer utopia, endorsing Taylor Mac's project of community building and dreaming our culture forward—the very goal of a queer DIY fashion designturgy.

Notes

1. Joel Schecter, "In the Beginning There Was Lessing . . . Then Brecht, Muller and Other Dramaturgs," *Dramaturgy in American Theater: A Source Book*, ed. Susan Jonas, Geoffrey S. Proehl, and Michael Lupu (Fort Worth, TX: Harcourt Brace College, 1997), 21.

2. Magda Romanska, ed., *The Routledge Companion to Dramaturgy* (New York, Routledge, 2014), 8.

3. The listed categories are to be covered in the author's book project on designturgy.

Postdramatic as a notion is established in Hans-Thies Lehmann's *Postdramatic Theatre* (2006) to refer to theater and performance events in which the dramatic text is no longer the focus, and the goal is to produce an effect among the spectators/participants through a combination of heterogeneous styles. Hans-Thies Lehmann, *Postdramatic Theatre*, trans. Karen Jürs-Munby (New York: Routledge, 2006).

4. Judith Butler, *Bodies That Matter: On the Discursive Limits of "Sex"* (New York: Routledge, 1993), 230.

5. According to David Román in *Performance in America*, "archival drag" refers to "the nature of contemporary performances that draw on historical reembodiment and expertise." Román, *Performance in America: Contemporary U.S. Culture and the Performing Arts* (Durham, NC: Duke University Press, 2005), 142.

6. Elizabeth Freeman, *Time Binds: Queer Temporalities, Queer Histories* (Durham, NC: Duke University Press, 2010).

7. Sara Warner, *Acts of Gaiety: LGBT Performance and the Politics of Pleasure* (Ann Arbor: University of Michigan Press, 2012).

8. Sean F. Edgecomb, "The Ridiculous Performance of Taylor Mac." *Theatre Journal* 64, no. 4 (2012): 549–63; Sean F. Edgecomb, *Charles Ludlam Lives! Charles Busch, Bradford Louryk, Taylor Mac and the Queer Legacy of the Ridiculous Theatrical Company* (Ann Arbor: University of Michigan Press, 2017).

9. David Román, Kalle Westerling, and Dan Venning, with Jennifer Buckley, Miriam Felton-Dansky, Kim Marra, César Alvarez, and Erik Patterson, "Subjective Histories of Taylor Mac's 'Radical Faerie Realness Ritual' History," *Theatre Journal* 69, no. 3 (2017): 403–15, 404–7.

10. Machine Dazzle, personal interviews with the author. 15 June, 15–27 Sept. 2017.

11. In this essay, the costumes I write about are from the *24DH* performance in San Francisco, from September 15 to 27, 2017, during which I closely observed Machine Dazzle's working process and had personal interviews with him. I address Taylor Mac the writer/co-director as "Mac" and the performer on stage as "Taylor." I use "Machine" throughout as a shorthand for Machine Dazzle.

12. For "chrononormativity," see Lee Edelman, *No Future: Queer Theory and the Death Drive* (Durham, NC: Duke University Press, 2004); J. Jack Halberstam, *In a Queer Time and Place: Transgender Bodies, Subcultural Lives* (New York: New York University Press, 2005); José Esteban Muñoz. *Cruising Utopia: The Then and There of Queer Futurity* (New York: New York University Press, 2009).

13. Freeman, *Time Binds*, 95–96.

14. In the performances in New York City, an audience member played Foster, and Taylor himself was the poet.

15. David W. Moore, "Headlamp History and Harmonization," Transportation Research Institute, University of Michigan. 1998. https://deepblue.lib.umich.edu/bitstream/handle/2027.42/49367/UMTRI-%2098%20-21.pdf?sequence=1, accessed 20 September 2017.

16. In the New York City performances, James Tigger! Ferguson's show-stopping striptease contributed a most sexually explicit moment of the show.

17. Taylor Mac, interview with KQED News, 15 September 2017. Web. https://www.kqed.org/news/11617367/berkeley-protests-political-analysis-the-vietnam-war-and-taylor-mac, accessed 16 October 2017.

18. John Hartley,. *The Uses of Television* (London: Routledge, 1999), 178.

19. Matt Ratto and Megan Boler, eds. *DIY Citizenship: Critical Making and Social Media* (Cambridge, MA: MIT Press, 2014), 18.

20. Dazzle, interviews.

NINE

Sing the Revolution!

Lin-Manuel Miranda, Taylor Mac,
and the Great American Songbook

David Román

I. Songbooks

> Look around, look around at how lucky we are to be alive right now!
> History is happening in Manhattan and we just happen to be
> In the greatest city in the world!
>   Lin-Manuel Miranda, *Hamilton*

On the night of 11 January 2012, I went to hear the public premiere of a hotly anticipated new genre-defying work-in-progress by an artist of increasing interest to the larger public. The event kicked off the new season of New York City's Lincoln Center's American Songbook series, a program committed to "celebrating composers and performers of American popular song."[1] The completely sold-out performance—a one-night-only event at the intimate Allen Room—a premiere jazz venue based on the design of a Greek amphitheater, with a huge wall of glass providing sweeping views of Central Park and Columbus Circle—would prove to be historical.[2] It was the first time Lin-Manuel Miranda performed what we now know as *Hamilton*, perhaps the most celebrated cultural event of the twenty-first century.

Hamilton transformed the American musical, and in the process reshaped the business of Broadway, all the while returning Broadway's

Fig. 28. Lin-Manuel Miranda and friends performing *The Hamilton Mixtape* at the Allen Room at Lincoln Center in New York City, January 11, 2012. Photo: Brian Harkin, *New York Times*/Redux.

relevance to American culture. Miranda himself became an iconic household name, one of the most significant and influential artists of his generation, and certainly the most famous Latinx theater artist of the twenty-first century. Miranda's presence at one of the country's most iconic venues for the performing arts, Lincoln Center, his affiliation with the American Songbook series, and the idea of situating himself deliberately within this audience and this tradition, challenged preconceptions about the venue, American popular music, and the role of artists of color in the history of the American Songbook. Lincoln Center gave Miranda the platform to debut his new musical and immediately place the work in the tradition of canonical American popular music; Miranda gave Lincoln Center an opportunity to reach a more diverse audience and expand its programming to include new voices, especially those of color. It was a mutually beneficial arrangement that literally set the stage for *Hamilton*'s ongoing success. The Allen Room was, to cite one of the catchphrases now made famous by the musical, "the room where it happened."

Lincoln Center's American Songbook series, which premiered in

Lincoln Center presents

American Songbook

Wednesday Evening, January 11, 2012, at 8:30

Lin-Manuel Miranda

Empire State of Mind (Remix) *(Shawn Carter, Angela Hunte, Alicia Keys, Jane't "Jnay" Sewell-Ulepic, and Alexander Shuckburgh; Stephen Sondheim; John Kander; Billy Joel)*

Passin' Me By *(Trevant Hardson, John Martinez, Romye Robinson, Derek Stewart, and Emandu Wilcox)*

Medley
   Juicy *(The Notorious B.I.G.)*
   You Ain't a Killer *(Richard A. Frierson and Christopher Rios)*
   Renegade *(Shawn Carter and Marshall Mathers)*

Get By *(Talib Kweli Greene, Nina Simone, and Kanye West)*

From *The Hamilton Mixtape* *(Lin-Manuel Miranda)*
   My Shot
   Right Hand Man
   You'll Be Back
   Helpless
   Valley Forge
   What Comes Next
   Dear Theodosia
   Jefferson vs. Hamilton #1: The Debt Battle
   Jefferson vs. Hamilton #2: The French
   Say No to This
   Jefferson vs. Hamilton #3: The Aftermath
   Alexander Hamilton

All vocal arrangements from this evening's program by Alex Lacamoire. Songs from The Hamilton Mixtape *coarranged by Alex Lacamoire and Lin-Manuel Miranda. Music and lyrics credits in parentheses. Song list is subject to change.*

Lin-Manuel Miranda would like to thank Ron Chernow, Luz Miranda-Crespo, Wendy Kail and Tudor Place, Tom Kitt, Luis and Luz Miranda, Vanessa Nadal, Owen Panettieri, Stephen Sondheim, John Weidman, and Jeff Zorabedian.

The Allen Room, Frederick P. Rose Hall
Home of Jazz at Lincoln Center

Fig. 29. Program for Lin-Manuel Miranda at the American Songbook concert at Lincoln Center in New York City on January 11, 2012. Photo: Courtesy of the author.

2010, promotes a generous understanding of American popular music, covering styles ranging, as their mission statement says, "from country to rock, from bluegrass to jazz, and from cabaret to Broadway." That night, though, was devoted to Lin-Manuel Miranda's musical lineage. He started off with a mash-up of Jay-Z's "Empire State of Mind" and Stephen Sondheim's "Another Hundred People" from *Company*, and also included segments of songs by Kander and Ebb, Billy Joel, and others, immediately positioning himself at the intersection of Broadway, hip-hop, and popular music, and more obviously, given his song choices, as a champion of New York City itself.

For "The Hamilton Mixtape" section, Miranda sang through a concert version of thirteen songs from what would become the musical *Hamilton*. At that night's concert, several singers and musicians of color accompanied Miranda—the people on the stage looked like the people of New York, which is to say they reflected the racial and ethnic diversity typical of the city but rarely seen on its stages. Already in the earliest incarnations of *Hamilton*, such as this one at Lincoln Center, Miranda was casting performers of color to embody the founding fathers of the nation, a choice that would become one of the most striking interventions associated with *Hamilton* throughout its history. *Hamilton*, which premiered off-Broadway at the Public Theatre in February 2015 before moving to the Richard Rodgers Theater on Broadway later that summer, is nearly exclusively cast with actors of color performing the iconic historical figures of early American history, beginning with Lin-Manuel Miranda as Alexander Hamilton, the musical's namesake, subject, and protagonist. Miranda, who was born in New York City, is Puerto Rican; the rest of the cast includes other Latinx, African American, and Asian American performers.

I was drawn to the Lincoln Center event for several reasons. The fact that Miranda, who had previously written *In the Heights*, one of the most exciting musicals of our time, was introducing new work to the public was reason enough to attend. He's among the most dynamic and charismatic performers I've seen, and his talent is irrefutable. His success as a Latinx composer and performer is extraordinary. *In the Heights*, which premiered on Broadway in 2008 after a limited off-Broadway run, was the first Broadway musical written by a Latinx creative team and featuring a diverse Latinx cast. Miranda wrote the music and the lyrics, and Quiara Alegría Hudes, the 2012 Pulitzer Prize–winning dramatist for *Water by the Spoonful*, wrote the *In the Heights* book. *In the Heights* focused on the economic and relationship challenges of an intergenerational community of pan-Latinos living in Washington Heights, a predominantly Latinx neighborhood in New York City. Strikingly and deliberately, and in direct contrast with the iconic *West Side Story*, *In the Heights* includes no violence or criminality, and the only death in the story is from natural causes. The musical was intentionally festive and celebratory of the Latinx experience. The cast was composed of an intergenerational group of pan-Latinx performers, which included Lin-Manuel Miranda as Usnavi, the Dominican bodega owner who's at the center of the musical. The concert debut of "The Hamilton Mixtape" featured many of the artists associated with Miranda's artistic circle, including *In the Heights* Broadway cast members Christopher Jackson, Mandy Gonzalez, and Jon Rua, along with other Broadway performers such as Rebecca Naomi Jones and James Monroe Iglehart, and Gavin Creel as King James of England, the one role that has since been consistently played by a white actor. The cast itself was reason enough to get excited, especially given the rarity of opportunities to see these actors perform on stage together.

Miranda's American Songbook concert was a thrilling night of original music reimagining the early history of the United States through contemporary popular musical idioms such as hip-hop and rap, and equally thrilling for recasting these early American historical figures with the voices and bodies of actors of color. The first half of the concert gestured toward the musical genres that influenced and shaped "The Hamilton Mixtape," showcasing the versatility of the performers, who, while cast in Broadway shows, rarely get opportunities to perform non-Broadway material at such prestige venues. Miranda's concert was bold and audacious for several reasons other than the *Hamilton* casting. During the first half of the concert, his choice to sing songs such as "Juicy" by the Notorious B.I.G., "Renegade" by Shawn Carter and Marshall Mathers, and "Get By" by Talib Kweli (which samples Nina Simone's version of the traditional Negro spiritual "Sinnerman") broke down the fences gatekeeping what constitutes the American Songbook. And yet for Miranda to insist that we hear these songs in relation to Broadway veteran songwriters such as Kander and Ebb and Stephen Sondheim, and popular music composers such as Billy Joel and Alicia Keyes, suggested that what was up next would be radically innovative in its musical hybridity. Anyone who has seen Miranda perform knows about the massive charisma of his stage persona, as well as the virtuosity of his talent. His energy, which builds momentum from song to song, is infectious and irresistible. His confidence seems impenetrable to doubt and self-consciousness. Miranda's American Songbook concert at

Lincoln Center dramatically shifted our understanding of American popular music by insisting on placing songs never previously affiliated with the American Songbook in conversation with canonical Broadway composers who are readily identified as such. Miranda's specifically curated program placed "The Hamilton Mixtape" as the direct heir of these traditions, the Songbook's next generational iteration, a performative prophecy fulfilled within only a few years of its debut. *Hamilton* was recognized with eleven 2016 Tony Awards including Best Musical, as well as being awarded the prestigious Pulitzer Prize for Drama in 2016.

I was also interested in attending this event at Lincoln Center because of my ongoing research on the American Songbook.[3] Traditionally, the American Songbook—sometimes even referred to as the Great American Songbook—is understood to be a roster of songs pulled primarily from the musicals of Broadway's so-called golden age and from Hollywood's iconic early-twentieth-century musicals—in other words, songs from the 1920s to about the 1950s. These songs were mostly recognizable to the American public through their circulation on radio and film, two mediums that in the early to mid century enabled singers working with jazz and swing bands, for example, to move the songs from live performance to record albums. The popularity of the songs also led to their circulation into the lives of many Americans, offering the nation a set of standards that formed the soundtrack to their daily lives.[4]

While the songs from these musicals and films were originally introduced as isolated numbers from Broadway or film, they began to cohere as the American Songbook soon after World War II. In the mid-1950s, Verve Records set out to record these songs as standards by organizing them according to the composer and lyricist, a decision that highlighted the role of the song's creative team and not its context. The idea of the songbook could also be understood as an archival project linked as much to historical preservation as to national identity and nationalist ideologies, given that the two words chosen for the name were "American" and "Songbook." The curation of the American Songbook in the 1950s was one of the most imposing practices of canon formation in American cultural history. Emersonian in its insistence on securing and promoting an indigenous American cultural practice, the establishment of the American Songbook was also symptomatic of the US's nationalist impulse in the wake of World Wars I and II. As Ralph Waldo Emerson famously called for in "The American Scholar," his mid-nineteenth-century essay declaring independence from inherited European and classical artistic traditions and literary forms, the mid-twentieth-century establishment of the American Songbook defiantly differentiates itself from European aesthetics and influence.[5] And while the establishment of the American Songbook set out to coordinate a set of musical standards pulled from Hollywood and Broadway to stand in for the American experience, it also reinforced the normative racial and gendered ideologies promoted by these mainstream representations. In its nation-building bias, the American Songbook defiantly promoted the idea of an American identity, which only bolstered the inherited social norms of who and what constituted that identity. The songwriters, for example, were predominantly white and male, and the songs, which were primarily incorporated into the songbook because of their mass appeal, reflected those experiences.

For this reason, I think its also telling that Verve Records chose the singer Ella Fitzgerald to record the American Songbook. Beginning with her 1956 recordings, *Ella Fitzgerald Sings the Cole Porter Songbook* and *Ella Fitzgerald Sings the Rodgers and Hart Songbook*, she went on to become the voice most associated with the American Songbook; in essence, she became the voice of the nation. By 1964, she had recorded six other songbooks with Verve: Duke Ellington, Irving Berlin, George and Ira Gershwin, Harold Arlen, Jerome Kern, and Johnny Mercer.

Interestingly, too, Fitzgerald did not come to sing the songbooks through the theater, which she had no previous history with beforehand. Other singers who were her contemporaries, such as Rosemary Clooney, Nat King Cole, Judy Garland, Billie Holiday, and most famously Frank Sinatra, also helped popularize the American Songbook. Lee Wiley, the popular 1930s radio singer, recorded 78s devoted to some of these same composers throughout the 1940s, beginning with a set of Gershwin songs in 1939. In mid-twentieth-century America, nearly everyone was singing these songs, but no one was more associated with the American Songbook than Ella Fitzgerald. Her recordings of the songbook composers remain enormously popular and are critically recognized as definitive editions. The Ella Fitzgerald Verve collections, along with the recordings by other popular singers, helped secure the sense that there was such a thing as the Great American Songbook, solidifying a set of composers, songs, and performers who would form its core.

The idea of the American Songbook raises several important questions worth considering: Is the American Songbook, as traditionalists argue, a closed set of songs determined by period and genre? And if so, what do we make of classics since the mid-1960s that have also been absorbed into

Fig. 30. Ella Fitzgerald Verve Records collage. Photo: Alex Luu/ALUU Productions.

the national consciousness, songs by Bob Dylan, Carole King, Stevie Wonder, or Paul Simon, for example, or songs from later Broadway composers such as Stephen Sondheim or Lin-Manuel Miranda himself? And what about other indigenous musical traditions in the United States, such as folk, blues, and gospel? Generally, the Songbook grew out of recognition of the extraordinary songwriting talent of the 1920s to 1950s and the mass popularity of the songs in various interpretive renditions. The ubiquity of the songs—on radio and television, at concerts and public events—also contributed to its acceptance in the canon; these songs were inescapable, sung by nearly everyone. But how has the songbook functioned for Americans since the 1950s, and who are its current interpreters? Is the interest in the American Songbook primarily nostalgic, or one that provides opportunities to build on this legacy for more contemporary purposes? These questions lead the debates between those who see the American Songbook as specific to the 1920s–1950s and those who view it as a more open and porous system that continues to evolve and grow, allowing each generation to contribute to its archive.

The Lincoln Center series clearly favors the latter interpretation, and the Lin-Manuel Miranda concert proved that point. Miranda is one of the many contemporary artists interested in placing himself in conversation with this tradition while at the same time altering it. When Ella Fitzgerald performed the Songbook, she did so in a segregated country that, while more than happy to hear her sing, refused her fundamental rights of citizenship. This paradox of Fitzgerald's social marginalization and national prominence calls attention to the dynamic between the performer and the Songbook itself. She was refused front-door entry to clubs and concert halls where she performed, she was denied contracts and gigs throughout the racist South, and she suffered humiliating micro and macro racial aggressions because of her race. And she endured all this abuse at the height of her international success in the 1950s and '60s. Yet despite these personal and professional setbacks, and the racist antiblackness sentiments that enabled them, Fitzgerald persevered to secure her place as the preeminent voice of the era.[6] Since its midcentury golden age, artists of all backgrounds have performed or recorded songs from the American Songbook; virtuosic singers such as Barbra Streisand, Aretha Franklin, and Linda Ronstadt immediately come to mind. Many, like Franklin and Ronstadt, are also social outsiders, who, like Miranda, revitalize the songbook by incorporating their own specific cultural and musical lineages into their recordings.

Consider Aretha Franklin in her 1970s concerts and recordings mixing standards, gospel, and popular songs such Carole King's "Natural Woman" or Paul Simon's "Bridge Over Troubled Water." In *Amazing Grace*, her 1972 live gospel album—which sold over two million copies and is still the best-selling gospel album of all time—Franklin sang traditional gospel songs such as "Amazing Grace" and "Never Grow Old"; standards from the classic American Songbook such as Rodgers and Hammerstein's "You'll Never Walk Alone" from *Carousel*; and contemporary songs written by Marvin Gaye, Carole King, and George Harrison. Consider, too, her role as an interpreter of the American Songbook and her standing in American history as one of the defining voices of the American people. President Barack Obama, when asked to place Aretha Franklin in context, wrote

> Nobody embodies more fully the connection between the African-American spiritual, the blues, R&B, rock and roll—the way that hardship and sorrow were transformed into something full of beauty and vitality and hope. . . . American history wells up when Aretha sings. That's why when she sits down at a piano and sings 'A Natural Woman,' she can move me to tears—the same way that Ray Charles's version of 'America the Beautiful' will always be in my view the most patriotic piece of music ever performed—because it captures the fullness of the American experience, the view from the bottom as well as the top, the good and the bad, and the possibility of synthesis, reconciliation, transcendence.[7]

Obama was responding to Franklin's tribute to Carole King at the 2015 Kennedy Center Honors, where she brought Obama, then president, and thousands of viewers to tears with her rendition of King's classic "(You Make Me Feel Like) A Natural Woman." Obama's assessment of Franklin, that "American history wells up when Aretha sings," points to the power of American popular music in the national psyche, a tradition that begins way before the Great American Songbook's arrival on the scene and, as Obama insists, moves well beyond it. Given her national prominence, it's no wonder that Obama asked Aretha Franklin to perform at his first presidential inauguration.

Artists such as Aretha Franklin expand the repertoire of what constitutes the American Songbook even as they continue to honor the songs most traditionally identified with it. Linda Ronstadt is another excellent example of this particular cultural phenomenon. Ronstadt, who by the end of the 1970s, was among the most successful performers in popular music, recorded three albums of standards with Nelson Riddle in the 1980s—*What's New* (1983), *Lush Life* (1984), and *For Sentimental Reasons* (1986). According to music critic and historian Stephen Holden, "Miss Ronstadt has formed a valuable bridge between two sensibilities that the myth of the '60s' 'generation gap' very nearly destroyed."[8] Holden is describing the tension between the American Songbook and rock 'n' roll, a tension promoted by generational divides and not merely musical tastes. Ronstadt's *What's New* was the first album by a rock singer to have major

Fig. 31. Aretha Franklin performs at fifty-sixth presidential inauguration ceremony for Barack Obama as the forty-fourth president of the United States on the west steps of the Capitol, January 20, 2009. Photo: Pat Benic/UPI/ Shutterstock.

Fig. 32. Linda Ronstadt's "What's New" and "Canciones de mi Padre" album covers. Photo: Alex Luu/ALUU Productions.

commercial success in rehabilitating the American Songbook since the rise of rock 'n' roll in the 1960s.

Holden sees Linda Ronstadt's entire career as an effort to "canonize songs and songwriters of enduring quality, while opening up connections between past and present." Rather than being a direct departure from her earlier albums, the Riddle trilogy places the American Songbook in direct conversation with the music most affiliated with Ronstadt's critical and commercial success: pop music, rock 'n' roll, and country. All of these songs—those from her previous albums and those from the Songbook trilogy recorded with Riddle—are part of the rich, expansive continuum of American popular music. And these songs cohere collectively through Ronstadt's generous curatorial vision and her extraordinary interpretive voice.

Shortly after publicizing these standards through her concerts and recordings, she moved to reintroduce yet another set of classics. In the 1980s, Ronstadt began recording a collection of Mexican folk songs in a sequence of albums, beginning in 1987 with *Canciones de mi Padre* and *Mas Canciones* in 1991.

These recordings, which proved to be immensely popular, selling millions of copies internationally, became the most successful non-English albums in the history of American popular music. Ronstadt, who was born and raised in Tucson, grew up listening to her father, who is part Mexican, sing these songs at home. Through her fame and status as a preeminent voice of her times, Ronstadt was able to introduce these songs to a larger general public. In her memoir, *Simple Dreams*, she writes that she was drawn to recording mariachi classics from the 1930s through the 1950s—*La Epoca de Oro* (the Golden Age). "I had grown up loving those recordings, mostly high-fidelity monaural recordings made in the RCA Victor studios in Mexico City," she explains. "They had a warm, natural sound, and I was hoping to capture some of that tradition on my own recording." Ronstadt's lifelong intimacy with these classic Mexican songs, which she performed with a full mariachi band and dressed in traditional folkloric costume, enabled her to return to her roots. She writes:

> The Mexican shows were my favorites of my entire career. I would sing two or three songs at a time, change costumes, and be back in time to watch the dancers. I never tired of them. The musicians were stellar and included a number of talented singers. I learned from them every night. The members of our touring company became close immediately, and I didn't feel the loneliness that I had experienced in previous tours. Riding on the bus late at night, I would doze off to the sound of rich voices speaking in a mix of Spanish and English, just like in my childhood. After the surreal experience of being caught up in the body-snatching machinery of the American celebrity juggernaut, I felt I was able to reclaim an essential part of who I was: a girl from the Sonoran Desert.[9]

Artists such as Aretha Franklin and Linda Ronstadt did more than merely publicize the established American Songbook for their generations and for their diverse multigenerational audiences. Unlike earlier singers such as Ella Fitzgerald, Franklin and Ronstadt had the means to expand the songbook to include material from other musical idioms and traditions that influenced and shaped their artistry.

II. "Taylor Mac Sings the Revolution"

Beginning around the same time as Lin-Manuel Miranda's 2012 Lincoln Center concert, Taylor Mac originated *A 24-Decade History of Popular Music*, an extraordinary durational performance project where Mac sang songs from 240 years of American history, from 1776 to 2016. Beginning in 2011, the initial concerts were performed at Joe's Pub, the famous cabaret venue in New York City affiliated with the Public Theater. Eventually, the concert grew, decade by decade, to become *A 24-Decade History of Popular Music*. In twenty-four separate hour-long sections, each devoted to a specific decade, Mac provided a counter-historiography to the conventional story of the nation. The performance was a history of popular music in the United States—although the songs were not necessarily the most "popular" of their time, they were selected based on their importance to a specific community featured during the decade being performed. *The 24-Decade Project* was not conceived as a show about the greatest hits of the past 240 years; the songs were selected for their relevance to the nation's social history and its various progressive movements. Each decade featured a specific community vulnerable to the political forces of its time and showcased its struggles against those forces. These communities included antitemperance activists, early suffragettes, Jewish tenement dwellers, 1960s Freedom Riders, and radical lesbian feminists, among others. The songs selected from the period revealed the struggle and resistance of the community under siege. The featured songs included immediately recognizable classics as well as many that were obscure or forgotten. Songs from the early decades of the concert, from the late eighteenth and early nineteenth centuries, were especially likely to be unfamiliar. The concert's archival goal was most pronounced in these sections, given the historical distance between the songs and the audience. Mac brought the earlier music into the present by summoning the songs' historical contexts and their importance to the communities involved.

As we moved forward in time, the songs became more familiar, and eventually, during the sections devoted to the 1940s, 1950s, and later 20th century, the song choices had a more direct link with the music of the audience's lifetimes, so the emotional connections with those songs were more pronounced. Sometimes Mac exploited this nostalgia, rousing the audience with popular hits only to abort the nostalgia for more politically poignant commentary. One example worth noting: Mac's cover of Laura Branigan's 1982 platinum-selling hit "Gloria," which invited the audience to sing along, and they did so enthusiastically. The catch: the song was completely re-contextualized and deconstructed from its original dance-club version. While Mac invites the audience to stand up and dance along, he breaks the song into three distinct versions with distinct choreographies and tonalities, distancing the audience from the immediate sentimentality that the song's opening chords and catchy chorus invoke. At one point, Mac reverses the logic of the performer/spectator dynamic, pulling a member of the audience to stand alone on stage as the audience sings the song. All eyes are on the audience member, who Taylor instructs to remain still and receptive to the audience's performance. Nearly every time I have seen this section, the audience member self-consciously begins to perform, as if they were required to entertain or at the very least participate in the audience's revelry. Eventually, though, they readjust and very movingly absorb the room's energy. Rather than indulge the song's nostalgic pull, Mac restages the song as a commentary on performance and reception, and on nostalgia's conservative impulses to imagine history as ideal.

Another example: When Mac sings Elton John's immensely popular "Goodbye Yellow Brick Road," the song's arrangement pretty much follows John's original, immediately familiar recording. However, the staging of the song deliberately and radically repositions the song as a queer requiem. Mac selects four members, sometimes more, from the audience to carry someone else from the audience over their shoulders and through the performance space. They are meant to symbolize and conjure Judy Garland's funeral, which Mac explains led to the Stonewall Riots. This repurposing of the song allows Mac to politicize "Goodbye Yellow Brick Road" and therefore realign the song to Stonewall, particularly the mythology that many queers have constructed around Garland's death and gay liberation.[10] The songs performed during the 1970s and 1980s decades might be the most familiar to the audience, but they are never performed in the style of a cover band determined to play the hits of the era. Mac reroutes the audience's nostalgia and invites us to hear these songs anew. This is true of all the material.

Songs are pulled from a wide range of musical traditions, including those from folk music, Negro spirituals, saloon songs, war ballads, labor tunes, Tin Pan Alley, and the American Songbook, to name only a few of the genres included in the project. Mac's musical director, Matt Ray, arranged all of the 246 songs, and led Mac's band. Taylor Mac sang all of these songs, and did so in full voice. There are moments of superb vocal virtuosity, where Mac's vocal skills are on full display. I was most impressed with Mac's rendition of "Soliloquy" from Rodgers and Hammerstein's *Carousel*, one of the most challenging songs for a male performer for its mini-operatic plot line and vocal intensity, but I was equally wowed by his moving version of Bob Dylan's "Hard Rain," which demanded an extraordinary level of lyrical memorization and ongoing delivery. These moments appear late in the full *24-Decade History of Popular Music* concert, all the more impressive given that Mac had been singing for many hours already.

Taylor Mac is a multitalented performer whose interpretations of American popular songs are sung with elegance and flair. Each decade also included an entirely original costume designed by Machine Dazzle specifically for Mac with that decade in mind. The flamboyant costumes link Mac to a particular artistic genealogy, which can be traced back to Charles Ludlam, whose Ridiculous Theatre of the 1970s combined radical drag, camp aesthetics, and gender nonconformity.[11] Machine also studied the historical contexts of the decades and created what he calls "immense sculptures" for Taylor Mac to "live inside for a moment in time." Machine dresses and undresses Taylor Mac on stage during the musical transitions between the decades. The costumes are then displayed in the theater's lobby in an exhibition of Machine's creative contribution.

Taylor Mac and his musical accompanists toured the *24-Decade History of Popular Music* throughout the world, generally performing sections of the concert in three-decade installments. In October 2016, he performed the entire *24-Decade* sequence at St. Ann's Warehouse in Brooklyn, New York, in a twenty-four-hour period. The performance began on a Saturday at noon and ended the next day at noon. For that event, Mac was accompanied by twenty-four musicians, one of whom would be eliminated each hour as the event moved forward. The loss of musicians decade by decade marked the passage of time and the sense of loss and renewal featured throughout the concert. This sense of perseverance and resilience was both a theme of the performance's spoken narrative and one of the performance's major rituals. By the end of the performance, which is to say at 11 a.m., twenty-three hours later, Mac was alone onstage. The gradual elimination of the core set of musicians marked Taylor's vulnerability as well as his achievement.

This extraordinary durational performance takes a toll on the artist and the audience. There were no intermissions, although audience members, who were asked to commit to the entirety of the performance, were free to leave the space when necessary. The audience was also fed throughout the performance's twenty-four hours, including a full meal at around 10 p.m. and a Depression-era type of soup kitchen line several hours later. For people to take breaks if needed, the balcony at St. Ann's Warehouse was designated as a resting place and set up with cushions and pillows. The event was deliberately designed to be physically exhausting. Mac had sought to find an art form that would simultaneously be about potentiality and limitations. The audience is central to this mission. Mac set out to build a tangible community from these concerts—one transformed by the event's demanding structure, which we each experience individually and also as a collective group. This sense of communal energy in the midst of exhaustion lies at the heart of the project. Mac identifies the AIDS crisis as the primary influence and inspiration for the project:

> I can pinpoint the catalyst to an AIDS action I attended in 1987. This action was a profound experience for me, a fairly isolated suburban queer kid who had never met an out of the closet homosexual, as I was suddenly exposed to thousands of queers. What has struck me from that day was experiencing a community coming together—in the face of such tragedy and injustice—and expressing their rage (and joy at being together) via music, dancing, chanting, and agency. Not only was the community using itself to destroy an epidemic, but the activists were also using a disease, their deterioration, and human imperfection as way to aid their community. In many ways, my entire career has been about reenacting this experience on stage, in one form or another, but a couple years ago I decided to consciously go at it. The result is a durational work that explores the various ways imperfection can foster community.[12]

I attended Taylor Mac's performances for several years during their gestation, experiencing the decades in various configurations in cities throughout the United States: New York, San Francisco, Ann Arbor, Los Angeles, Santa Barbara, Chicago, and the twelve-hour concert during the summer of 2016 in Poughkeepsie, New York. I also attended the entire twenty-four-decade performance performed in Brooklyn in 2016.[13] In each of these cities and on each of these occasions, I witnessed firsthand Taylor Mac's singular ability to forge—often against the audience's own will—a community, however imperfect. "Perfection is for assholes," he stated often at these concerts, a rejoinder to the demand by most theatergoers for a polished final production. Mac's performances, while not necessarily works in progress, allowed the toll of performance on the artist's body and the audience to be displayed.

The performances included moments of striking intimacy, moments when spectators interacted with one another and with Mac and the company of artists on stage. It was more than mere audience participation, although it was definitely that too. At one point in the show, Taylor Mac admitted that he himself feels abused by mandatory audience participation; that is, when artists are "forcing their fun on me," his immediate response is "fuck you, I don't want to have fun!" But he sees his version of audience participation as different: "When I ask—I want you to be uncomfortable." Most audience members comply, eager to be on stage. Others, while they may be more reluctant or "uncomfortable," participate in part out of trust, sensing Mac's genuine community-building impulses.

Mac insists on establishing a community by casting his audience in various roles throughout the concerts, or as Jennifer Buckley writes, "physically shuffling the audience" so that we participate in different configurations. At times we reenact major historical wars, albeit with ping-pong balls or pillowcases as weapons.[14] During the American Civil War, for example, we were divided into two groups: the Confederate and the Union soldiers, and were required to drop to the floor if we were hit in the head or heart by ping-pong balls tossed by soldiers on the opposite side of the space. By the end of this sequence, and after acknowledging the loss of soldiers from both sides of the war from combat and disease, Mac sang a soaring version of "When Johnny Comes Marching Home"—an 1863 ballad written by an Irish-American named Patrick Gilmore, that was sung by both sides of the battle anticipating their soldiers' return:

When Johnny comes marching home.
Let love and friendship on that day,
Hurrah, hurrah!
Their choicest pleasures then display,
Hurrah, hurrah!
And let each one perform some part,
To fill with joy the warrior's heart,
And we'll all feel gay
When Johnny comes marching home.[15]

The song serves as the transitional moment between the decades of the Civil War and the decade of Reconstruction, and moves the audience into the tenth hour of the performance. While the decades are full of highly theatrical moments, the performance included various moments that also foreground Mac's vocal agility—Taylor Mac unplugged, as it were. The antiwar sentiment of "Johnny Comes Marching Home" resurfaces during the World War I sequence when Mac has all the men in the audience under forty join him on stage to re-enact that war while he sang, "Keep the Home Fires Burning," a popular British war song from 1914.

Keep the home fires burning,
While your hearts are yearning.
Though your lads are far away
They dream of home.
There's a silver lining
Through the dark clouds shining,
Turn the dark cloud inside out
Till the boys come home.[16]

He invited the women in the audience to sing along and provided the song's lyrics on an enlarged banner to facilitate participation. The audience sang this song of hoped-for reunion while the young soldiers were left on stage. In this moment, we experienced the sentiments, not of the soldier, who we were told "dream of home," but of those who must "turn the dark cloud inside out" until the boys come home. The boys on stage were serenaded by an audience decidedly marked as unlike them; the audience was cast as those left behind by the war anticipating the young men's return.

Or we were asked to differentiate ourselves by age. During the decades of the 1920s, the youngest person in the audience was invited to come on stage to join the oldest person in the audience; everyone over fifty was asked to raise their hand, and those under fifty were asked to lock eyes with someone fifty or older. The younger person was told to dance the movement of the older person while Mac sings Papa Charlie Jackson's bawdy 1926 blues song "Shake that Thing":

Now the old folks like it: the young folks too. The old folks showing: the young folks how to do
They call it shake that thing, aww, shake that thing[17]

This choreographic mandate was required of the over-fifty/under-fifty pairings throughout the theater, making palpable the idea that intergenerational connection is necessary for community survival. Or, during a sequence in the 1956–1966 decade, all the white people in the audience were told to leave their seats and stand in the aisles to represent the mid-century white flight to the suburbs, while the few people of color in the audience were invited to take whatever seats in the center sections they choose. Throughout this upheaval, Mac sang "Don't Let Me Be Misunderstood," the Nina Simone song of 1964 that was a major hit for the Animals the next year. Taylor's audiences, despite outreach efforts for more diversity, are heavily white. It's intense to see the main seating area emptied out; suddenly the aisles are blatantly congested. Taylor is well aware of his audience makeup, and this moment strikes me as a moment of shared communal self-consciousness. Happily, for some of us, we are not asked to relinquish these seats once the song ends.

These moments of involved audience participation both contribute to the performance's intimacy and call it into question. The audience differentiated by age, gender, or race, for example, calls attention to who's in the theater and who is not, and how we self-identify or are categorized by others along these marks of difference. The performance builds intimacy by giving the audience an intense shared experience that is generally meant to bring us closer to one another, yet by shuffling the audience into different groups throughout the performance's twenty-four duration, a level of anonymity is preserved given that the intimate groups switch up and change, making it more difficult to maintain ongoing connections. The person who fed you grapes early in the performance was probably not the person you slow danced with at the same-sex prom later on. And given that the grape-feeding occurred during a decade when the audience wore eye masks, we might not have known who that was in the first place. Throughout the performance, the audience was physically moved through the entirety of the space, including the main stage itself. Spectators were pulled from the audience to the stage directly by Taylor Mac, while at other times Mac abolished seating entirely and had the audience sit on the theater's floor. This heightened audience participation was inescapable; spectators were forced to relinquish any sense of traditional theater decorum that they might transport into the space. At times, we were even put to work to help bring the performance to life. During the twenty-four-hour concert, the audience was transformed into stagehands, moving chairs, setting up tables, and serving food. For Mac this type of participation breaks down social resistance and builds bonds, bonds that outlast the performance and model a possible world available to all of us if we just did the work to make it real. Like the AIDS walk from 1987, we built community in the midst of its dissolution through song, dance, and agency. And, like the AIDS walk of 1987, the performance demands a lot of communal work and commitment to succeed. Throughout *A 24-Decade History of Popular Music*, Mac reminded us of his practice: "you honor the past, by doing it to the best of your ability; you honor the present moment, by deconstructing it; and you honor the future by making something out of it that moves the culture forward."

A 24-Decade History of Popular Music is at once a repository for resistance to white supremacy, hetero male cisgender dominance, and nationalist fanaticism. But that sounds heavy-handed—the work is so much more joyful than that. It's what Mac calls a radical faery realness ritual, a place for community building and communal sacrifice. What Mac reminds us is that the history of the nation is one of resistance and rebellion led by those most vilified in the status quo. Taylor Mac sings the revolution that has been at the heart of America's history, locating and reviving the country's radical spirit to retell the story of the nation from a more inclusive and imaginative perspective. Like Lin-Manuel Miranda's *Hamilton*, Taylor Mac's *A 24-Decade History of Popular Music* insists on the reclamation of this history by those least identified with political power. Its radicality, like that of *Hamilton*, is in its audacity to take over the space and claim the stage of American history.

Taylor Mac—along with Lin-Manuel Miranda—joins a growing list of performers who have over time revisited the question of the American Songbook and its significance and responded in turn with their own sense of purpose and skill. There is no shortage of talent devoted to performing the American Songbook—this has been true since it origins. But each generation produces its own unique and distinct set of interpreters, who challenge the American Songbook's canonicity even as they build on it. The simultaneity of this defiance and adherence keeps the songs meaningful and relevant to new audiences, audiences often (and most likely) unimagined when the Great American Songbook was first established. It's not surprising, then, that the best of these performers emerge from multiple underrepresented communities and that their song selections amplify and expand what's understood to stand in for the nation's musical set list. These performers, beginning with Ella Fitzgerald, give voice to the nation and its sentiments through song. That these artists are outsider figures, singers not always fully recognized as normative national subjects when they emerge onto the scene, makes their contributions all the more remarkable and profound. They ask: What can we do with this history? They answer: Sing the revolution!

Notes

I wrote this piece during the period when Taylor Mac was touring *A 24-Decade History of Popular Music*. It was initially conceived as a lecture. I started writing about Taylor's work in 2015, and I started lecturing on the *Decades* project in the following year, 2016. I decided to write up something that linked Taylor Mac with other interpreters of the American Songbook while addressing issues of race, sexuality, and citizenship in contemporary US culture. I am grateful for the opportunities I have had to speak about Taylor's work to various audiences, especially the University of London's Royal Central School of Speech and Drama, who hosted me as a visiting scholar in 2018 and invited me to present the talk as my inaugural lecture. My thanks to Professor Joshua Abrams for making that happen. I'm also grateful to audiences at Brown University, where I last spoke about Taylor's work in the fall of 2019 during Taylor's residency. My thanks to Professor Patricia Ybarra for making that happen. The Brown University event was the last time I saw Taylor and company perform sections of *A 24-Decade History of Popular Music* before theaters shut down.

1. This quote and the one further down the page are pulled from the Lincoln Center website: http://aboutlincolncenter.org/programs/program-american-songbook

2. The Allen Room was renamed the Appel Room in 2014 after a $20 million donation from Herbert Allen.

3. David Román, *Performance in America: Contemporary US Theatre and the Performing Arts* (Durham: Duke University Press, 2005).

4. On the history and debates surrounding the American Songbook, consider Ben Yagoda, *The B-Side: The Death of Tin Pan Alley and the Rebirth of the Great American Song* (New York: Riverhead Press, 2015); Rob Kapilow, *Listening for America: Inside the American Songbook from Gershwin to Sondheim* (New York: Random House, 2019); Max Morath, *The NPR's Curious Listener's Guide to Popular Standards* (New York: Berkeley Publications Group, 2002); and Alec Wilder, *American Popular Song: The Great Innovators, 1900–1950* (New York: Oxford University Press, 1972), among many other volumes on the topic.

5. Ralph Waldo Emerson, "The American Scholar," in *The Essential Writings of Ralph Waldo Emerson*, ed. Brooks Atkinson (New York: Modern Library, 2000), 43–59.

6. Stuart Nicholson, *Ella Fitzgerald: The Complete Biography*, offers an in-depth history of Fitzgerald's time with Verve Records and her experiences with racism throughout her career (London: Routledge, 2004).

7. Barack Obama, quoted in David Remnick, "Soul Survivor: The Revival and Hidden Treasure of Aretha Franklin," *New Yorker*, April 4, 2016.

8. Stephen Holden, "Linda Ronstadt Celebrates the Golden Age of Pop," *New York Times*, March 5, 2016.

9. Linda Ronstadt, *Simple Dreams: A Musical Memoir* (New York: Simon & Schuster, 2013), 179.

10. See Charles Kaiser, *The Gay Metropolis: The Landmark History of Gay Life in America* (New York: Grove Press, 2007); Martin Duberman, *Stonewall* (New York, Plume, 1994); and Marc Stein, *The Stonewall Riots: A Documentary History* (New York: New York University Press, 2019) for starters.

11. Sean F. Edgecomb, *Charles Ludlam Lives!* (Ann Arbor: University of Michigan Press, 2018).

12. Taylor Mac, interview.

13. My review of this performance appeared in *Theatre Journal*. See David Román, "Subjective Histories of Taylor Mac's 'Radical Faerie Realness Ritual' History," *Theatre Journal* 69, no. 3 (2017): 403–15.

14. Jennifer Buckley, "Taylor Mac, Walt Whitman, and Adhesive America: Cruising Utopia with the Good Gay Poet," this volume.

15. "When Johnny Comes Marching Home," lyrics by Patrick Gilmore, 1863.

16. "Keep the Home Fires Burning," Ivor Novello and Lena Guilbert Ford, 1914.

17. "Shake That Thing," Papa Charlie Jackson (1887–1938).

TEN

The *Walk Across America for Mother Earth*

Paul Zimet

In January 1992, Taylor Mac joined a hundred political activists and walked across the United States. For nine months this group of aging hippies (reliving their glory years), baby hippies (trying to discover the glory years they missed), punks, anarchists, dykes, radical fairies, men, women, senior citizens, and children walked an average of eighteen miles a day, through every weather imaginable—camping in parks, farms, churches, community centers, and schools—from New York City to the Nevada Nuclear Test site just south of Las Vegas. The Walk carried the subtitle, "From 1492 to 1992: 500 Years of Genocide on Native American People." The Nevada Nuclear Test site is on Western Shoshone land. The US government signed a treaty with the Shoshone people in 1863 telling them it was theirs for all eternity, but when the government needed land to test nuclear bombs, they decided the treaty had expired. The Walk traveled from community to community in America to spread the history of the test site and gather a movement of resistance that would force the US to give the land back to the Shoshone people.

Eighteen and eager to flee his suburban conservative upbringing, Taylor joined the Walk. Others joined because they had no place else to go, because lovers had joined, because political action was part of who they were, because they wanted to sightsee, because they had a disturbing fixation on Native American culture, because they were mentally ill or homeless, or because they truly did believe they could shut down the test site. The play *Walk Across America for Mother Earth* is Taylor's retelling and re-imagining of this journey.

In 2008 Talking Band commissioned Taylor to write a play for the company.

Fig. 33. Greeter (James Tigger! Ferguson), Kelly (Taylor Mac), and Nick (Will Badgett) in *Walk Across America for Mother Earth*, 2011. Photo: Darien Bates.

The company was founded in 1974 by Ellen Maddow, Tina Shepard, and myself. One advantage of having a long-lived company is that in working with artistic collaborators over many years, you develop a common language: you acquire, invent, and share techniques, you learn some things that work and some things that don't. A danger, though, is repeating oneself and becoming too comfortable in what you do. So the company has tried to throw itself off balance by seeking out artists whose work excites us, who have different visions and approaches to creation, and who will push our own work in new directions. Morgan Jenness—literary agent, dramaturge, teacher, activist, and a central figure in New York theater—suggested that we work with Taylor. Ellen Maddow and I had already seen and admired some of Taylor's work, and Morgan brought Taylor to see ours. On the surface our theatrical styles were quite different, but Taylor, Ellen, and I sensed that we shared an underlying aesthetic: what Taylor jokingly referred to as "Neo-Romantic."

We were not interested in the cool, ironic distancing that had become popular in downtown theater; we embraced the heightened theatricality of experimental theater. Taylor's work was political, passionate, exuberant, funny, humane, and immediate.

Ellen and I met with Taylor to discuss a commission, and he proposed writing a play about the journey across the United States that had been such a formative influence on his identity as an activist, a gay person, and an artist.

Taylor wrote,

> What the Walk ended up being for me (and many others) was a coming of age saga and an exploration of community. The walk was an embrace of the present moment with all its conflicts and possibilities for new paradigms of love and family. I came out on the Walk, dyed my hair green, fell in love for the first time, had my life threatened at gun point on two separate occasions, learned how to dumpster-dive and feed a hundred people every day on the discarded healthy produce of Americans, performed in my form of drag for the first time (what I call being a Fool), and learned about grass-roots action and the kind of activist and American I wanted to be.
>
> I saw the beauty, the wild variation, and the oppressive homogeneity of our country on a level that few people ever get to see: step-by-step. I'm interested in using my true-life experience as a springboard to creating a play written in the genre of pastiche (squishing many different genres together to create a post-modern theatric) which explores the joys and sorrows that come with a desire for community. I want the play to ask the question: what does it mean to be an American activist?

However, Taylor was in the midst of putting together another epic project—*The Lily's Revenge*—so *The Walk Across America for Mother Earth* would have to wait.

The Lily's Revenge, a five-part, five-hour show, premiered in 2009 at HERE in New York City. Taylor envisioned each part as stylistically different, so he invited five different directors. Rachel Chavkin directed Part II, the choreographer Fay Driscoll Part III, video artist Aaron Rhyne Part IV, and David Drake Part V. Taylor invited me to direct Part 1, *The Deity*. For me, working on *The Lily's Revenge* was an invaluable introduction to a new community of artists. Taylor is deeply interested in building community, and one of his impulses in bringing different directors and their frequent artistic collaborators into the same project was to connect artists from different niches of the downtown performance world. The cast of *The Deity* was a mix of Talking Band members—Ellen Maddow and Tina Shepard; alternative theater luminaries—Rae C. Wright and Muriel Miguel (Miguel is artistic director of Spiderwoman Theater); up-and-coming theater makers Haruna Lee and Heather Christian; and performers from the gay burlesque and cabaret world—Lady Rizo, James "Tigger" Ferguson, Bianca Leigh, Darlinda Just Darlinda, and Taylor. *The Lily's Revenge* also introduced Talking Band to Machine Dazzle, one of Taylor's key collaborators. Machine designed the costumes for the show that defined the fantastic theatrical realm of *The Lily's Revenge*, although his creations were more than clothes—they were sculptures, assemblages, scenic elements.

The Walk Across America for Mother Earth had many permutations. I have at least twenty-four drafts of the play. Taylor undoubtedly has more. The full production that premiered at La MaMa in January 2011 was very different from the first version of *The Walk Across America for Mother Earth*, which Taylor, Ellen, and I developed with students at NYU's Experimental Theatre Wing in the spring of 2010. In the period between those two productions Taylor worked the show through many frames: Chekhov's *The Three Sisters*, a beauty pageant, and commedia dell'arte. Each added a layer to the realized show. Some elements remained visible, others metamorphosed, and others dropped out, but even those that were not readily apparent to the audience remained as an unseen scaffolding for the work.

The earliest version performed at NYU's Experimental Theatre Wing drew deeply from Taylor's actual experience of the Walk and the people who went on it. There are gay and lesbian activists; Belgians who "have an unnatural fixation for all things Native American"; Kelly, a character modeled on Taylor; Professor Creekwater, a "homeless by choice casualty of a Reagan administration mental hospital cutback"; Red Blanket, who claims to be a Native American Vietnam vet; and Helga, an older woman dying of cancer. The characters walk through all seasons and weathers, they protest, they stage die-ins, they hold consensus meetings (which never reach consensus), they fall in love, they switch partners, they tell each other about their pasts and why they are here, they wonder and argue about what it means to be an activist; they reach the test site and lock themselves down to the cattle guards. The draft is loose and has an anarchic feel, much like the walk itself. This first presentation—especially as performed by the youthful student cast—captured the exuberance, doubts, longings, and determination of the marchers.

In June 2010, Taylor, Ellen, myself, and two performers—Suli Holum

Fig. 34. Angie (Daphne Gaines) and Rainbow Carl (Jack Wetherall) in *Walk Across America for Mother Earth*, 2011. Photo: Darien Bates.

and Steven Rattazzi—were invited to a residency at the Orchard Project in upstate New York to further develop *The Walk Across America*. During this residency Taylor started to work on a new draft modeled on *The Three Sisters*. (Taylor had used a similar writing process in writing Part III of *The Lily's Revenge*. Early drafts closely followed *Waiting for Godot* but eventually Part III transformed into something quite different, with *Godot* providing a hidden structure.)

In the "Three Sisters" draft of *Walk* Taylor took a major step to giving structure to the play and definition to the characters.

Irina, the youngest of Chekhov's three sisters, becomes Kelly. As Irina longs to leave her provincial town for Moscow, Kelly longs to leave his suburban background and "the ugliness of Real America." The Nevada Nuclear Test site is Kelly's Moscow—a destination that will give his life significance.

Chekhov's Masha is Angie, Kelly's close friend from high school who persuades him to go on the Walk "to do something of consequence with ourselves."

Tuzenbach, the young lieutenant of *The Three Sisters*, is Greeter, an aging radical fairy and activist since the sixties, who has lived most of his life on an all-male commune in Tennessee. As Tuzenbach is in love with Irina, Greeter is smitten with Kelly.

Vershinin, a military officer newly arrived in the sisters' provincial town, is Rainbow Carl, one of the several Belgians on the Walk. He dazzles Angie with his eloquent talk of the future, and she, despite being a lesbian, decides to leave her partner Marsha for him.

Marsha is modeled both on Kulygin, the husband of Chekhov's Masha, and also on the old nanny Anifisa. Like Kulygin, she is both loving and repulsive to Angie.

Natasha is Flower, a loud, uncouth hippie who smells of patchouli oil. The others make fun of her, but she tenaciously wields whatever power she has. Just as Natasha tries to persuade the sisters to get rid of Anifisa because she is too old to do her job, Flower argues that Marsha, who is ill with cancer, should be kicked out of the march.

Andrei, the brother of the three sisters and Natasha's husband, is King Arthur, the unofficial leader of the leaderless Walk. He is a fabulist who has claimed to be, among other things, a Vietnam Vet affected by Agent Orange, an ex-Weatherman now committed to nonviolence, and an AIDS activist who once put a giant condom over a senator's house.

Solyoni, Chekhov's sarcastic, jealous outsider, is Nick. He makes bizarre pronouncements and clings too closely to Kelly, who he claims raped him in a former life.

The overlap between Chekhov's characters and the characters in *WALK* is clearly not exact. Taylor used *The Three Sisters* as an armature. What the characters in both plays have most in common is their desires—for change, for love, for purpose. Unlike Chekhov's characters, who seem immobilized in their desires, the walkers take action. They reach their destination. The tone of act 4 in the *Three Sisters* is elegiac. Everyone is leaving. Nothing has been accomplished. No dreams are realized. The final section of the *Three Sisters* draft of *The Walk Across America* captured this mournful tone, but at the expense of losing some of the raw energy and immediacy of earlier versions. Even while working on this draft, Taylor recognized the need to explode it.

In subsequent drafts Taylor assigns commedia dell'arte equivalents to his characters: Kelly and Angie are the Inamorati, the romantic, vain, and often foolish lovers; Greeter is Pantalone, the old man who chases after younger women; Nick is Il Dottore, an angry, disruptive busybody; King Arthur is Sandrone, a crude, clever, and cunning peasant; Natasha is Columbina, a flirtatious and wily comic servant; Rainbow Carl is

Fig. 35. King Arthur (Steven Rattazzi) and Greeter (James Tigger! Ferguson) in *Walk Across America for Mother Earth*, 2011. Photo: Darien Bates.

Arlechino, the witty, nimble, acrobatic servant; Marsha is Pulcinella, the intense, mean forebear of Punch in Punch and Judy shows. So, while some genes of *The Walk* characters are Chekhovian, their presentation is not: they are physically animated, extreme, vulgar, boldly colorful, and comic.

An example of how Taylor distills *The Three Sisters* into commedia dell'arte is Andrei's monologue in act 3. Speaking to his unseen sisters, Andrei defends his marriage to Natasha, and then confesses that he mortgaged the family house without their knowledge. Finally Andrei says, "When we got married, I thought we'd be happy . . . all of us . . . But oh my God . . . (*Weeps*) My dear sisters, don't believe me, don't believe me . . ."

In the parallel moment in *Walk*, King Arthur breaks down crying after being accused at a consensus meeting of sexually assaulting one of the women on the march:

> KING ARTHUR. I've told you who I wish to be and not who I am. I am no activist. I am nothing but lies. Even these tears are lies.

> (He takes off his long-haired biker wig, revealing a short-haired wig underneath.)

WALKERS. Huh! *(ARTHUR takes off his short-haired wig, revealing a bald head underneath that.)*
WALKERS. Huh! *(ARTHUR takes off his bald-cap, revealing his normal hair underneath that.)*
WALKERS. HUH!

King Arthur's multiple reveals are akin to a commedia lazzo (a stock comic routine). There are lazzi sprinkled throughout *Walk*. When Marsha first appears alongside two Belgian walkers, Beeka and Jimica, they enter upstage on their knees as if they are specks in the distance. As they catch up with the other walkers they become taller—a trompe l'oeil of perspective. In a sequence of rapid-fire lazzi, sliding curtained panels reveal the characters in outrageous tableau vivant representations of events on the walk.

On top of the layers of the actual walk, *The Three Sisters*, and commedia dell'arte, Taylor introduced additional stylistic elements.

The stage directions for the Prologue's opening song call for the performers to walk as if in a beauty pageant. They do synchronized walks and solo turns. When Greeter moves downstage to talk to the audience, he walks and poses as if in a fashion show. Later, the actors' poses also borrow from Kathakali dance gestures.

These multiple layers were all filtered through an aesthetic honed by Taylor and the performers with roots in burlesque and cabaret. Their comedic style—broad and inclusive—immediately made the audience complicit in the action. A stage direction states, *"the characters talk to each other and the audience as if they are fellow walkers. There should be no attempt to look over the audience's heads, as if speaking to them, but actually talk to the people."* The actors treat the audience as confidants, witnesses, and partners. At times they address the audience directly, but even when speaking to another character they let the audience know they are performing for them as well. This mode of performance—as much a function of the performers' consciousness as a style—became integral to the theatrical world of *The Walk Across America*. The audience became part of the community Taylor wished to create.

The performers' skill in responding to the audience and to unplanned incidents came into particular focus during one performance when Nikki Zialcita, playing a spinning tornado, twisted her knee and tore a ligament. She suddenly collapsed onto the stage. The show was stopped, an ambulance was called, and for thirty minutes, as everyone waited for the emergency medical technicians to arrive, Taylor improvised a monologue for the audience. The EMTs, from an Orthodox Jewish ambulance corps, arrived, startled to be met by performers in fantastic costumes. In full view of the audience, they put Nikki in a wheelchair and agreed to let her finish the performance. The audience felt themselves to be participants in a richly expanded event.

The feeling of community was reinforced during the intermissions, which Taylor imagined as a rest day on the walk. Taylor describes the possible activities of the intermission in an appendix to the script:

> *tents are set up; the audience (if they brought their own mugs, as they should be instructed to do when they buy their tickets) is served soup that has been cooked during the first act; there is a talent/no talent show that audience members can sign up for, in which they can do up to 10 seconds of performance; rehearsed numbers. . . . are also performed in the talent/no talent show; laundry is hung; card games are played; literature is passed out; hair is hennaed or braided or beaded; fake tattoos are offered; two people in the men and women's bathroom are giving themselves whore baths. During the Intermission/Rest Day, the actors should be themselves, not in character, just having a good time with the audience.*

The Talking Band/La Mama production had no tents or soup, but there were nutritional yeast popcorn, hair braiding, tattoos, photo-ops with protest signs, and songs. The songs were mostly outtakes from earlier versions of the show, and the production stage manager, Robert Signom III, sang a sweet song that he wrote about stage managing.

The music of *Walk* is woven into the fabric of the entire show. Ellen Maddow, the show's composer (who also played Flower in the Talking Band/La Mama production), wrote, "The musical landscape is created by the sound of walking feet whose rhythms shift to support the text and reflect the state of the walkers—a community in constant motion. The music is portable. It is created by the characters from inside the action of the play. We used a guitar, played by an actor wearing a small amplifier, body percussion, plastic water bottles, melodica, hand drum, etc., but any portable instruments played by particular performers can be used in the score (accordion, ukulele, fiddle, pennywhistle, etc.). The singing should sound spontaneous, familiar, ragged, and powerful."

Walking is the central action. As director, I imagined the actors to be almost always on the move. We needed to create an inventory of walks "to support the text and reflect the state of the walkers." Throughout each developmental workshop—at NYU Experimental Theater Wing, at the Orchard Project, at the Playwright's Center in Minneapolis, and in the workshops leading up to the New York production—we made up, discarded, and refined a multitude of walks to add to our repertoire. The walks had different rhythms, tempos, shapes, facings, intentions, moods, and intensities. They moved in and out of counterpoint, the way walkers naturally move in individual ways, but then unconsciously fall into sync with their fellow walkers. We juxtaposed sections of text with different walks—sometimes wanting to see which walk best supported the text or, if we wished, contradicted it. We gave the walks names so we could remember them—Triplets, Cock Walk, Grapefruit Prance, Runway Walk, Fossy Cross, Kathakali, Belgian Frite, and so on.

In act 1, the characters stop occasionally to hold consensus meetings, to have a die-in, to greet a new arrival, or to stand on a soap box and make a speech, but for the most part they are walking. After the intermission, the movement changes. Act 2 starts with a tornado. The actors are whirled about, blown off stage, a small group of characters is left on stage trying to continue the walk, they are whirled about again, and another set of characters is blown onto the stage. In the second half of this act, the marchers are running. It is Columbus Day, 1992, and they have reached the Nevada Test Site. They race to be the first to the bowling alley at the center of the site. (It is all that remains of a fake village built by the bomb testers.) Then they run to escape the Wackenhuts, the private security force hired to guard the site. One by one they are caught and put in a paddy wagon. At the end, all that remain free are Kelly, Angie, and the Belgian guitar player, Beeka. They continue to walk.

Anna Kiraly's scenic design preserved the large open space of La MaMa's Ellen Stewart Theater. A brilliant yellow road curved for 60 feet from the cyclorama at the back of the playing area to the audience risers. It was a loopy road to Oz. The only movable set pieces were a map of the United States on which the characters periodically mark their progress with a red dot, a two-dimensional cartoon car and paddy wagon, and four rolling panels. On one side of the panels were gold draped curtains (used in the sequence of quick lazzi), on the other, painted views of the road and the roadside scenery. At first the marchers walk together, but later they straggle apart and walk in separate smaller groups in front of the painted panels, as if they have stretched out along different points on the road.

Anna's design for these painted panels was, in part, inspired by David

Hockney's "Pearblossom" Highway. Hockney's artwork is a photographic collage/drawing that layers 800 separate photographs of Route 138 in southern California. He took the photos from different angles and distances, including extreme closeups of the highway signs. There is no central perspective. In this way he enables the viewer to see the signs, the trees, the trash lining the road, and the sky, all from a multitude of viewpoints. Like the walkers themselves, Anna's roads can't be pinned down. One viewpoint can't contain them. Her brightly colored signs, clustered together and somewhat askew, clamor for attention.

The visual mix of 1992 ragtag activists, commedia dell'arte, beauty pageant, and kathakali were brilliantly realized in Machine Dazzle's costumes and Darrell Thorne's makeup design. The script describes the desired aesthetic mélange:

> All characters wear vibrantly colored foundation makeup (similar to a Kathakali look). Their faces have so much sequins and eye work it seems as if they are wearing color commedia dell'arte masks. They have extreme features: prosthetic noses, massive ears, protruding chins, and wild matted towering hair. They wear anarchist street clothes made to look like commedia dell'arte attire (cut-off jeans meet farthingales and patch-work pantaloons, political slogan t-shirts made into corsets and bustiers, fanny-packs that look like bum-rolls and codpieces). All outfits have an element of a deranged beauty pageant. It should be colorful but the color has faded from too much use.

The characters were decked out in "spectacularly tattered and layered and spangled thrift-shop couture." For instance, Greeter "sports butterfly wings, go-go boots, tassled knee bands, a cascading wig in multiple shades of purple, a crinkly blue beard, and a handbag shaped as a pair of fire-engine red lips." The Grass on the side of the road was played by a performer covered in long green grass festooned with soda cans, food wrappers and other discarded trash.

The vibrant colors of the costumes and set were echoed in the bold strokes of Lenore Doxsee's lighting design. The cyclorama provided a shifting backdrop of transparent blues, deep purples, yellows, oranges, and greens.

● ● ●

The *Walk Across Mother America for Mother Earth* is a comedy that's serious about its politics. The image of Marsha racing to the bowling alley, rolling her IV stand while pulling out her remaining clumps of hair, is grotesquely funny, but her fierce determination to shut down the test site is not. Shortly before they reach the site, Kelly says, "Greeter was talking about how people who live in St. George, Utah, downwind of the test site, have the highest cancer rate in America, and I thought, 'Fucking move!' Why is it my problem? Why can't they just fucking move?" It's a funny moment—an extreme reversal of Kelly's idealistic sentiments—and at the same time, a painfully honest expression of his despair. He goes on, "I try to change the world, but why? Why would I want to change the world and make it a better place for these people? I can't stand these people. I'm one of these people."

As the play ends, Kelly and Angie continue to walk, while in the distance the other walkers sing a protest song from the paddy wagon.

KELLY. Angie?
ANGIE. Yeah?
KELLY. It's not stupid, what we're doing is it?
ANGIE. Maybe.
KELLY. But it's not pointless?
ANGIE. No.
KELLY. There are stakes, right?
ANGIE. Yes.
KELLY. Even if, in all the mess, you fail to address it?
ANGIE. When things are wrong, people should at least try to make them better.
KELLY. Even if they make things worse?
ANGIE. I think so.
KELLY. Because failure is just success biding its time?

(They start to run again)

ANGIE. Kelly?
KELLY. Yeah.
ANGIE. If decades do go by . . .
KELLY. And nuclear bombs still exist?
ANGIE. And people continue to be destroyed?
KELLY. And peace never comes?
ANGIE. What then?
KELLY. They do sing beautifully.

The 1992 Walk Across America for Mother Earth was one of 500 demonstrations held at the Nevada Test Site between 1986 and 1994, involving 37,000 protestors and more than 15,000 arrests. In neighboring Colorado, beginning in 1978 and continuing through the 1980s, thousands of protestors occupied the Rocky Flats Plants, which produced the plutonium triggers for atomic bombs, and hundreds were arrested. The Rocky Flats Plant was shut down in 1992 after the EPA and the FBI raided it for criminal violations of environmental law. The same year the Nevada Test Site stopped explosive testing. However, the site did not shut down. It still operates on Shoshone land, where it conducts tests on the United States's aging nuclear arsenal.

Nuclear bombs still exist. Global warming threatens catastrophic upheaval and is already bringing misery. As I write, a global pandemic destroys lives and livelihoods, and accentuates enduring economic and racial inequalities. Police violence against people of color continues to reveal how deeply embedded racism is in the structures of our society. The list is long.

In a moment of despondency, Rainbow Carl speaks of his panic that "success is just failure biding its time, this is what it feels like to be an activist." But at the end of *Walk*, Kelly understands that the reverse may be true: "failure is just success biding its time." At different moments in struggles for justice and equality both formulations are true. In either case the walkers, and others like them who feel they have a stake in their society and world, have no choice but to act. It is a matter of both faith and necessity. Representative John Lewis, one of the original Freedom Riders and marchers in Selma, who was beaten by mobs and the police and was arrested twenty-four times, put it this way "Be hopeful, be optimistic. Never, ever be afraid to make some noise and get in good trouble, necessary trouble. We will find a way to make a way out of no way."

ELEVEN

An Interview with Taylor Mac

Kevin Sessums

The first time I ever saw Taylor Mac perform was at the Afterglow Festival in Provincetown, Massachusetts. I think that was in 2011. I had heard that he was sort of a combination of that other Taylor—Laurette—along with, oh, a little Liberace and a lot of Ethyl Eichelberger with some Genet sprinkled in like ginger then peppered with some Peter and some Paul and marinaded with a mess of Mary. And even with all that, I still wasn't prepared for the "all that" he turned out to be. He was performing his *Comparison Is Violence or the Ziggy Stardust Meets Tiny Tim Songbook*. It was transcendent. The last time I felt like I did that night was when I was twelve years old and answered the altar call at a little Methodist church in Mississippi at a revival service when "Just As I Am" was being sung and the Holy Ghost was stirring. Taylor Mac's art is in its devoutly secular way about redemption and revival and transcendence. It is about changing us in order to accept ourselves just as we are. It is about on some deeper level doing just that: leveling the altar and elevating the alter.

The last time I saw him was during the pandemic, when we called each other on FaceTime on September 15, 2020. We were each at our homes upstate. He was wearing overalls. I wasn't. We had this conversation. —Kevin Sessums

> KEVIN SESSUMS: Have you been up in the Berkshires the whole time since the pandemic lockdown began?
>
> TAYLOR MAC: Since March, yeah. I've been to the city two or three times. But other than that, I've been here. It's the longest stretch I've

ever been here. It's nice. Meditative. I'm not getting more done. But I'm not getting less done.

KS: So that's means you're still productive because your normal output is rather productive.

TM: Yeah. I wrote a play. I'm also trying to write a book for a new musical, but I'm dragging my feet on it. I can't talk about it to the press yet. So it depends on when this interview will be published. Off the record right now, I'm writing the book for the musical version of "Midnight in the Garden of Good and Evil." Jason Robert Brown is writing the music. It's for Broadway. I've done a detailed outline. Everyone is happy with it. Rob Ashford is the director. We've done the first two scenes. I've just got to get to that third scene.

KS: It's all about the third scene.

TM: Not really.

KS: Okay. Then it's all about the fourth scene so you have to write the third scene to get to it. So why did you go down to New York for those few trips? What got you out of the cabin?

TM: Dental work. I had to go pick up some more clothes. I'd been wearing the same two pants and three shirts for three months. I wanted to get my ukulele. I went the first time to do some chores. Get the mail. The second time I went down to do a recording session with Matt Ray. We're making a holiday album.

KS: Very Andy Williams of you.

TM: But it was so nice just to see friends. I saw friends. I miss seeing friends.

KS: I miss live culture. I've been to a few things at PS21 over in Chatham. I know we say that theater and music and dance nourish the soul but they also heal the body in some way. My body has viscerally missed paying witness to art being conjured. I didn't realize how much my body missed being in the presence of it.

TM: Yeah, yeah. The wonderful thing about Brooklyn—especially when everybody was getting their $600 a week—is that it was a little bit like the government was finally paying for the arts. All these musicians were just performing for free on the street. It was just heaven. There was free art everywhere. Vanderbilt Avenue was shut down and it was open for people to walk and it was so civilized. For me, Brooklyn is just where it is at right now.

KS: Are you moving there?

TM: No. I'm not moving there. I'm hunkering down. I'm one of those hunker-down people. I just let the world change around me. I used to live in Brooklyn. But I moved because it was so boring. Really boring in the '90s. But when I moved to the East Village, everybody moved to Brooklyn.

KS: To get away from you?

TM: Yeah, but I didn't take it personally.

KS: What kind of artist are you if you don't take it personally?

TM: The healthy kind—unlike some other artists I could tell you about.

KS: How has the pandemic affected the arts and artists? There is the concrete everyday aspect of it, which is artists having to try to find a way to support themselves and just to eat. But how has it affected the art itself? We are living in dystopia.

TM: Yeah, I guess.

KS: Or are we? Is it instead a kind of warped version of utopia? Because what you just described in Brooklyn sounded more utopian in its way.

TM: It's a combination of everything. It's awful to walk around with masks on. It's awful that the West is burning. It's awful that we have this president and white supremacy is rising. It's awful. All of these things are awful . . . and . . . well . . . and . . . it would be also irresponsible not to recognize that there is also some really good stuff going on despite all that. That is the human challenge. I just read something recently that said that if you are going to worship anything then worship compassion. So I see that happening all over the place: people digging into their compassion as much as I see a lot of people who are hateful. So whenever there is horrible stuff there is also good stuff with it. I believe in what Justin Vivian Bond says about the end of the world: It is not happening because it is not that easy. The end of the world is going to be slow. It is going to be slooooooooow.

KS: Well, maybe it has been slow all along and we're at the endgame.

TM: I can tell you that the world is going to last a lot longer than my life. I'm learning Italian right now.

KS: Those are two interesting sentences to string together. Why are you learning Italian as the world slowly ends?

TM: Because it's a dying language. But I can guarantee you that I will die before Italian does.

KS: Let's keep tying this conversation into the pandemic and the lockdown: Are you working on a play about the 1918 flu epidemic?

TM: It's not really about that. There was a parade in Philadelphia where it spread pretty wildly. It starts the day of that parade and is set in Philadelphia. Then it goes forward in time to the 1950s. So it's sort of set in both those time periods.

KS: I talked to you once and you cited your first gay rights parade in San Francisco as being seminal to your life—a kind of starting point for you—when you saw AIDS patients being pushed in wheelchairs in the midst of all that celebration, and now you're writing this play that has this parade as a starting point that was seminal to the flu epidemic. There is something about you and parades and a kind of heightened incongruous sadness within a celebration. Next you'll be playing Dolly Levi and singing about such a parade passing by. I'd love to see you as Dolly Levi, in fact.

TM: There is something about the festival. It's all about the day when normal society celebrates the fact that men can wear high heels and perhaps dresses. To me, theater is all about why is today different than any other day. So, of course, since I gravitated toward theater, I also gravitate toward those days that are different than every other day. And those are celebrations and funerals and memorial services and election days . . .

KS: Ritual. You're talking about rituals and the ritualized.

TM: Big ritual events, yes. And also that moment when the release valve is opened and you can let out the steam and how in that moment the culture sits on you and "the etiquette" sits on you and your own personal judgment sits on you, but you can let some of that stuff go. That's a real queer survival technique, how we latch ourselves onto those kinds of days, those kinds of moments.

KS: How do you think the institutional theaters that have supported you will survive this pandemic era we are living through? I miss my trips to London and all its institutional theaters and their productions. I thought of you when I just signed onto the Royal Court's website yesterday because there was a durational piece on its site called *The Caretaker* by Hester Chilingworth which has been up since May 8th. It's a camera focused on the bare stage and the ghost light and every now and then a voice will come into the piece with a message. The Young Vic just put up an interactive installation called "The Undiscovered." There is a huge banner with an image of Marsha P. Johnson draped over the front of the building. Also the Royal Court is doing a living newspaper starting in November that will employ playwrights and actors and directors. It will be topical with a satirical edge maybe. It all reminded me of you in its varied ways.

TM: Is the government paying them to do this? They do seem a little more creative in how to pay artists over there. I wish our government would get creative. I wish our theatrical leaders would get creative. It feels like everyone is just trying to work in the same models that they did before just only slightly limited. It's just so boring. What I am longing for is more creativity in the field of creativity. That's always been the case though.

KS: Have you come up with any new paradigms since you have always been about breaking old ones in your work—or reinventing them. You don't just break the fourth wall. You break paradigms.

TM: I did come up with a new financial model. But my art is not arts administration. Somebody else would have to take it and turn it into the thing it can become. But TricklupNYC.org is definitely a model that existed before—but didn't exist in the theater world, I don't think. This is what I keep saying to people: If we had a million subscribers we could be giving away $10 million every month. That's more than the National Endowment of the Arts. How much would it take for all the regional theaters in America to come together and put all their content up on one site and charge probably more than the million people who would subscribe $10 a month to see it? Then as an organization they all could collectively give out $10 million a month. How hard could it be? You'd have to get someone to organize it because everyone would want to syphon it off into their own group. And everyone wants control. There's not a lot of team playing in that industry. But it's a model that's working. We've given $70,000 away and we only have about 1,000 subscribers. Every month we give another $10,000 away. And it's just a bunch of videos basically of a bunch of people reading poetry.

KS: I have been reading poetry in videos I post on Facebook and Instagram. It gives me something to do during the pandemic. Maybe the pandemic is making us all artists. Maybe artistry has always been a way to ward off being stir-crazy.

TM: I think we all were artists already.

KS: You just used the term "team playing." Isn't a lot of the arts world in competition? Isn't being competitive part of being an artist?

TM: Or they think they are in competition. I guess they are because if you think you're in competition, you're in competition. I mean, that is the thing I didn't like about Broadway actually. I realized at the Tony Awards that I had unconsciously signed myself up to be a cast member—just by going to Broadway—to be a cast member in a reality TV show competition. You know: Who's gonna win? Here I was, I thought I'd never go on RuPaul's show. I'd never do anything like that. And there I was at the Tony Awards thinking: I'm on RuPaul! It's just called the American Theatre Wing.

KS: And yet, you're going back to Broadway because you're writing this book for this musical based on "Midnight in the Garden of Good and Evil."

TM: Well, yeah. Yeah.

KS: So there is a place in your life for RuPaul's show.

TM: I don't know. I guess that's an interpretation of it. I'm just trying to get away from competition and make this stuff. I will try to figure out how to balance having to participate in the rat race and just make my stuff.

KS: I think of you as a singular artist, Taylor, who makes singular stuff. The first time I had ever heard of you was the first time I ever saw you at the Provincetown Theatre during the first Afterglow Festival. You were doing your "Comparison Is Violence or the Ziggy Stardust Meets Tiny Tim Songbook." I thought: this is church. It was that kind of transcendent experience. I don't go to Ptown anymore really. Not enough people of color, as you sing in one of your Instagram Ptown songs you've posted.

TM: That's all I really want to do anymore. Write sing-along songs that take me a day to write. I want to write a hundred of them. So there you go. That's me right now.

KS: Sounds like a sequel to your twenty-four-hour durational history of the twenty-four decades of popular music.

TM: When it's ten, it's like they're just semi-okay songs. But when there's a hundred of them then it's really amazing.

KS: That was Shakespeare's attitude about his sonnets. I think he made it up to around 150 or so.

TM: That queen knew how to write.

KS: That's the same line I've heard about you. Not because of competition, but based on how we gauge things, you've had a lot of success. You've been acknowledged. You've been affirmed.

TM: I've been affirmed!

KS: For your art, yes. A lot of artists create art in the hopes of attaining that kind of affirmation. Artists like an audience. You certainly engage yours and make them at times even a part of the art being conjured in real time. How do you keep creating art once the acclaim has happened? Does it come from a different place?

TM: You have to learn that if you want longevity in this business. Although I've met some old people who are still doing it for the applause. So maybe I'm wrong on that. For me personally at a certain point I had to learn a different way of being an artist. I couldn't keep my thirteen-year-old self who was happy when someone told me I was good at something. As Quentin Crisp said: Find out who you are without praise or blame and be it. When I heard that quote, it became a kind of organizing principle for how to work my life. It's okay if they love it. It's okay if they hate it. Just make. Just figure out a way you can enjoy making. That's where it's really at for me. But there are other people who love to have the audience stand and cheer for them. I always feel sad at that point. I feel happy for about five seconds. And then, I go, ". . . oooohhhh . . ."

KS: There is something inherent in applause signaling the end of something that is deathlike. Something has died in that moment of applause.

TM: Yeah, yeah. They are applauding the end. It's lovely and dear. I like the ritual of that. But it's not my favorite part. Being in the moment and making—I'm more that kind of queen.

KS: You're also in your overalls-wearing-phase kind of queen. We're doing this interview by FaceTime and you are sitting there in your overalls. It's like you're doing a Larry Kramer homage.

TM: Covid has done this to me. It has turned me into Larry Kramer. Nothing like a pandemic to turn you into Larry Kramer.

KS: You are old enough to have lived through two different pandemics. How is this one different to you as an artist and a person and a queer?

TM: Well, I'm a solid adult in this one. I grew up during the AIDS epidemic. AIDS really hit the national attention around 1984 maybe. Is that about right? I was eleven. But I came into my sexuality during AIDS. Then as a young adult in the early 1990s I had my first dating experiences during it. So I think I had a slightly different experience of it than even people ten years older than me who went through that epidemic. This one feels less dramatic. It feels like there is less stigma. It feels like less people are getting it even though I don't know what the numbers actually are. It just feels that way. It feels like people are dying less excruciating deaths. It doesn't feel like it's focused on one demographic. It doesn't feel like we're losing an entire generation of leaders. It is a lot less traumatizing for me personally. If I had lots of loved ones who died of it, I'd feel differently.

KS: I had an uncle yesterday die of it. He was 93 but he wasn't sick until he got it and then he was gone very quickly.

TM: But that is different than if it took every friend you had. It's just different. I find the comparison to be . . . well . . . it's similar in that I stayed out to 5:30 in the morning the other night and had a lot of fun. I had not done that in over a year. I was with everybody. We were outside. We were on picnic benches. We were drinking. Everyone was wearing masks. People were socially distanced. But then as happens when you're outside dining and you're with people, somebody will always have a different level of boundaries than you do and they cross your boundaries before you even know they're doing it. You know, people without masks are getting up in your face. Then you take your mask off to drink. Suddenly someone is sitting right next to you and doesn't have a mask on. So I did have a little bit of that concern. It was my first time in six months that I had been with that many people. But I had so much fun. But then the next morning, I thought, oh, I've got to go get tested. I've got to tell everyone I know that I'm going to be in contact with that I've had this experience. So I was having all those kind of flashbacks to the 1990s. My personal life has to be private and I have to hold a little bit of guilt about fun and shame about having fun beyond just the puritan weight. That's the thing I find the most similar about this time. I feel like this is much less of a big deal—although it's a bigger economic deal.

KS: I was going to ask if you had been lonely. But you've been up in the Berkshires with your husband. So has it strengthened your marriage?

TM: It has. He's been very good through this whole thing. I've been a little bit more emotionally up and down and up and down—oddly manic depressive even though I'm not a manic depressive. I've had lots of energy and then no energy. Really happy and then totally depressed. And all in the same day. It's very odd for me to be that moody. But, yes, it's been really beautiful and I am really lucky to have him. And yet I do miss stimulation from other people.

KS: Do you miss city life?

TM: I didn't. I was sort of hating the city before all this started. So I was really actually happy to get out. I thought: maybe I'm done with New York. Because I just hate the way it's become. I hate the capitalism of it. I hate how overpopulated it is. Nonstop construction everywhere. Either the noise level has gone up or I've gotten older and I can tolerate it less. It was all of that at the same time and I was ready to leave. But with COVID and everybody leaving it, New York is now heaven.

KS: But the only thing is the lack of a cultural life.

TM: But there is culture.

KS: It's just not $200 a ticket.

TM: Yeah. $200 tickets to see something you don't even like. It's now free jazz on the street. It's free rock 'n' roll on the street. It's salons. And activism. It's everything I care about.

KS: I've only been down to the city once since February and that was for the queer march in June. I was sort of shocked at how empty it was. It was as if a bomb went off and left the buildings standing. I kept thinking, where are the people?

TM: Yeah. I hope it stays that way. I'd like the indoor culture to start happening again but I don't need the people. I don't need all the money. I feel like money has killed that city. I can say that Manhattan feels sad right now. It felt gross before. So between sad and gross, which do you want? But Brooklyn just felt so fun. I'm loving it. But I also realize that none of this will stay the same. One thing you can count on about New York: it will change.

KS: When I first got to New York in the 1970s, I had mentors who told me that I should have been around in the 1950s in New York when it was filled with artists and apartments were cheap and it was grittier and it was the real New York. Now I hear myself telling young people you should have been in New York in the 1970s when Times Square was sleazy and sex was really sex and apartments were cheap and it was filled with artists. Kids now will later tell kids in the future that they should have been in New York in the first couple of decades of the 21st century when the High Line went up and everyone was fucking with masks on and marriage equality happened and we fought back at fascism and a reality TV star was the damn president and you could get a studio apartment for $3000 a month. We are all just saying we miss our youth.

TM: I don't miss my youth. I much prefer this moment to my youth.

KS: I do too honestly. But I just went though a beloved dog dying and it broke open something in me. It lanced the grief I've carried around with me my whole life—through a childhood in which I lost both my parents and then my youth and my adulthood which were both imbued by AIDS. I think gay men of a certain age just carry this grief around with us from that other pandemic. Does grief inform your work at all?

TM: I think so. My dad died when I was four. So I think my understanding of loss is a little more calloused than most people I meet. I was at the funeral for an acting teacher of mine and I was sad. We're sad when people pass. But the young people in the room in their early twenties—I was in my early thirties at that point—were responding to it in the way that people do when they have never experienced grief before. And I realized, oh, I have grown up with expecting people to die as opposed to being surprised by it. You just have a different approach to life when your parent goes early. You become very aware of death and how it works. I don't know if that is good or bad. It's probably just made me a little more cynical. But that's okay. I'll take it.

KS: On the flip side of that, is joy important to your work? I know as someone who pays witness to it, I feel joy while experiencing it.

TM: I guess that's what I really mean. We're all dying. We're all going to die. None of us is getting out alive. So let's live. Let's enjoy each other. Let's try to figure out a way to have a good time. I don't discredit delving into sorrow as a good time. We just watched *Chinatown* the other night. It's the most tragic movie you can ever watch. It's sooooooooo tragic. Everything bad happens in that movie. And yet, I don't know . . . it's just so good.

KS: But that is one of the things I love about the art you make: its embrace of the incongruous. You acknowledge disintegration in all its forms and yet you mine it for joy. I like how it always keeps me a bit off-balance.

TM: Yeah. A lot of people mine joy for joy. But I go, you don't have to mine joy for joy. It's joy. You don't have to deconstruct it. You don't have to transform it. It's great already. You don't have to turn it into a drug and then shoot it and ruin it. Because by overworking joy, you end up ruining it. The more interesting thing for me—the more purposeful thing—is to work sorrow. How can you transform sorrow?

KS: You're not just an artist. You're an alchemist.

TM: Oh, well. If it's not broke, don't fix it. But if it is broke . . .

KS: . . . make it more broken and make it more of a prism.

TM: Sometimes that is the way to make it more fun—to break it even more.

KS: Do you think "Gary"—although set in ancient times—was prescient for what we are going through now with COVID with all these bodies piling up?

TM: I think it was right at its time. I think it was about the Trump administration and it was about the polarization of America for me and it was about the degree of the history of casualties through powermongers. It was about essential workers. I guess if it had opened right before the pandemic, it would have been shut down like everything else. But "Gary" is a long conversation that is hard to have honestly. Sometimes I just don't want to have it because I can't really have it honestly. I mean, I can in twenty years. But not right now. Not while people are still alive.

KS: The production or the play itself?

TM: The production. I'm really proud of the play. I think the play is remarkable. I think it is the best thing I've written. I wish it would get a whole bunch of other productions and that people would dive into it and see beyond just the surface level of it because I think it is much more profound than just a gimmick. That is how it was treated by the press when it was on Broadway. It was gimmick—and it's too bad.

KS: Do you think Trump is a clown? And if he is the clown, then who is the fool?

TM: I don't think Trump is skilled enough to be a clown. He's actually not funny.

KS: He's a vulgarian. He's seriously vulgar.

TM: A clown is someone who wants what they want when they want it. So in that sense, yes, he's a clown. But clowns have to have pretty good skill.

KS: At least go to clown school down in Florida.

TM: Clowns are attracted to study. He's not a professional clown, I'd say. But maybe he's a clown in terms of insult. I just don't think he's happy enough to be a clown.

KS: My term for him is the Tacky Know-Nothing Fascist Vulgarian. His vulgarity underlines everything.

TM: Yeah, yeah. I call him the Heckler in Chief.

KS: He's just so unserious about the job. He defiles everything.

TM: He's just heckling everybody. Look, he's a child of privilege and probably was abused. There's something wrong with him, something mentally wrong with him.

KS: I think he's a sociopath.

TM: Yeah. When you realize that, you go, oh, it's not really his fault. It's our fault for letting him take charge.

KS: It's the Constitution's fault because of the electoral college. We didn't let him take charge. We voted against him in the popular vote. He was installed after winning fewer votes.

TM: But he was still allowed to be in charge. Why do we allow a sociopath to be in charge, a person not mentally fit? We just do it again and again and again. It's up to the culture to change. He can't help it. Even though I don't like him and I don't want him to exist in the world, I can't really focus my attention on him because it is the culture that needs to change.

KS: And what do you think will happen to your world in which you exist as an artist if he is somehow re-elected and we have four more years of this chaos?

TM: I used to get so annoyed with my mom when she would say this but she'd say, "This too will pass." He's going to die eventually. Did we ever think the Reagan era was going to end and change? And it did. We're still suffering as a result of it. But things move on. Things move on. It will move on again. People definitely will be harmed as a result and it will get uglier for a while. But then that too will change. I just hope I live long enough to see it change. I keep going back to John Lewis. John Lewis didn't get cynical. And if he didn't get cynical then we don't have a right to be cynical. If people who got spit on and beaten up and killed just trying to get served lunch didn't get cynical, then we don't have the right to get cynical. We just have to keep working. That's what we have to do. Keep working.

KS: What do you think the Black Lives Matter movement means to the theater realm? I know that there are coalitions of BIPOC working toward more equity and work in the theater. You're a queer but the theater realm is one sphere where being queer can maybe equate to belonging to a sphere of power and it can work in your favor.

TM: It's odd. Everyone says we're privileged because we're gay men. I mean, I'm kind of a man, I don't know what I am. But everyone says there is privilege with that. I recognize that. And I also recognize that I have gotten opportunities because of it and I have not gotten opportunities because of it. So knowing that information, I go, okay, I am going to try and remove myself from that equation altogether and just make my own shit. That's been my approach. I've rarely worked with any of the institutions within the theater world. You said earlier that the institutions that had helped me in my career are having a hard time now. No. They're actually not. HERE Arts Center helped make my career. But that's the only one I can really claim that has helped me.

KS: The Magic Theatre in San Francisco?

TM: It came onboard later after I was a thing. It wasn't that I didn't get help here and there from PS122 or Dixon Place or different places like that. But these are low, low, low-to-the-ground theaters. I think they are more likely to survive than the midrange ones. I'm not too worried about it. I think that some things will fall away and some things will build back up. I am hopeful that if they do, then it will be more interesting. And I hope that the ones that get built back up will be built in more equitable ways.

KS: A moment ago when you said, "This too shall pass," wasn't there some sort of inherent privilege in that? If you can survive for another four years waiting for it to pass, aren't you privileged in some way?

TM: I said that as part of it going back to my dad dying when I was four. I am much more cynical than you think I am.

KS: Oh, honey, you have no idea how cynical I think you are. That's how cynical I am.

TM: To take it back to John Lewis again. I have to remind myself not to be so cynical. But I am more and more all about "this too shall pass." Yeah, people will die and I might be one of them. Friends and loved ones and people I admire. And then there will be a whole other group of people in the world.

KS: We are replaceable.

TM: We are replaceable. We are not special no matter what your mother told you.

KS: Now, Taylor, I think you're pretty special.

TM: I'm not special.

KS: I do think that. You are.

TM: I'm not.

KS: Well, it's not for you to say you're special. But I can say you're special. Although where I'm from down south saying "Taylor's special" means something else.

TM: Well, I'm that kind of special, too. I'm a little off.

KS: Endearingly so. Are you still writing the play that is all entrances and exits?

TM: Yes. I am. I thought it was something that we could rehearse on Zoom actually. So we might start doing that in January. I am busy doing something else in December.

KS: Which is?

TM: I won the Ibsen Award.

KS: How many fucking awards can you win, bitch?

TM: I know. It's this Norwegian award. The Norwegians have given it to me. It's sweet. It's quite sweet. They are giving me a first edition of *A Doll's House.*

KS: Wow. Oh, my God.

TM: So we're doing a virtual performance for the Norwegians online.

KS: That's quite a sentence. A performance of what?

TM: It's a performance of our holiday show. I'm not sure if we're going to open it up to other audiences or not. It's going to be my first Zoom show.

KS: So now you've won the Herb Albert and the MacArthur and the Ethyl Eichelberger and the Doris Duke and the Ibsen.

TM: Right?

KS: That sums you up. When I knew I was going to talk to you today I went and looked up Ethyl Eichelberger's obit in the *New York Times*.

TM: Ethyl Eichelberger had an obit in the *New York Times*? I didn't know that. That surprises me. I wouldn't think they would have done that then.

KS: I didn't realize that Ethyl was the son of Amish parents.

TM: I didn't know that either. Wow. So was Ethyl raised in the Amish world and left it?

KS: Yes.

TM: Wow. That's amazing.

KS: So thank you for talking to me today. Because of you and doing my research beforehand, I discovered that about Ethyl. You were a conduit to Ethyl—which too is a kind of summing up.

TM: To circle back about some of the love that I have gotten—the overabundance of love that I have gotten—it is because there was a missing generation. I can acknowledge that and through me they too can acknowledge that. They can say, well, we can't bestow this on Ethyl but we can on you. For whatever reason my art is a little more attuned to that missing generation than what is happening now.

KS: So let us end this conversation, Taylor, with an acknowledgement and remembrance of Ethyl Eichelberger. Let her make an entrance as we make our exit.

TM: Yay.

KS: Let us end on incongruity. Sorrow and joy. Entrance and exit. You and Ethyl. Cynicism and hope.

TM: Yes.

KS: Thank you, Taylor. I love you.

TM: Maybe I'll come visit you in Hudson.

KS: I'd like that. You're always welcome.

TWELVE

Collaborations

Matt Ray

In 2007 I moved into a 900-square-foot loft in Williamsburg directly above the Bedford L train stop. It was a time when artists in New York could still afford that kind of thing, and it was a bare-bones space with a lofted bedroom, Modine heater, and 20-foot ceilings. I made it into a decent home recording studio, and it became a true live/work space. It was a rustic old wood frame factory with cement floors; the landlord had cut it up into rentable units. It had no windows (but two skylights), and during the time I lived there it flooded, vagrants used the hallway as a toilet, and a blizzard covered up the exhaust vents and nearly gave me carbon monoxide poisoning. It was old school and off the books. It was heaven for a while.

It was there that I was living when I first met Taylor Mac. My phone rang one day and it was the great downtown accordianist/songwriter/chanteuse Rachelle Garniez asking me if was available to come play piano for a reading of some new music she had written with Taylor for a new play. I wasn't familiar with Taylor's work at the time, and I was pretty wiped out from a run of gigs, but it sounded so kooky and exciting that I immediately said yes and got myself together to go to the reading. That turned out to be the first read-through of the music for *The Lily's Revenge*, and the beginning of the most thrilling artistic collaboration of my life.

I had started out my career as purely a jazz musician, but after the turn of the millennium I had begun to drift away from jazz and more into other music worlds—singer-songwriter, cabaret, folk, indie rock, etc. The mainstream jazz world in which I had been immersed was exciting, dynamic, and rewarding, but straight-male-dominated and quite rigid in its expectations of what types of expression one could present. I remember musicians telling me "Don't play so many arpeggios, you sound like Liberace," or "You play too pretty," or "Don't play that, it sounds too 'man-on-man.'" As a queer person it could feel lonely and stagnant. I had become grateful for any opportunity to step away from it, and during the 2000s I had had quite a few opportunities to branch out. Music-directing *The Lily's Revenge* was the next step toward upending my artistic process and life. When I started working with Taylor on that production I walked into a world of Machine Dazzle costumes, durational performance, and queer concept work that altered my entire view of myself and what I could be in relation to my art. That is what Taylor Mac does when you enter judy's world.

With *Lily* I began as a pianist and music director, then arranger, and then as the years rolled by I moved into a full-time collaborative relationship with Taylor as we developed *A 24-Decade History of Popular Music*. Collaborating with Taylor is exciting because the process feels stable and yet flowing. It starts out as a task, like "Hey, learn these twelve songs and let's get together and see how to make them fit into what we're doing," and becomes, "Hey, we're in this room and these are the songs that sound the best, how can we make what we're doing fit these songs?" Then come the rehearsals, and then public performances (which are workshop-style), and then more changes and adjustments. There are always rules and structure because Taylor is detailed in that way, but within that structure there is so much chaos and excitement.

For *24-Decade* Taylor had a rule that judy had to sing on every song in the show. Sometimes we would be featuring one of our other talented vocalists and it was up to me to figure out how best to work Taylor into the arrangement. We also had a rule that we had to lose one musician every hour of the show, but I wanted to change up the sound from hour to hour, so sometimes I would bring a whole mess of new musicians onstage and we would just make sure the count went down by one. Taylor let me do whatever I thought was best for the show. The rules were made to be bent and broken.

The true chaos would come when we would parachute into a new theater and attempt to present twenty-four hours or six hours or twelve hours of show with only a few days of rehearsal. The shows themselves were both planned and unplanned, wild and contained, with Taylor hovering over or disappearing into the audience to alter their viewpoint, unsettle them, focus them, and create an ever-growing community that would metastasize and grow after that day's show was finished.

The most exciting thing about collaborating with Taylor is the feeling that you are collaborating with the whole world. We'd have a performance of *24-Decade* scheduled for a city, and we'd be bringing in local artists—dozens of musicians, Dandy Minions, guest singers, acrobats, a choir—to join us in the show. Their lives would be altered by the experience. The twenty-four hours of show was so large and impossible to perform without mistakes that it allowed us to give the local guest artists the opportunity to bring their art to us, to succeed and fail and laugh and watch the show while on stage and have an *experience*. That was and is the magic. Their friends and families would come. Gaps would be bridged. The community octopus would sprout a ninth leg.

After nearly every *24-Decade* performance I would come to Taylor's dressing room and we'd discuss what had happened onstage and in the audience, and what changes we could make. We'd also take note of happy accidents that we wanted to make permanent fixtures in the show. Our collaboration always feels constant yet fluid, and I love that. We are always talking, always exploring, always adjusting. People have asked me to be involved in traditional theater work many times over the last decade, and I've almost always said no, because how can you go from community engagement, political awareness, and constantly changing work to music-directing a work where the goal is for the show to become "fixed"?

One time we were in Australia on tour as a duo, and we were in the dressing room pre-show and there happened to be a piano in there. We were about to play one of the worst and least-favorite shows we've ever done—a Sunday matinee for an audience of people who didn't know who we are and who were accustomed to classical music performances. That made it all the better that one of our best collaborations came out of that day. One of the techniques we'd use to learn material for the twenty-four-hour show was to create theme concerts. Taylor had been promoting an upcoming theme concert called "Songs of the American Right," where we would compile and perform a two-hour concert of all the conservative songs from the larger show. We had songs like "It's Time for Every Boy to Be a Soldier," "Don't Fence Me In," and "Masculine Women, Feminine Men," but we didn't have enough material to make a full show. We needed more. I started looking up Ted Nugent songs and reading the lyrics out loud. The lyrics were so bad we couldn't bring ourselves to listen to the actual songs. We came across "Snakeskin Cowboys," which was a Nugent song that appeared to be encouraging queer-bashing (which we later confirmed to be true when our guitarist Viva DeConcini sent us an old Nugent radio interview). The song has horrible lyrics. So we decided to turn it into a sweet slow dance ballad and we wrote new and original music for it right then and there in the dressing room. That was the first time we went from singer and arranger to co-composers. Now we write songs together all the time, and it took refusing to listen to Ted Nugent to make that happen.

Later on, Taylor and I were talking about being children of the 1980s and never getting a queer prom to go to, so we decided to turn that Nugent song into a queer prom in the show, both to get back at Nugent, and to live in the beauty of what a queer prom experience might have felt like as a teenager. It became this intimate moment in the shows where everyone in the audience is holding each other (largely in same-sex coupling) and being completely silent. The beauty of that moment came out of the ugliness of the song. The ever-changing nature of our collaboration and Taylor's constant openness to new ideas allowed that concept to become a reality. Every time we perform that song and I look around at the audience members surrounding me on the stage having genuine intimacy with each other, I am deeply moved. I think of myself and draw inward toward my own coming-of-age, and then am pulled back out of myself toward the energy of the room, and then I can clearly see all the myriad personal experiences people bring to the theater, and how unearthing them is both personal and cathartic.

Moments like that are why people come into Taylor's world and stay awhile. I always feel like if one tries to find a continuous thread to exist on in this capitalistic and deeply unsettling world, it should be a combination of the metaphysical and the visible. Religion doesn't get there for me, but we all want to be a part of something. We all yearn for meaning. We all need to make a living. Where is the thread? For me it's been sticking to the community that is willing to learn and grow together. No matter what happens, we in Taylor's world are connected by our personal growth, our art, and our deeply interesting common experiences during judy's shows.

Yet it goes deeper. It becomes like some kind of a swaddling. A group energy exchange. Yes Taylor's work is about building community through shared experience. Yes it's about reminding us of things we've forgotten, dismissed, or buried. Yes it's about reframing history in a queer context with queer language. All of those beautiful literary descriptions fit. However, it's also about Taylor's unique ability to trust, to adjust, to care, and to curate. It's truly a personal and transformative artistic connection, especially for me. I will always be indebted to Taylor for showing me that more is possible, more is available, more is outside, and more is inside. The art never stops, and our Taylor Mac community becomes like a mushroom's hyphae where the connections are always more vast than what appears on the surface.

Machine Dazzle (Matthew Flower)

I often wonder what would have happened to me if I hadn't met Taylor Mac. As an artist and designer, I value context and meaning—a reason to make art, not for myself, but for a greater good. I've sometimes heard that work comes through an artist rather than from an artist. This is how I describe my working process with Taylor . . . I think he sees in me the same qualities that I see in him, a voice with purpose, a queer identity, and a vision that challenges the status quo. And Taylor thinks BIG! Perfection!

When Taylor and I first met in the post-9/11 downtown re-emerging club scene, REVOLUTION was in the air. That word continues to change meanings and my work. If there's work to be done, the artists will show up. Artist *as* Activist. Now I wonder, when has revolution NOT been in the air?

When we first met, I was experimenting with my own gender-nonconforming drag and was part of a queer dance troupe called the Dazzle Dancers, hence my nom de plume. We danced and stripped in all the downtown queer bars and clubs. I designed and made the removable costumes. We often shared a stage with Taylor Mac. He was different. Painting his face in unusual ways, gluing things to his head, wearing found objects and playing the ukulele . . . instant family.

One night, Taylor asked if I would make him a "Lily" costume, I was honored and gladly got to work. About a year later he asked for another Lily costume (after wearing the first one to shreds). Taylor also asked for a few daisy costumes . . . with "removable" petals. That's when I knew he was building a much larger show, *The Lily's Revenge* at HERE. Forty cast members, five directors, one self-taught costume designer . . . Taylor didn't tell me how to make things, only why. There were stock characters and more: brides, grooms, flower girls, flowers, bees, and an incurable disease. I could make the costumes however I wanted; the crazier it was, the more Taylor liked it . . . creative paradise! It was exhausting and a huge success.

I knew Taylor truly appreciated my work when he asked me to do his next show, *Walk Across America for Mother Earth* at La MaMa. This show was based on true events that also loosely included characters from the commedia dell'arte . . . at least that's where we started. Taylor is very careful about what he gives to me as a collaborator. He knows that I go to work as soon as we start talking, so he is selective about the information and the words he uses. Not too little and not too much—just enough to send me on my creative path.

Less than a year after *Walk* . . . Taylor asked if I'd make a 1790s-inspired outfit, that's it, nothing more. A year later he asked if I could make a 1930s outfit, and then a 1970s. Then, maybe half a year later, we had the meeting. Taylor asked for a 1770s-inspired costume, and then he explained to me his concept for a twenty-four-decade-inspired show as a long-term project. Thrilled beyond belief, I was in ecstasy at the prospect of crafting twenty-four period costumes *my way*. We had the luxury of time. As we started workshopping different decades, it became clearer what the show was actually about: *community*. All of that information was flowing through me and coming out on the other side as a sculptural realization of history, America, revolutionaries—and all through a queer lens. *A 24-Decade History of Popular Music* is certainly our greatest collaboration.

My costumes are work. And Taylor loves to work. What I make can be heavy, and uncomfortable. Sometimes it's a balancing act, all for the sake of community, change, and art! He puts a lot of trust in me, and I return that trust with faith. Taylor also works for me. He knows that I wouldn't ask him to wear a costume that I wouldn't wear myself. He sees my potential and nourishes it. This is what Taylor offers all of his collaborators—he feeds them opportunity and cultivates magic to share.

One of my favorite collaborative moments happened in Melbourne, Australia. The theater had a large fire curtain with the image of an Art Deco angel. During chapter 4 of the *24-Decade* extravaganza we decided to start the show with the fire curtain down. We thought it would be amazing to raise the fire curtain and a harnessed Taylor would be "flying" in air, replacing the angel in that space. "Hey, Machine, do you think we could make some wings?" Hell yes! So chapter 4 starts in 1956 and goes to 1966 and the decade focuses on the first-ever march on Washington for civil rights. At the height of Pop Art, using iconic images, I decided to dress Taylor in Jackie Kennedy–in-Dallas "realness." The outfit included Jackie's pink suit, which I made out of an old American flag. I rendered it pink by painting pink dots on it in a Roy Lichtenstein manner; Campbell's soup cans hugged the shoulders and around the back to represent Andy Warhol. Barbie was invented during this time, so I had her represented in various forms on the costume. Taylor even starts with a large bouquet of red roses—but what wings were appropriate?

Just days before, we heard of the mass shooting in Las Vegas. As an antigun gesture, I created two large "wings" in the form of human hands mimicking a gun. I made them in a Roy Lichtenstein way, with dots just as with the pink suit. It was an ode to JFKs assassination AND a reaction to tragic recurring events in America. The crowd went crazy! We have used the hands in that section of the show ever since.

Viva DeConcini

Interview conducted by Sean F. Edgecomb on August 17, 2020.

SFE: Hi Viva, so can you tell me about when and how you first met Taylor Mac?

VD: Well, I was a refugee of the musical patriarchy, having had to leave some bands I'd worked in for years after, you know, one rape joke too many. I met Miss Saturn out on the fantastic NY nightlife scene and we put together a show which was, to my knowledge, the only queer female-led live music show with strippers, called Viva's Rock 'n' Roll Burlesque. In the fall of 2009, I had called Darlinda to do a show and she said that she couldn't do any shows for the next two months, because she was in this other really great show. "You should come—I think you would like it." I had never even heard of Taylor and I was nervous about making it through all five hours, but I was also very excited because it had so many of my favorite performers in it so I went and I wasn't bored for one minute! In fact, my mind was completely blown. I like to paraphrase Taylor: I thought two things when I saw *The Lily's Revenge*: number one, Taylor is one of the finest minds of our generation, and number two, here is someone who hates Ronald Reagan as much as I do! People say Trump is worse and I know it's different, but for me Reagan was just as bad. I was struck by the virulence of Taylor's passionate hatred for Reagan and I was overjoyed to experience how he transformed it into this hilarious, fun show that created this big community.

That show had four intermissions where you could meet the cast in a place called "The Discussion Disco" and that's where I met Taylor with my standard line at the time (and still!), which was, "Great show, do you need a guitar player? I'm a guitar player—and hey, you need a rock band? I've got a rock band." He doesn't remember but he gave me his email! So a few months later, I reached out to invite him to a variety show I was doing at Joe's Pub. He said yes, but then never told me what songs he wanted to do, so I bought his album on iTunes and picked a few of his original songs, including "The Palace of the End" and "Practice" and we arranged them for my band. After that he asked me to be in *Walk Across America for Mother Earth* at La MaMa and then the *24-Decade* show and *Holiday Sauce* and the rest is history.

SFE: What have you learned from Taylor or the experience of collaborating with him over these several projects?

VD: Oh man, I learned so much from Taylor. I'm very theatrical and have always been involved in theatrical things, but I had never really done—you know—theater. I was a Latin nerd and an English major, so I love poetry and the use of language but the way Taylor combines standup comedy, music, and theater, with its kick-ass lights, sets, costumes, and audience participation, into a totality of spectacular experience ignited my thoughts and feelings in ways I never before thought possible.

Machine Dazzle's costumes are crucial for this. Their glittering beauty and out-of-this world-ness combine often incongruous things in ways that change what you think is possible. This can put you in a place of hope even in the face of terror. His Civil War costume for Taylor had a hoop skirt with fake barbed wire and hotdogs, with ketchup and mustard dripping like blood. It's really horrifying, but because it has this garish comic effect it gets inside your mind in a way that is very, very new because you know, yellow blood. It sets your brain askance. You look at and you think—it's blood, it's ketchup, it's mustard, it's blood but blood isn't yellow, wait—what's happening? And then poof, your mind pops open and you're able to think about history in a new way. And of course all this is happening while Taylor is singing and talking and the audience is re-enacting the Civil War with ping-pong balls. As if all of that weren't enough, *A 24-Decade History* uses music as a time machine to show how us queers have always been a part of American history. That is, as we say in burlesque, a big reveal. Dandy revenge! Like with rock 'n' roll it takes anger and transforms it into joy. This, I think, is one definition of queer: Resist with Pleasure.

SFE: I love Taylor as a friend and as a performer who I respect and enjoy so much, but as I'm sure you know, *A 24-Decade History* has received some criticism, particularly around the way it presents race through American history, considering that as the sort of performative interlocutor and tour guide, Taylor is still a white man of some privilege. As a scholar and teacher I'm always encouraging my students to work from an authority based in their own experience and to question everything that they see, but, in this case, I think criticism often comes casually from people who might not necessarily be willing to take the time to engage in the work. What do you make of this criticism?

VD: Well, Taylor's stated intention is to subvert the very idea of perfection and so I think it welcomes criticism. Community is messy and full of humans, and therefore mistakes. The show exhorts us all to take agency, Taylor quotes Maxine Wolf at the NY Act Up meeting when people are trying to figure out how to pay to Xerox some flyers for an event, she says "Pirate the fucking copies!" And of course, the Larry Kramer quote, "You don't have to ask permission to participate in the creativity of your own survival." So yes, I think if you take the time to meaningfully engage with the show, you will see that it is open to criticism and is embracing imperfection on purpose to reveal biases where they are and not just where we want people to see them. It is a very honest show.

Also, Taylor uses his privilege to help people. He may in fact get more attention than nonwhite females (because the theater world, spoiler alert, is racist and sexist) but he's committed to and excels at sharing the spotlight. And he does this at a personal cost in a sense, because I think he could easily have a great career on his own, just with a ukulele or piano accompanist. He doesn't need all of us to become famous, but he wants more than to just become famous so he puts his grant money where his mouth is and hires women, BIPOCs, and other marginalized peoples, and then we all get to play, you know, the Barbican. He wants to change the culture because he has suffered under the culture. Again, this is what it means to be queer.

Niegel Smith

I will never forget the first time I witnessed Taylor perform. It was judy's world premiere of *The Young Ladies Of . . .* at The HERE Arts Center in New York City. I was immediately taken by Taylor's ability to take us into the deeply personal while locating the personal in a global political space. They did this while lifting us with music and while centering a glittery queer perspective. And that was just the writing. Taylor also embodied those themes—judy's stagecraft found transcendent beauty in decay and detritus. I was hooked.

Fast forward to 2011. I'm directing Lady Rizo, *Ordained*, at Joe's Pub and Rizo asks if we should bring Taylor on as a performer in the work. I didn't hesitate. Yes, yes, yes.

One day in rehearsal, I stopped everything. I made us hold. The collaborative conversation had veered off the rails, and I wanted us to refocus on Rizo's intentions and aims. We did that and took a break. In that break, Taylor walked over to me and said, "I think you're my director." That was the invitation that has led to an incredible series of collaborations, including *A 24-Decade History of Popular Music: A Radical Fairie Realness Ritual, HIR, The Fre,* and now *The Hang.*

Taylor is a total theater artist. Judy is equally comfortable writing, performing, and directing. It makes for deeply nuanced collaborations. I love that by the time we get to presenting the work for an audience there's been a total blending and co-ownership of the vision. So whether I'm directing or codirecting, I'm looking for ways to get judy's perspective fully articulate so that I can digest it, interpret it, and lead the rest of the team toward a shared understanding of the work. With *24-Decade*, that was fascinating—because early on our codirection looked like Taylor making a ninety-minute performance for a particular decade.

Before rehearsing judy would ask me some questions about theme and songs and participation, but we decided that we didn't want me to get into the weeds right away. I needed to be the outside eyes. So Taylor would go away with Matt Ray, Machine Dazzle, and the musicians and make a version of the decade. I purposefully would not see a lick of rehearsal or performance until the first audience. Whoa—unheard of. But we had this innate trust about how the work needed to come into being. I would see that first performance, take in its beauty, and note where it could lift—be more cutting, think about whether the song order was really landing the emotional or narrative arc, consider how the moments of participation

Fig. 36. David Román, Morgan Jenness, and Niegel Smith before a performance of *The Fre*, the Flea Theater (2020). Author's photo.

and banter were effective. And after the makeup and costume had come "mostly" off we would begin to work—usually right in the dressing room. We would chat about my insights and impulses, and then we would come up with what was most pressing to implement for the next performance, the next night!

It was a joyous challenge to be making the work with the audience. That impulse to put my part of the direction in the space and the stakes of a paying audience allowed Taylor to follow their initial creative intuition before I came in with a true director-as-audience point of view to lift it.

That was our process for nine of the decades. In 2015, Taylor, Matt, and I were invited to spend several weeks at the Sundance theater residency, where we were sequestered with our dear dramaturg Jocelyn Clarke. We broke down all twenty-four hours looking at everything from the narrative arcs in each decade to dramaturgical basics.

We then examined each chapter, considering how participation evolved over the twenty-four hours and how that related to time of day and where the audience would be physically or emotionally. Matt was also working out which musicians we were losing each hour and how that formed the interpretation of the music. We had two huge walls running the length from the back door to the front door that had every song, meal, banter idea, costume change, and participatory move all mapped out.

Before that residency, I knew I could wrap my mind and arms around three to six hours of material, but I was always nervous about how we would mentally and conceptually hold all twenty-four hours. The Sundance residency solidified our shared understanding of what we were setting out to do and became the spine for all that followed.

Because we have been co-making so intensely from the outset, when I take on the role as director solely, there's no fear or sharp lines about what our roles are as collaborators. In staging the world-premiere productions of *HIR* and *The Fre*—the execution of the physical world has always been the greatest opportunity for blurring our roles. Our aesthetic and queer experience is so aligned that I can easily intuit our performance style, the music, and our dynamic with the audience, whether proscenium, immersive, or whatever else might serve the experience best.

Taylor's plays ask us to consider new ways of looking and participating in a theatrical act. That means I have to get deep into judy's mind and invite judy into the scenic design process *very* early in the process. For *HIR* we were working on what Taylor was calling "absurd realism." Now this was a brand new concept birthed out of Taylor's impulse to queer realism because—as always—the form of the play needed to match, lift up, and support the content. When we started designing the set, we were taking realism into the territories of symbolism and deconstruction, which kept bringing in a heaviness. And I wasn't happy. Taylor wasn't happy. We knew we were making a deeply funny work, and the humor had to come from how absurdly high we took the situations and physical embodiments. Taylor was right there with me and the scenic designers—at the design meetings, at the load-in, and at the previews—pushing the physical setting where it needed to land.

One day in rehearsal, an actor pushed a huge pile of laundry out of the way so their cross from downstage to upstage would be easier. Taylor leaned over and said, "that's not the play." We were learning that the obstacles which were "real" would create situations that were "absurd." By having a huge piles of laundry in the space, the actor would now need to high-step, climb, scoot over them to make the cross. Absurd realism.

I love working with Taylor. I'm convinced every new play director/playwright relationship should be as bonded. When you're setting out to put a new performance in the world—how do you get to unity in design, performance, and text? Because we are working out a shared vision—Taylor primarily focusing on the text, and I'm primarily focused on the execution—and while honoring and insisting on a slippery middle, where we are all up in each other's business, we can more confidently point our collaborators toward the finish line. We are all working together toward the ideal introduction of a new work.

Tigger! Ferguson

I always remember meeting Taylor at the fagulous farewell party for our mutual friend, Jonny Woo. (Maybe late 2001 or early 2002? Whenever Jonny was planning his return to London and Taylor was still new in town . . . or downtown.)

It was a costume party at Marion's restaurant on the Bowery, and Jonny gave each of us different instructions for our lewks. I came as Tiggarabia, my trashy drag version of a fin-de-siècle fantasy Salome. Across the table from me was a bewitching bald beauty dressed as . . . maybe a battered wife? I didn't know this person, but I was mighty curious. Then Taylor got up and sang the most hauntingly touching rendition of "Nothing Compares 2 U," which was made all the more haunting in judy's battered drag. Right after that memorable performance I said, "Wow! Sit back down here and tell me EVERYTHING, darling. Where did you come from?"

Taylor has since reminded me that we had met once before that, in

Provincetown. I'd forgotten this because I was busy chatting with this hot guy I'd hooked up with before, who had once again become his boyfriend (and now husband) Patt.

There is also a kind of meeting that happened even earlier, in a way.

Here is how Taylor described it, both onstage in *A 24-Decade History of Popular Music* and several years earlier, when he officiated at my nude wedding on the beach at Fire Island:

"Years ago I was sitting backstage with Tigger! telling him about this documentary film I'd heard about in the 1990s. Apparently some guys went around in a pink Sodomobile to all the states where it was illegal to have sodomy and well . . . did some political action. I said to Tigger! that it seems my whole life I've wanted to know those people. The people who do those kinds of things. Who take hatred, oppression, and shame and make joy, celebration, and love. Those are the people I'd like to surround myself with. At which point Tigger! said, 'Um, that was me. That queen in the Sodomobile documentary? I was one of them.' I'd been a friend with Tigger! for a few years at that point, and I didn't know that I was already surrounded by those people. You get what you ask for in this life. You get what you make. You may not know it until someone tells you to look around."

We've collaborated frequently since.

The collaborative process has varied from show to show, but I'm honored and tickled that Taylor considers me a Muse.

Judy often devises a show and leaves spaces for me to do my thing, whatever that may be. It depends on each show just how specific the demands of the framework might be. But judy is incredibly generous and perspicacious in creating a framework for collaborators to shine according to our various strengths. For shows like *Holiday Sauce* or *Live Patriot Acts: Patriots Gone Wiiiiildd!*, there's a clear theme and function as parameters, but I am given free reign to create my own acts in my own style. That's why you're cast. In one script the stage direction was "Tigger!: WERRRK!"

And back in the day, when I booked Taylor in my burlesque/performance art shows at Coney Island or Slipper Room, the whole point (and the joy) of it was to just let judy do whatever the fuck judy wanted. I'd give the context for the show, and then discover onstage along with the audience just what Taylor would do. That's the delight of casting your favorite talents in unscripted shows: you say as little as possible and then enjoy the stunning surprises.

In more tightly scripted shows, such as *The Walk Across America for Mother Earth*, I played the role as Taylor had written it. Especially since I jumped in to learn and perform the role just one week before opening night. But even then, Taylor leaves room for actors to interpret judy's marvelous words as they resonate with us. And when you have the chance to say such words, you want to make damn sure you give them life but do not get in their way.

My favorite role that I have ever played, in fifty years of show biz (counting childhood church pageants), was the Great Longing, the living stage curtain in Taylor's Obie-winning *The Lily's Revenge*. It was a fabulously over-the-top villain role that was written especially for me! How could I help but revel in such a gag-worthy golden opportunity? But even then, amid the elaborate fantasy plot structure that spanned five acts and six distinctly different directors, judy scripted the space for me to create my own striptease as a key dramatic point in the transformation of my character. In a musical with a different actor, it would surely have been a song. But Taylor knows my strengths and gives me the spaces to lean into them, all while offering delicious challenges and still supporting the story judy needs to tell.

We always share the common dream of creating community and sharing good stories, while telling the awful truth but still offering some measure of hope.

We're all wary of the tendency to blow smoke up the ass of celebrated artists, but this is the goddamn truth. Taylor is my favorite performing artist AND one of my favorite friends and human beings. I wouldn't love judy any less if judy was still strumming a ukulele in sleazy downtown bars. And in a way, judy is always doing just that. What's not to love?

Barbara Maier Gustern

As a voice teacher long associated with the New York downtown arts community, I was aware of Taylor Mac. They had appeared in a Weimar New York show I coproduced. But as a student, Taylor's lessons started when they conceived of the *24-Decade History of Popular Music*.

Our work began after my husband Joe, a Broadway singer, was in declining health and given to falling. He and Taylor often talked a bit before a lesson. During one session, Joe fell off his chair. Taylor stopped midphrase, picked Joe off the floor, and settled him back in his chair. Taylor always made Joe smile with a cheery greeting. Although I never had to call on Taylor, it was comforting to know that they were just across town and offered to hop on their bicycle and come if I needed.

The thought of singing twenty-four hours seemed an impossibility to me. I was sure it would lead to vocal damage, perhaps permanent. It seemed my duty to warn Taylor, but they were fully aware of the risks. Even knowing, Taylor was dedicated to their vision of an uninterrupted twenty-four hours. In 2016 we began weekly sessions working on breath, range, stamina, flexibility, and kinesthetic awareness. The diverse styles Taylor performed had specific demands. We expanded range, found healthy ways to produce a variety of timbres, and devised buzzwords to remind Taylor to relax if they felt tension. We consulted a laryngologist, who underscored the importance of hydration. Guest artist performances allowed for a bit of break time.

By attending all the shows leading up to the marathon show, I was able to pinpoint potential problems. I would email if I had any comments. By the time the first show was over it was clear this twenty-four-hour show would be a reality. Taylor wrote me into the show as Mother. I sang a hymn from his childhood, "Shepherd Show Me How to Go." We had some scripted dialogue and some impromptu. What a thrill to stand beside Taylor in those high platform shoes and me at 4′ 11″. Being part of the diverse community of artists that Taylor brought together made coming to the theater each time a moment of intense joy. And to realize that our two years of hard work had provided a technique strong enough to support extraordinary vocal demands was a dream come true.

Taylor's favorite saying is "perfection is for assholes." This surely resonated in our work. Taylor knew what they wanted and they did it. Our job together was to make the dream possible and Taylor's job was to make it happen.

This remains one of the highlights of my life. Thank you Taylor.

Linda Brumbach

In 2009, I went to see Taylor Mac's *The Lily's Revenge* at the HERE Arts Center. It was a six-hour community fantasia with a soaring spirit the likes of which we had never experienced. I go to see a lot of performance work, and, even so, it was unusual for me to encounter an artist with such bravery and generosity, who understood the functions of community, had an innate sense of justice, demanded awareness, and brought great joy into the room . . . all at once. I was glad to be introduced to Taylor's work, and to spend the next several years getting to know him as a performer, a maker, and a friend.

I founded Pomegranate Arts, a performing-arts production company, in 1998, with my longtime producing partner Alisa Regas. When we met Taylor, we were in the midst of independently producing a remount and international tour of *Einstein on the Beach*, the durational contemporary opera by Philip Glass, directed by Robert Wilson. A hallmark of Pomegranate Arts is that we are invigorated by projects that anyone else might deem impossible. By many standards, the work it took to bring that *Einstein on the Beach* back to the stage, on the scale that we did, could be considered the most challenging and meaningful project of a producer's career. And it was! But, as we were planning our final tours of *Einstein*, Alisa and I were eager to identify our next project to champion. It was around that time that Taylor shared with us his ambitious vision to create *A 24-Decade History of Popular Music*, which he wanted to pursue with his longtime collaborators, the costume designer Machine Dazzle and music director Matt Ray. The idea was inspiring and terrifying at the same time—and we knew we had to be involved.

Coming out from under *Einstein on the Beach*—a work that requires precision and repetition—there was a level of chaos and messiness at the heart of Taylor's process, endemic to beginning something so ambitious from scratch, that was not in our comfort zone. However, it was completely refreshing and challenging to dream about how we could help Taylor create an infrastructure to build *A 24-Decade History of Popular Music* through workshops, touring, experimentation, and performing-arts-presenting partnerships.

It sometimes seemed like a risky experiment to create a sustainable producing model to align with the scale of Taylor's concept within pre-existing and traditional presenting platforms. The reason it worked was because we were able to absorb and appreciate the chaos, while centering Taylor's ideals of unearthing buried truths to sing a new and more perfect America into existence.

From 2012 to 2016, Pomegranate Arts organized ongoing workshops, rehearsals, tours, and marathon training for Taylor and the broader creative community of the project. The culmination of these developments was the world premiere of a single twenty-four-hour-long marathon performance of *A 24-Decade History* at St. Ann's Warehouse in Brooklyn in October 2016, just one month before a crucial presidential election in the United States. The community of artists, guests, and activists had expanded during the development of the project. Over 200 performers participated in the premiere, and an audience of 700 very lucky people were present for what became a generation-defining immersive event.

After the devastating results of the 2016 presidential election came to bear, we knew that we needed to find a way to bring *A 24-Decade History of Popular Music* to a broader audience, so we established a touring model that presented the work over four six-hour evenings across two weekends. We were able to bring the piece, in its entirety, to five cities between 2017 and 2019. Our tour began in San Francisco, where we were presented at the Curran Theater in collaboration with Stanford Live. Engagements then followed at the Melbourne International Festival, LA's Ace Theater with CAP/UCLA, the Philadelphia International Festival of the Arts at the Kimmel Center, and finally at the Berliner Festspiele in 2019. We captured the performances on film in two cities and hope to offer it to more audiences on screen someday.

To present the entire twenty-four hours on tour, we traveled with 35 consistent company members, and also invited approximately 150 local performers and activists to join us in each city. The building of each show in every unique community was an integral part of the experience and the work. Taylor never stopped responding to what was happening politically in America and analyzing how he could shift elements of the show to resonate in the communities where we were performing——always leaving space for a local perspective.

Taylor had met the Seattle-based artist Timothy White Eagle who, after his participation as a Dandy Minion at the Brooklyn premiere, assumed the role of "Dandy Minion Artistic Director" on tour to help cultivate the Dandy community in each city going forward. Our music director Matt Ray worked closely with us to identify local pickup musicians in each city to incorporate into our orchestra.

There were several featured-guest moments throughout the production, which required a great deal of research and coordination for each city; some parts involved audience members, others invited individual artists, activists, small groups, and larger community ensembles that reflected the fabric of each hosting city. These guest performers were sometimes people who had never been invited onstage or backstage at a large-scale performing-arts center. Others of them had never entered a markedly queer environment. This was not a traditional "casting call"! It takes time and care to identify the right people to join Taylor on stage and to expand the *24-Decade* community. Those connections, while not always initially obvious, often begin to appear inevitable once Taylor has had his way with them. Through these collaborative, community-driven moments, the work had room to change, and the narrative became even more impactful because they were imprinted by localized contributions.

One of my favorite examples of how this worked was in relation to the song "Love Will Tear Us Apart," by Joy Division, which Taylor performs in the hour of the show focused on the 1980s, an era when AIDS ravaged the queer community in America. Before the 2016 marathon performance, while we were developing *A 24-Decade History*, we had the opportunity to perform a section of the work at Celebrate Brooklyn, a free outdoor music festival with an audience of over 3,000 people. We were introduced to the incredible Brooklyn United Marching Band, an all-Black community youth marching band, and invited them to join Taylor on the aforementioned song for a surprise guest appearance. The young musicians in Brooklyn United had participated in many exciting events, but they had never shared the stage with a drag performer before. The Celebrate Brooklyn show remains one of the most inspiring moments in the development of the piece—cementing an unlikely relationship and finding similar causes within different forms. When the Brooklyn United Marching Band joined Taylor again at the St. Ann's Warehouse marathon performance, the young musicians arrived to the theater wearing pink berets in solidarity with Taylor and the queer community.

When Taylor next performed this section of the show, during its development phase, at CAP UCLA's Royce Hall, he invited the first all-female mariachi ensemble, Mariachi Reyna de Los Angeles, to perform with him on "Love Will Tear Us Apart." These powerful Mexican immigrants, female activists, and spectacular musicians gave new meaning to the song through their empowerment, lived experience, and work.

In 2019, when we brought the show in its entirety to Berlin, a fourteen-member all-accordion band Akkordia was our featured guest on "Love Will Tear Us Apart." The group formed in 1935, before World War II. Including them in the performance of this song, in the context of a work about communities rebuilding themselves after being torn apart, was profoundly moving in Germany.

These three community groups—Brooklyn United Marching Band, Mariachi Reyna de Los Angeles, and Akkordia—performed the same song, expressed and interpreted in vastly different ways, but each group responded deeply to the core of the Taylor's message about the strength that communities are capable of and how they rebuild themselves after being torn apart.

Then love, love will tear us apart again.

Love, love will tear us apart again.

—Joy Division (1980)

Taylor is a multifaceted artist of vast intelligence, with a terrific improvisational wit, and the ability to pay constant attention to craft. But at the core, he is a community organizer. He has the ability to provoke and embrace his audience, regardless of their age or affiliation, and hold their attention in the palm of his hand. I often think of Taylor as a twenty-first-century Dolly Parton—one of the rare artists who somehow manages to connect and bring together the most unlikely range of people and build bridges to reimagine the world together, even when we are uncomfortable doing so. As he constantly hones and defines his own craft, he is exploring ways to make room for others. Though it is important for him to create a structure, Taylor's awareness of the potential transformation that can happen by giving up a level of control and delving into the unknown is singular.

He messes with us and then he loves us . . . and this is Taylor's unique magic.

THIRTEEN

"It's going to go on a lot longer than you want it to"

A Conversation about Taylor Mac, Covid, and Collaboration

David Román and Sean F. Edgecomb

DAVID ROMÁN: Sean and I wanted to include a more personal chapter in the volume, one that showcased our individual investments and subjective responses to the work of Taylor Mac, which has touched us both deeply and yet very differently. We also wanted to demonstrate something central to Taylor's aesthetics and politics: collaboration. One of the things I admire most about Taylor is their willingness to bring other artists into their creative practice. Our conversation invites others to share their own stories and impressions and models one way to talk about an artist's work outside the rigidity of critical objectivity as the primary discursive mode for scholars. We started off with a set of questions about when we first encountered Taylor's works and from there let the conversation flow more organically. The conversation was conducted totally through email, as Sean lives on the East Coast and I live in California, and we were unable to meet in person at any point given pandemic restrictions during the period when the conversation took place. The core of the conversation took place during the summer of 2020 when the impact of Covid was only beginning to be fully revealed and the growing anxiety surrounding the 2020 US presidential election was inescapable. Suffice to say that we were, like everyone else, under tremendous duress! Finally, let me add that we tried to incorporate as many of Taylor's pandemic and postpandemic projects as possible herein. Taylor and their collaborators are especially prolific, and new creative projects continue to announce themselves with frequency.

SEAN F. EDGECOMB: I've known Taylor Mac personally for almost fifteen years, so I've kind of had a front-row seat for the evolution of their career from quite early on. I first became aware of Taylor's initial solo performances in the East Village in around 2002 or 2003 when I was spending a good deal of time expending youthful queer energy in New York City (read between the lines). It was during this period that Taylor was experimenting with solo cabaret style and gender-fuck drag in dingy clubs like the Slide Bar and the whole scene had a kind of queer, anarchist energy, largely in response to the 9/11 terrorist attacks and a growing disenchantment with George W. Bush's presidency. It wasn't until 2007, however, that I started seriously following Taylor's work—before the "judy" pronoun was introduced to the public. It was that same year, after completing my PhD exams at Tufts University, that I decided to focus my research on Charles Ludlam, which fortuitously brought me back to Taylor. Ludlam, who arguably invented queer theater in midcentury America through a pastiched style and midcentury genre called "Ridiculous," was at the time not often studied outside of a class on LGBTQ+ theater. Partly influenced by the fact that Ludlam had been largely forgotten and partly inspired by an ongoing conversation about President Bush's precarious legacy that was a constant in the media, I started to think about what Ludlam's legacy looked like. Beyond the fact that Taylor's drag aesthetic was reminiscent of Ludlam's (among others', such as Ethyl Eichelberger's), early on, Taylor openly referred to their style as "Ridiculous" (in a direct homage to Ludlam). I knew that, along with Charles Busch and Bradford Louryk, Mac had to be a chapter-based case study in my dissertation.

It was in late summer of 2007 that I saw a performance of *The Young Ladies of . . .* at HERE Arts Center in Manhattan. *The Young Ladies of . . .* is Taylor's autobiographical solo play that, among many topics, deals with the complex personal grief surrounding the death of their father. I distinctly remember how uncomfortable I was when I first saw Taylor's makeup and costume—a baby-doll dress tacked to a filthy muslin sack and a white face awash with messy glitter and sequins—but by the end I was stunned. I still hold that performance, in HERE's tiny, stuffy theater, as one of the most special of the productions I've attended. Mac's charisma was

Fig. 37. Matt Ray, Taylor Mac, and Sean F. Edgecomb before a performance at the Powerhouse in Brisbane, Australia, August 2013. Author's photo.

like nothing I had ever experienced in theater. They were born to perform. The following spring, still enamored, I took a break from my teaching at Tufts and headed back to New York on the train to interview Mac for my dissertation. I sat on their couch in the East Village and we ate apple pie and chatted about their past and their work and their goals. We've pretty much been in conversation ever since, whether in New York; Brisbane, Australia, where I was a faculty member at the University of Queensland for three years; or wherever our paths have crossed. I have seen as many of their plays and performances as possible since.

DAVID ROMÁN: I came to Taylor Mac so much later—the first piece I saw was *The Walk Across America for Mother Earth*, which was running at La MaMa during one of the Under the Radar Festivals that Mark Russell curates. It was during the winter of 2011. Of course, I had heard of Taylor's work before—so many people I respect were telling me about Taylor's performances, but I kept missing them over the years. I live in LA and while I am in New York all the time, it doesn't always work out for me to see things. I remember wanting to see *The Lily's Revenge* a year or so earlier during another festival run, but my schedule wouldn't allow it. There was also a run at San Francisco's Magic Theater shortly after that, that I also missed! For a few years, I thought I'd never be in New York or San Francisco during one of Taylor's shows! It was so frustrating. Still, Taylor was on my radar and not under it, so to speak. So when I learned that Taylor was on the schedule for the 2011 Festival I immediately booked my ticket. I went with my friend Holly Hughes, herself a veteran East Village performance artist. Holly and I have a long history of friendship, which includes going to see plays and performances. We coedited *O Solo Homo*, an anthology of queer performance texts a few years back, and we were in the habit of meeting up in New York every January for the Under the Radar Festival and the COILS Festival too. We were both excited to see Taylor's play.

It was an incredibly special night for so many reasons. First, and most poignant, I saw *The Walk Across America for Mother Earth* only a few days after Ellen Stewart's death. To be at La MaMa, a sacred space that Ellen Stewart so beautifully cultivated over long decades of devotion, and to be among her extended community of artists and activists, felt already to be immersed in a ritual of mourning and remembrance. I associate La MaMa with theatrical experimentation and innovation, local and global diversity, and a strong political consciousness regarding social justice issues— all things that mattered deeply to Ellen Stewart. Before we even entered the formal performance space, there was the palpable energy of community. The atmosphere was relaxed, inviting, and festive, and there was an air of mystery permeating the space that, while probably true of all pre-performance time, had a more anticipatory excitement than usual. These qualities, I would soon learn, are staples of a Taylor Mac performance. The play, directed by Paul Zimet, who offers an informative explication of the piece in this volume, itself is a very sweet picaresque piece about a group of idealistic people marching to protest the US's taking back Western Shoshone Nation land to repurpose it for use as a nuclear plant. We meet a disparate group of characters united through their radical commitment to progressive social issues—as well as to flamboyant costume. I should add that this was also my first experience with the mind-blowing genius of Machine Dazzle, Taylor's in-house costume designer and collaborator.

The Walk Across America intensely moved me. I don't mean to be provocative when I say that I am most drawn to performances of sincerity. That's not to say I can't appreciate irony or even sarcasm, but queer performances that lack heart and compassion and traffic mainly in blunt one-liners and overwrought wit, tire me to no purpose. I no longer have the patience for those kinds of works. I found the *Walk Across America* to have so much heart and purpose, so much artistic integrity and aesthetic beauty, and yet still be a bit messy too. At intermission, the performers took to the lobby and improvised short musical segments to entertain us, suggesting that the play's intermission was for the audience and not necessarily for them, or maybe it was an extension of the performance and not an intermission at all. Regardless, I was totally won over by what transpired on and off the stage that night.

There are moments when I experience a performer and immediately recognize a kindred spirit—I felt that with Holly and with Tim Miller, when I first saw them perform years ago. And also with Luis Alfaro and Chay Yew, artists whose sensibilities and aesthetics immediately align with my own. Something about *The Walk Across America* registered as deeply familiar to me. The funny thing is that, unlike you, Sean, I have spent little time with Taylor outside of the theater. We've had no apple pie together! But I think of Taylor—and Machine, Viva, who was also in the cast of the play, and many of the extended artists affiliated with Taylor's world—as part of my extended community.

SEAN F. EDGECOMB: Absolutely. I agree that *community* is an essential term and concept when thinking through all of Taylor's works. Obviously, many contemporary theater artists continue to build coteries that attract collaborators and audiences, but Taylor has always had that *je ne sais quoi* that acts as an invitation to join judy's community. I first experienced this "thing" in the lobby of HERE after *The Young Ladies of . . .* where people stayed after the show to process and converse in the lobby—that's pretty remarkable in general, but even more so for a New York City audience used to staying in their lanes and speeding expeditiously through the day. In fact, it was in moments like these that I forged friendships with musician Matt

Ray and other downtown queer performers in attendance (many of whom beautifully relate their own relationships with Taylor in the artists' section of this book). This almost magical something Taylor possesses has even inspired a constellation of more distant communities that hold judy as a spark of inspiration—even if they have not experienced the work in person. I've been teaching Taylor's plays since 2008 and I continue to be delightfully surprised when I run into former students at performances and scholarly events that focus on the work. I also know a handful of young artists in Australia making exciting queer work who consider YouTube videos of Taylor's early solo performances, videos that we watched in my lectures at the University of Queensland, as foundational to their practice.

I surmise that part of what I might call the "Taylor Mac phenomenon," as you mention, David, comes from that spirit of sincerity that Taylor radiates. I also think that Taylor's charismatic power to attract others comes from a sense of vulnerability evoked in each performance. In my chapter I think about Taylor Mac (the performer) as a modern-day fool, an outsider who carries with them the weight of the world and employs laughter and often self-deprecating humor to exorcise feelings of oppression and marginalization. While Taylor's positionality and authorial perspective may hold a special attraction to members of the LBQTQ+ community, there is something universal about their message of kinship that is achieved through such intersectional community-building—a place for processing sadness, joy, and as you related, not afraid to get a little messy, like Taylor's now-iconic makeup (I think the slippage of queerness as a form renders it inherently messy).

Although I would argue that all of Taylor's works embody a sense of fellowship toward the community formation we're discussing, *A 24-Decade History of Popular Music* is a culmination of all of those ideas on the grandest of scales. As mentioned earlier in this book, the seeds of *A 24-Decade History* were planted when as a teenager Taylor attended an AIDS Walk in San Francisco and simultaneously felt the loss and grief of the gay community while watching it gain strength by banding together. The *24-Decade History* concert, in all of its forms, seeks to find common ground and celebration in the shadow of over 400 years of American oppression. There is something quite cathartic about entering a curated space dedicated to listening to the stories of Others, which is, in large part, what I think the concert is about.

Beyond its message of diversity and inclusion, formed by creating space for suppressed voices to be heard and celebrated, *A 24-Decade History* quite literally builds community as part of its process and performance. I have greatly respected your work for years, David, and you were a foundational support and mentor in getting my first book published, but our shared experience at the twenty-four-hour concert at St. Ann's in 2016 was really the impetus for this book project. I also met many of our contributors there, including Kim Marra, Lisa A. Freeman, and Jen Buckley, during or soon after the concert. For me, it has been a delight building a scholarly subcommunity that is directly related and in response to Taylor's art. I know that you traveled to follow the concert as it developed in the years before the twenty-four-hour show—what was that experience like?

DR: Well, I certainly didn't anticipate following Taylor while they were on tour! I saw an early installation at New York Live Arts on the early decades of the twentieth century—and was quite moved by the entirety of the project. I am trained to think historically, and I was drawn to the intensity of the archival project behind the event—the excavation not only of the songs, some of them so obscure as to be nearly forgotten, but of the stories of the marginal subcultures that Taylor describes before, during, and after the songs are sung. I was also drawn to the dynamic between Taylor and Matt Ray, his musical arranger, who is on stage throughout the entire performance and leads the band. Matt appears so unassuming and totally unembellished, he's usually dressed simply in a monochromatic dark casual suit, whereas Taylor is dressed in these spectacularly theatrical and colorful costumes that are impossible to ignore.

I think it's telling that Matt, unlike Taylor and Machine, appears so normative throughout the performance. His apparent lack of flamboyance, his conventional masculine handsomeness, and his general submission to Taylor and Machine's high-voltage theatricality, complements Taylor and Machine's vivaciousness, as if they were meant to be antithetical points on a queer continuum. On first impression, they don't look like they would be in the same show! And yet they are entirely joined at the hip through the music. I was fascinated by their relationship as artistic collaborators. I think Matt Ray is a genius. I loved hearing his arrangements and watching him guide the various musicians on stage. Their level of talent, and

I refer to the entire company—so impressive! And furthermore, on first viewing, Taylor's performance had a level of unpredictability that was enormously seductive to me. It was as if anything could happen in the space—there was so much suspense and surprise.

Finally, I was drawn to being in a room with a majority of queer people, people like me who felt summoned to the event for the guaranteed queerness of it, even if the audiences were mainly in their forties, predominantly white, and certainly middle class. That wasn't true everywhere I traveled, obviously, and it especially wasn't true on college campuses when students attended, but the racial dynamic was predominantly monochromatic. There's a moment when Taylor discusses the mid-twentieth-century mass exodus of white people from the cities to the suburbs. It's a segment I've seen performed several times, and it always plays out the same way, regardless of the city. Taylor asks all the white people in the audience to give up their seats—and often these seats are the most expensive!—and stand in the aisles while the people of color in attendance can move and occupy any of these front-and-center seats. Consistently, the center section remained underpopulated, given the paucity of people of color in the audience, but the aisles— they were jampacked with white people! The only city where I found the demographics more diverse was San Francisco. The Curran Theatre, where Taylor performed six-hour segments from the *24-Decade History* over several weekends in the fall of 2017, nearly a year after the Brooklyn marathon, was completely sold out. And it's a huge venue! By then, word of mouth on Taylor's performances had grown substantially, and San Francisco's incredibly robust and lively queer community came out en masse to be there. People showed up! I found those audiences to be much more diverse, and during the "exodus to the suburbs" section, the center section up front had a range of people of color taking over the area.

A year or so before, in early 2016, when Taylor first performed at this venue, and before the Curran was fully renovated and way before the St. Ann's Warehouse event, Taylor performed an evening of the earliest decades here. Then, however, the audience was seated on the stage, since the theater proper was being renovated. There were no seats in the auditorium. It was a much more intimate crowd, and we could generally see everyone in attendance, which wasn't true in other cities. The night I went, Taylor serenaded Nancy Pelosi, maybe even while sitting on her lap! I can't recall if Taylor sat on Pelosi's lap or her husband's lap, but during one of his many excursions into the audience—"Move your shit! Move your shit!"—he ended up parked on top of them. It was always a thrill to see who would be in the theater for the shows.

Mainly, though, I followed Taylor's performances for more personal reasons. My life had fallen apart around that time; I was going through one of the most difficult emotional times in my life, and I wasn't sure how I was going to get through it. Taylor's performances were perfect for me—not only were they phenomenal distractions, but they went on and on for hours! There was something perversely comforting in Taylor's chronic refrain that the performance would be going on a bit longer than it should. This idea that the performance—like my anguish—couldn't be contained within an expected temporal logic or anticipated contractual time frame weirdly helped me find my way through a seemingly interminable heartbreak.

I found the collective energy of endurance and affirmation that Taylor and company engendered to be quite healing. I don't want to overly romanticize Taylor's work, but I will say this: the *24-Decade History of Popular Music* concerts helped me move out of the darkness I was experiencing during that time. And at the risk of overindulgence—or worse in our culture, over-sharing!—Taylor helped me begin to rebuild the brokenness of my heart and spirit after an unanticipated and devastating intrusion of drug addiction, an experience that wreaked tremendous havoc in my life—and this despite me not being the one who used. I was blindsided into anxiety, depression, and grief. And I was uncertain how to imagine a future different than the one I had been building for so long. I'm generally a happy positive person, and I am not one prone to depression, but I was in a very fragile emotional state during the years Taylor was on the road with the *Decades* project.

I should add that I usually went to these performances alone precisely for these reasons. Only a few times did I go with friends, carefully inviting only those who knew my story and whom I could trust with my process. I even went alone to the St. Ann's event. Of course, I knew people at the Brooklyn event and at one point, dur-

Fig. 38. A poster advertising David Román's invited guest lecture at the University of London, 2018. Design: Alex Luu.

ing the Mikado section, which I had seen staged many times before, stepped out for nearly an hour to commiserate with a writer friend, who was also rebuilding their life after a similar breakup.

In part, the ritualistic aspect of the performances (and Taylor's persona as radical fairy shaman) provided a safe structure for me to emotionally unload. I found the performances cathartic. And I don't think I am alone in feeling that. I find the generative spirit of Taylor's work to be love, something I talk about in my contribution to this volume. So, given that context, I chose to attend Taylor's performances across the United States as a form of self-care. I went to performances throughout the Northeast, the Midwest, and throughout California. Of course, the scholar in me was drawn to documenting the performances, but if I am being honest, my investment in Taylor was much more personal than professional. The professional angle enabled the personal. That said, I was nonetheless invested in tracking the differences in venues and audiences, and also in how the work was received. Also, as you know, Taylor rehearsed the show by performing the show on stage—so if you wanted to hear the new decades they were working on, for example, you might have to go to Chicago or Poughkeepsie to experience the new work. Taylor and Matt also worked with local musicians when they were in a city for an extended stay. The shows in Ann Arbor, for example, took advantage of the multitude of talented session singers available from nearby Detroit, two of whom—Thornetta Davis and Steffanie Christi'an Mosley—who performed at the Michigan shows actually ending up joining the entourage for the next few years. They first came on board, however, to enhance the 1966–76 decade, which was one of the most soulful of the entire show, with songs from Curtis Mayfield, the Supremes, and so on. I can't imagine their cover of "Gimme Shelter," one of the highlights of the project, without hearing Steffanie singing "it's just a shot away, it's just a shot away." Taylor always creates space for other talent to share the stage, fully aware of the racial and gendered politics of who gets to sing when and where. I think it was important for the company, which, other than Bernice "Boom" Brooks (drums) and Gary Wang (bass), was primarily white, to have more talent of color visibly on stage. While Many of Taylor's collaborators are people of color—Niegel Smith, who served as codirector; Mimi Lien, who worked on scenic design; Timothy White Eagle, who coordinates the Dandy Minions; Jawole Willa Jo Zollar, who choreographed the most recent work beginning with the *Decades* project—they generally remained offstage.

One of my favorite moments in the several years I was tracking Taylor's performances was right here in Los Angeles, when Taylor invited the Mariachi Reyna de Los Angeles, a local company of all-female Latinx mariachi singers, to perform with them at Royce Hall. After performing a short set of their own, they accompanied Taylor on the devastatingly beautiful Joy Division song "Love Will Tear Us Apart," which was offered as an anthem to the AIDS era. This moment always overwhelms me; it moves the performance away from the archival history of the previous decades and segues the performance into the era of my own lived experience. The song itself is enormously charismatic even without the bells and whistles of Machine's gorgeous, eerily haunting costume and the visual spectacle of a dozen female mariachi singers dressed in traditional costume. This seemingly impossible harmonious grouping turned out to be among the most authentic performances I've ever seen. Unfortunately, it wasn't replicated anywhere else.

SFE: Thank you so much for sharing a really personal anecdote about what the concert means to you, David. Your story resonates with

me on so many levels and I think it reiterates not only the vulnerability that Taylor brings to each and every performance (regardless of the venue), but also the vulnerability and openness that this
kind of performance requires—or even demands—from an audience. For me, the most dynamic example of an exchange between
Taylor as performer and the audience took place at the finale of the
24-Decade marathon concert in Brooklyn. The attendees (including
a few of our contributors) had varying responses to the full concert,
and I can speak directly about mine—and as much as I treasure
every moment of the event, I can also report that it had both highs
and lows. I attended with my now-husband and his sister, and although we all were fans of Taylor and thrilled to be there, suffering
from early October head colds, we all relied on each other to pull
through the exhaustion of the full marathon experience. As I recall,
it was around 6 a.m. that the Brooklyn United Marching Band—a
community-based organization that provides inner-city youth with
opportunities for academic support, skills building, character development, and performance—came into the space. My companions and I had been sleeping in a makeshift communal bed deemed
"the Dandy Loft" that was a jumble of mattresses set up in a balcony,
overlooking stage right (a photo of us lounging actually appeared
in the New York Times), and with the pounding of the drums there
was a palpable shift of the energy in the room. For the final six
hours, this energy became more intense, even frenetic, and then
for the last hour, something magical happened. In the final sixty
minutes of the concert, which took place on Sunday morning between 11 a.m. and noon, Taylor was alone onstage, almost nude and
accompanied only by a ukulele. After performing for a full twenty-
four hours, and giving everything of themself vocally, physically,
and emotionally, is was clear that even the act of holding up the
ukulele was a challenge for Taylor at that point. I'd like to believe
it was the audience that gave them the strength to finish—we had
in effect formed a collective over the past day and night, unified by
the experience, but even more so by the vulnerability, compassion,
and gratitude held in that moment. I've written about this before—
and it reminds me of the legends surrounding Judy Garland "being
held up by the audience's adoration" as she struggled to sing Over
the Rainbow at her legendary Carnegie Hall Concert in 1961—but
this is a moment in live performance that I will remember forever.
It almost felt like time had stood still.

Fig. 39. Sean F. Edgecomb and his companions take naps in the early morning hours of the marathon *24-Decade History of Popular Music* concert at St. Ann's Warehouse in Brooklyn. Photo: Sara Krulwich. With permission of the *New York Times*.

In stark contrast, I can think of a couple of examples where Taylor's work didn't land as well, partially because of an audience's unwillingness to take on what the work required of them. In autumn 2019, when Taylor was completing a tour of New England with an abridged version of *A 24-Decade History*, I had a dramatically different experience at Wesleyan, a small, selective liberal arts college in Connecticut. When Taylor appeared for a hosted conversation on the evening before the performance, only twenty people showed up. I found this particularly shocking, because I know so many people in New York—and beyond—who would jump to have such an intimate experience with judy. The following night, at the concert, the energy was, well, bizarre. Half of the campus audience showed up already suspicious—in performing a kind of value signaling toward self-declared wokeness, they had chosen to reject what Taylor offered in performance before ever receiving it. For example, when Taylor referred to "liberals," this particular group was aggrieved that judy didn't say "progressives." I believe that part of this was an unpreparedness to accept Taylor's trademark messy style, an embrace of the imperfect as a form of queer expression. In fact, an ongoing, oft-repeated motto for Taylor in performance is "Perfection is for assholes." I can see how an institution that built its identity from a place of excellence could struggle with the elevation and celebration of the less-than-perfect, but it also pulls the curtains back on the challenges academia will face in the coming years and the socioeconomic privilege and subsequent elitist, class-driven entitlement that so often continue to radiate from its historical core. The other half of the audience seemed to be wealthy, older white subscribers from the surrounding area, and they largely refused to participate. During the now well-known "gay-prom" segment, where audience members are asked to dance intimately with a same-sex partner regardless of their sexuality, a couple of silver-haired men sitting behind me not only flat-out refused to participate, but also made homophobic comments through gritted teeth. I bring up this experience because I think it underscores how a willingness to engage, or even let go of one's preconceptions, is essential to the kind of work Taylor creates, regardless of one's politics.

That being said, I have certainly preferred some of Taylor's works more than others. When I attended the premiere of *Holiday Sauce* in December 2017, I wasn't immediately sold. As an extension of the *24-Decade History*, but composed of various holiday tunes, it felt less thought out, even a bit tacked-on to the success of the previous marathon. The auditorium of Manhattan's Town Hall, where the concert took place, was seemingly packed with every person who had missed out on the marathon the year before—attending a Taylor Mac concert suddenly had a different kind of cachet, at least among New York's self-declared patricians of cultural trends. The energy of the production felt even more frenetic and haphazard than usual, and I think that a huge part of this came from the fact that Taylor was grieving for both the passing of his mother the previous year and the death of his drag mother, Flawless Sabrina, only a couple of weeks before. This was also less than a year into Donald Trump's presidency, and the city of New York felt like it was in a constant state of malaise (or at least in my regular haunts)—and the show felt like an extension of that sadness, even if we could be surrounded by politically like-minded people. That being said—I know others who

Center for the Humanities: 50th Anniversary (1969–2019)
Monday Night Lecture Series | Fall 2019

Wesleyan University

Sequel as Revolution:
Taylor Mac's Queer Time

SEAN EDGECOMB · CUNY

For almost twenty years, Taylor Mac has reformed queer performance in the United States, proudly unfurling the banner "the revolution will not be masculinized." This lecture critically considers his* magnum opus, "The 24-Decade History of Popular Music," among other works, to illustrate how Mac redefines the notion of the sequel as a productive form for queer continuance and its analysis. Declaring that "all stories are sequels," Mac consistently guides audiences to work against patriarchal notions of historicism, teleology and linear temporality, demonstrating how queer alternatives may be imagined to promote art as revolutionary social action, and giving voice to the marginalized, who have not been the beneficiaries of normative cultural patterns. The malleable, immersive nature of his work endows audiences with a broadly defined queer authority to assist in reforming not only homogenous and exclusive narratives of the past, but also the very work itself, spinning a limitless web of queer sequels and queer potential.

*When on stage and in performance Taylor Mac uses the gender pronoun "judy," but otherwise uses male pronouns in his daily and creative life.

SEPTEMBER 23 @ 6 P.M. | DANIEL FAMILY COMMONS, USDAN UNIVERSITY CENTER

CENTER FOR THE **HUMANITIES**   Supported by the Office of Student Affairs and the Usdan University Center

Fig. 40. A poster advertising a talk on Taylor Mac by Edgecomb at the Wesleyan Humanities Center, Wesleyan University, fall 2019. Poster design: Angela Fan.

had their first Taylor Mac experience with *Holiday Sauce* and they absolutely loved it. So, I guess what I am trying to say is that unlike most contemporary, professional American theater, which so often strives for consistency toward perfection (Broadway actors can be fined for glaring errors that would threaten a production's integrity and artistic vision), Taylor offers something unique—a different, refreshing perspective, which is admittedly sometimes more enjoyable at some times than others, but always provides audience members something to reflect on after leaving the performance space. In many ways that spirit of communal imperfection, following Taylor's aforementioned declaration that "Perfection is for assholes," was the inspiration for our book.

I would like to believe that we have co-curated these contributions from scholars and artists with diverse perspectives not only as a record of Taylor's oeuvre, but as a documentary analysis of what it means to openly engage with Taylor and the work at this specific moment in our history.

DR: Yes, I agree. The ecstatic endorsement of Taylor's work that all of our contributors promote—and probably the two of us most of all!—is definitely in line with the celebratory reception Taylor's work has received at large. This book came out of that spirit, and, as you suggest, sets out to capture it. I am fully aware that our volume lacks any critical skepticism of Taylor's career, unless it's our shared muted response to *Holiday Sauce*, which I too found underwhelming. But I'm not one for "the holidays" and I am not one for "the sauce," so I knew in advance it wasn't necessarily going to be for me. Still, I loved the surprising insertion of the Rolling Stones' song "You Can't Always Get What You Want"—one of my favorite rock songs of all time—and which ended up being for me, at least for that night, an ironic reminder that "you get what you need." And, yes, you are right Sean, so many others experiencing Taylor for the first time loved *Holiday Sauce*, as did so many of their veteran fans.

But I'd like return to the point of our enthusiasm, and the volume's unapologetic love for the work, and say that I'm not drawn to critical negation, or calling out anyone's failure, let alone an artist's, as a means to flex my own need for attention or power unless their politics are so heinous that my silence is complicit in provoking or enacting harm, however it manifests. I'm more drawn to what

Taylor embodies—generosity, empathy, affiliation. My intellectual impulses gravitate to those feelings. I am willing to risk the charge that we lack critical distance from the work, or that our enthusiasm compromises the academic integrity expected from a scholarly volume published by a university press. I've written about this "problem" in nearly every single book I've published, this sense that the scholar—and especially the queer scholar, the scholar of color, the scholar invested in the community—must somehow mute their feelings, especially those feelings most affiliated with love, to maintain their intellectual credibility. Neither one of us went out of our way to find someone to "balance" the anthology with a critique of Taylor's work. In fact, we basically did the opposite. We asked scholars to contribute who were already invested in Taylor, and therefore sympathetic to Taylor's work. In fact, Sean, you are the only scholar who has previously written on their work. Other contributors, whose expertise may lie elsewhere, are writing about Taylor for the first time. At the core of this volume are two interrelated claims. The first, that Taylor Mac deserves our scholarly engagement, is intertwined with the second, that the field of theater and performance studies needs to engage their work. Of course, every artist deserves critical attention, and of course the field should address whoever the field desires; this is not about gatekeeping. It's about using our resources to expand the field, especially to those figures who are relatively new to the scene.

The project's vulnerability, which I am well aware of, is that by focusing solely on the work of Taylor Mac, it plays into the idea of canonicity, that certain artists are so exceptional that they merit entrance into an already-set system of aesthetic and cultural values that determines great art. That's always the problem with single-artist volumes. The challenge, then, it seems to me, is to insure that the methods we use to explicate Taylor's work are generative to scholars working in the field (and even outside of it), and intelligible to readers outside the profession. I don't think either one of us is operating under the logic that Taylor is a genius—and this despite the MacArthur!—a person of such exceptional talent that they are more important than other artists. I think we are interested in exploring the phenomenon of Taylor Mac—their emergence as a figure of tremendous cultural power and influence, their facility across genres and venues, and their appeal to multiple audiences and spectators—even as we inevitably contribute to the ongoing celebrity of Taylor Mac. More to the point, we both felt it important to showcase Taylor's multitalented collaborators, the main evidence that the myth of the creative genius is a dated Romantic fallacy. Taylor's work is a result of the creative energies of an extensive web of artist collaborators and community affiliates.

On a different note, I want to address the context of the Covid-19 pandemic, which has shaped the final stages of our process with this book project, and more immediately impacted Taylor's career. As the virus continues to mutate and the pandemic continues to spread, history keeps changing. What we write today will be yesterday's news tomorrow, a product of a past moment in the pandemic, however it continues to mysteriously unfold. We are vulnerable to the changing contexts of the pandemic, obviously as people doing everything we can to live through it, and as scholars addressing the contemporary as it slides into the immediate past. When 2020 began, Taylor was still booking performances of *Holiday Sauce*, the concert performance of winter holiday songs, a sort of epilogue to the *24-Decade Project*, throughout the country and abroad; *Gary*, Taylor's 2019 Broadway debut, which had been nominated for several Tony Awards including Best Play, was primed to be a staple of the regional theater's upcoming seasons, and *The Fre*, Taylor's latest play, was set to hold its world premiere at the NYC's the Flea Theater. By March of 2020 everything changed. And it changed for everybody!

SFE: Boy oh boy, did it ever! On Saturday, March 7, 2020, I headed to downtown Manhattan to see the premiere of Taylor's play, *The Fre*, at the Flea Theater. News of the Covid-19 virus was really just starting to gain traction, but in retrospect, we had no idea of what was to come. The theater lobby was packed—and not a mask in sight. I gave the director, Niegel Smith, a hug and unreservedly shook hands with several people before heading upstairs to the Sam Theater. The gorgeous set, ridiculously designed by Jian Jung, took the form of a ball pit (representing a muddy swamp) where audience members could choose to literally immerse themselves in the production. I thoroughly enjoyed the play—a commedia-style spoof and queer love story about the geographical and cultural segregation that exists between rural, conservative Americans and the urban, liberal

Fig. 41. Taylor Mac, Steffanie Christi'an Mosley, and Thornetta Davis performing during *A 24-Decade History of Popular Music* (2016). Photo: Teddy Wolff.

elite—but I had no idea how it would prophetically speak to our
current situation in this country. Taylor wrote *The Fre* as part of
their ongoing Dionysia Festival, a series of four plays intended to be
performed for a full day, mimicking the theater festivals of ancient
Athens. Along with *The Fre* and *Hir*, which have already been produced, the repertory will include *Prosperous Fools*, a dance-theater
piece inspired by Molière, and another currently untitled piece that
will focus on the farcical entrances and exits of fifty clowns. Thematically, the four plays provide commentary on the "cultural polarization" of the United States, once again tying into the ancient
Athenian tradition, where theater was a space intended as a place
for debate, cathartic processing, and perhaps most importantly,
unity that surpassed the limitations of regional or national identity.
On the leadup to one of the nastiest and most divisive elections
in American history, the message of listening, openness, and unity
that Taylor evoked was particularly timely.

DR: I think the coronavirus is inviting us—some would say coercing us—to return to our core selves, or to at least explore more deeply who we are and what we value. I think it's great that you are pursuing your creative capacities as we work on this academic book together. I've been keeping my life simple—staying quiet, avoiding conflict, swimming laps. The closing of the theaters breaks my heart. It also forces me to spend my time differently too—I am reading more, streaming virtual theater, and taking long walks with my dogs. Funny, the last time I went to the theater was to see *The Fre*, probably the week after you; it was March 12, a Thursday, and Broadway had just been shut down and everything else in New York City closed the next day. I remember seeing Niegel in the lobby and also Carol the producer, and talking with them about our shared concerns for safety. Morgan Jenness, who often dramaturges for Taylor and serves as one of Taylor's mentors, was also there, as was Taylor, who was taking notes in the theater since they were still in previews. There was some confusion that night about whether the play would go on or not, and the level of stress in the lobby was palpable. The coronavirus was definitely on people's minds, we were only learning how to talk about it. The play was staged in a massive ball pit and audiences had the option to immerse themselves in the pit or sit outside of it. The night I attended, about half the audience sat in the pit, which might have helped with social distancing, come to think of it, although apparently plastic is known to harbor germs so there's that to consider! The Flea posted the following announcement on their website:

> The threat of COVID-19 is making its way into every aspect of our lives as New Yorkers. We assure you that we are taking the steps for a high degree of sanitation to ensure the health of every member of the company and each member of the audience.
>
> The balls in the pit are GermBlock antimicrobial balls. Before each performance, we sanitize the ball pit with a professional-grade disinfectant. This combined with washing your hands often and using the hand sanitizers provided before you enter the ball pit will help ensure the safety of us all. We strongly encourage all audience members to take these steps.

I sat in the third row, a few seats over from someone who flew in from Chicago to see their daughter who was in the show. It wasn't full, but it wasn't empty either. To be honest, I was pretty distracted by the unfolding stressful news of the pandemic. I was supposed to leave for London the next day for an extended theater run, and was having serious misgivings about international travel. I ended up flying back to California instead. Since I was so distracted, I don't think it's fair for me to write up an assessment, except to say that it was unlike anything Taylor had done before. The play was cast mainly with young people, over a dozen actors of different backgrounds, genders, and sizes, and I am not sure if that has more to do with the Flea's mission or with the nature of the play itself. The play was an allegory, and much like *Gary*, Taylor's debut play on Broadway, *The Fre* served as a commentary on the political stakes of surviving the Trump era. The heart of the play was a dialectical tension between ignorance and wokeness, and how one person can bring political consciousness into their community if only they are seen and heard. It's also a love story, as you described it, Sean. I do remember at the end, the ushers invited the entire audience into the pit if we wanted to be photographed immersed in the colored balls. I left right away, anxious to call United Airlines and ask about the status of my London flight and whether they were planning on cutting back service to the US or not. International travel was becoming an increasingly politicized issue in the United States, but also in Europe, including the UK. All of this is to say, I remember more about my conflicted feelings and anxiety-driven emotional state the night I went to see *The Fre* and less about the play or its production. I haven't been to the theater since. No one has, right? And yet our theater artists have continued to create work throughout quarantines and lockdowns. I do my best to keep up—mainly because so much of the work is designed as a benefit for theater and for theater people. It reminds me of the early AIDS years, when certain artists—some, but not everyone—used their talents and networks to raise money to support those most vulnerable in the community. Broadwaycares/Actors Equity still hosts benefits and even launched a specific Covid-19 Emergency Fund immediately once the theaters closed. Tom Viola, Broadway Cares: Equity Fights AIDS's executive director, is a hero of mine; he's always there to help.

Taylor too has done remarkable work to support artists since the pandemic broke. Taylor—with Niegel Smith, Morgan Jenness, Emily Morse, and Kristin Marting—founded the Trickle Up: A New York Artists Network—a grassroots program to support freelance theater artists without resources or a safety net. For $10 anyone can subscribe to their website and stream video content by some of the biggest names in the theater, who offer monologues, songs, or whatever, to raise money for the campaign. More than fifty artists have participated, including Dominique Morisseau, Lucas Hnath, Rachel Chavkin, Paula Vogel, Basil Twist, Lynn Nottage, and also Taylor, of course. Whenever they reach $10,000, they donate that money to an artist in need. The mission: artists helping artists. Taylor has also reactivated their Instagram account and uploads performances of original songs, generally written that day. Taylor calls them the Ptown sing-alongs, since they are about Provincetown and, well, are meant to be sung communally. The songs are generally three minutes or so and range in topics as bawdy as the notorious "dick dock" pier, which begins with the lyrics "There were fifty cocks beneath the dock, ebb and flowing with the tide," with each chorus losing ten or more cocks along the way to end with the "one lone cock beneath the dock," who will wait it out for another night, and the song renews itself again. "The Dock" was posted on August 3, 2020, but my sense is people will be singing this song for some time! My favorite so far, though, is the clever critique of Provincetown's "whiteness" problem posted a few days later, called "Where Are the BIPOC in This Town?" where Taylor asks "Were they run out of town or were they never around?" Most songs are performed on the banjo, but Taylor also sometimes sings without any instrumental accompaniment and offers his versions a cappella. Like the final decade of *A 24-Decade History of Popular Music*, where Taylor is alone on stage with a ukulele, the Provincetown Instagram songs allow Taylor to showcase their songwriting skills, which are a mixture of personal storytelling, whimsical charm, and political critique.

SFE: I think that, now perhaps more than ever, we need artists like Mac and the beautiful vision created by judy's collaborative team—the storytellers—to make sense of the world around us. This manuscript is going to press in the midst of a continuing global pandemic, and on the first anniversary of a failed coup on the US Capitol building by insurrectionist supporters of the forty-fifth president. This is an anxious time, an uncertain time, and often a frightening time.

A year ago, during an alarmingly quiet holiday season, with many people under strict lockdown restrictions due to Covid-19, I watched the *Holiday Sauce* virtual special, which Mac and collaborators recorded and edited in the fall. The virtual concert was a delightful opportunity to feel like a part of the community we had been sorely missing—the downtown theater community, the queer community, the New York City cultural community, and the hybrid community of theater artists and scholars—and although it wasn't quite the same as being nudged into the corner of Joe's Pub and didn't have the energy of a packed Town Hall, it was familiar and heartwarming. As this collection demonstrates, Mac's work often deals with difficult times, with anxiety and with melancholy, but the spirit of *communitas* that it engenders is undeniably linked to hope, and if I had to choose one word to describe an indescribable body of work, that is what I would choose—hope. For the 2020 *Holiday Sauce* special Mac appeared in a glorious costume designed by Machine Dazzle, modeled after the surrealist fruit-faced paintings of Renaissance great Giuseppe Arcimboldo. Mac appeared as a virtual cornucopia, covered in the fruits of the harvest (featured as the frontispiece of this collection). The symbolism of this incredible concoction by the brilliant Dazzle was clear—Mac embodied an abundance of hope for a brighter future when we can all be together again, sporting a suit of glorious bounty to sustain us all in the interim.

DR: Taylor and Matt's new project, also produced by Linda Brumbach and Pomegranate Arts, one of the great producing companies for contemporary performance, featured musicians affiliated with *A 24-Decade History of Popular Music*. Tentatively titled *Queer Icons*, the new performance of original songs devoted to queer icons from world history had its debut in New York City for one night only, as part of the Lincoln Center's Restart Stages program at a concert titled "Egg Yolk," designed to bring the performing arts back to the people of New York City with live outdoor programming at Lincoln Center's Damrosch Park. I flew in from Los Angeles, the first time back in New York since March 2020, to see the free public performance. The audience was seated in socially distanced pods, and we underwent temperature checks before we were directed to our seats. People were excited to be there, and the event felt celebratory, as if we were marking the collective transition to a new, less-frightening moment in the pandemic, one where we could return to live events and public gatherings with a sense of safety.

For the short window of time in early summer 2021, many people were finally able to feel more comfortable sharing space with others, including strangers. Most of the audience went without masks. I'm not sure I've ever hugged so many people at one event beforehand! The feeling at Damrosch Park was one of joyfulness and relief, and among Taylor's extended community, it felt like a reunion. All of this is to say that the Lincoln Center performance was a radical departure from the Flea performance at the start of the pandemic. For me, it was especially poignant that my return to live theater would be a Taylor Mac show, given that the last show I saw before the shutdown was his play at the Flea in March 2020. I'll be honest, Sean, and I feel like it's important to note this here, these last two Taylor Mac performances seem irrevocably attached to the pandemic for me. I should say, though, that I felt much more present at *Queer Icons* than at *the Fre*, where I was just too distracted by the unfolding of Covid-19 and its sudden and dramatic entry into our lives. *Queer Icons* celebrates key figures in LGBTQ history, and each figure—Larry Kramer, Marsha P. Johnson, Vita Sackville-West, and Bayard Rustin, to name only four—gets their own song, and each song is presented in its own musical idiom, which is to say that there is no musical coherency in the show, given that there is no uniform way of understanding or presenting queerness. Despite some technical difficulties at the top of the performance, which led Taylor to improvise a vulgar little ditty that took issue with the renaming of theaters and museums with the names of hyperconservative donors, such as David Koch, while the sound issues were resolved, the short performance, which ran a little over an hour, was sweet-natured in tone. Taylor even introduced themself as a "gentle soul"—shifting away from fierceness and ferocity and embracing their inner bear with a wild, nearly Whitmanesque beard! The Lincoln Center performance was the launch for the new project, which as it develops will include over fifty original songs written by Taylor and Matt. This one-night-only concert was the "small band" debut of what seems to be a much larger spectacle reuniting many of the collaborators from the *Decades* project, including Machine, who dressed Taylor for the event in a multicolor pasta concoction experience, while Machine was dressed accordingly—since "every good dish needs a doily"—as the doily itself: "I am an open invitation to serve those noodles, baby!" The theme for the night, at least from Machine's perspective, was culinary. Of course, the *Queer Icons* project can take many turns as it develops, but the Lincoln Center performance made one thing very clear: Taylor and their collaborators are forging ahead with highly imaginative, socially relevant, and wonderfully entertaining work.

SFE: I am envious that you were able to attend the Lincoln Center "Egg Yolk" concert as part of Pride 2021, as I also have not attended a live theatrical performance since *The Fre* in March 2020. Because I relocated to my house in rural Connecticut over the pandemic, the past year and a half have been primarily about reflection—running in nature, cooking and baking, painting and thinking about the performances that I typically attend in New York City three or four times a week. I think what this period has taught me is to take less for granted, to really take the time to think and reflect on the art that I am so privileged to encounter as well as the realization that more is not necessarily more. I'm not sure I will ever consume live theater and performance in the same way and at the same quantity and pace that I did before the pandemic. It feels like a paradigm shift.

As you mention, Taylor also spent much of the pandemic in more bucolic locales—namely the Berkshires in western Massachusetts and Provincetown on Cape Cod, growing out a full beard in the process (which I love, because I think it elevates their genderfuck aesthetic to an even higher level, on par with Charles Ludlam's hairy chest in a dress). Although I lived for many years outside of New York City, spending the past seven years there it was easy to forget that important theater and performance, and more specifically queer theater and performance, happen outside of New York all of the time. I recently read Stacy Wolf's book *Beyond Broadway*, which graciously highlights the history and ongoing importance of community and amateur theaters in the United States, and it made me realize that in many ways downtown theater in general, and more specifically what Taylor is doing, is a continuation of this tradition—and although it may take place in the city, it never really loses its roots.

While live performance remains magically ephemeral (though a discussion could be had around how the pandemic has inspired new forms of virtual theatricality), I realize that the roots we create through the process of theater-making and performance do not—they endure. Whether as performers and designers, as dramaturgs and producers, or as scholars and teachers, we remain connected in a glorious and complex rhizome of origins and growth through communities. I would like to think that this collection is evidence of that tenacity, queer resolve, and finding strength in chosen community.

Contributors

Kelly I. Aliano is the author of *Theatre of the Ridiculous: A Critical History* (McFarland, 2019). She has presented at numerous conferences in the field of video game studies and has a chapter in the *Bloomsbury Handbook of Posthumanism*. She has presented papers on musical theater at Association for Theatre in Higher Education conferences and serves as the LGBTQ+ focus group representative for the organization. She regularly collaborates with Dongshin Chang from CUNY Hunter about writing pedagogy in theater courses; they published a chapter in *New Directions in Teaching Theatre Arts* (2018) on the subject, as well as an article on low-stakes writing for *Theatre Topics* (November 2019). She currently teaches at Long Island University's Post Campus in the Department of Theatre and in the English Department at LaGuardia Community College, CUNY, and is a student in the Museum Studies MA program at CUNY School of Professional Studies.

Linda Brumbach founded Pomegranate Arts in 1998. It is an independent production company dedicated to developing international performing arts projects, working in close collaboration with contemporary artists and arts institutions to bring bold and ambitious artistic ideas to fruition. Productions include Taylor Mac's multi–award winning *A 24-Decade History of Popular Music*, the Olivier Award–winning production of *Einstein on the Beach* with Philip Glass, Robert Wilson, and Lucinda Childs, and the Improbable Theater's *Shockhead Peter*. She is the North American tour producer for Batsheva and Sankai Juku, and has overseen productions for Twyla Tharp, Spalding Gray, Roger Guenveur Smith, Diamanda Galas, Elizabeth Streb, Karen Finley, Richard Foreman, and many others. Linda received the 2016 ISPA Patrick Hayes Award for long-standing achievement in the performing arts, has served on the board of the Association of

Performing Arts Professionals, and is a founding member of the Creative and Independent Producer Alliance.

Jennifer Buckley is associate professor of English and theater arts at the University of Iowa, where she teaches courses in modern and contemporary drama and performance. In addition to *Beyond Text: Theater and Performance in Print after 1900* (University of Michigan Press, 2019), which won the 2020 ATHE Outstanding Book Award, she is the author of essays in several edited collections, as well as articles and reviews published in *Modernism/modernity, Theatre Survey, Theatre Journal, TDR: The Drama Review, SHAW: The Journal of Bernard Shaw Studies, Theater,* and *Comparative Drama.* Her current book project is *Act Without Words: Speechless Performance on Modern Stages.* Buckley serves as the vice president of the International Shaw Society.

Machine Dazzle has been dazzling stages via costumes, sets, and performances since his arrival in New York in 1994. Credits include Julie Atlas Muz's *I Am the Moon and You Are the Man on Me* (2004), Big Art Group's *House of No More* (2006), Justin Vivian Bond's *Lustre* (2008) and *Re:Galli Blonde* (2011), Chris Tanner's *Football Head* (2014), Soomi Kim's *Change* (2015), Pig Iron Theater's *I Promised Myself To Live Faster* (2015), *Bombay Ricky* (Prototype Festival 2016), Opera Philadelphia's *Dito and Aeneus* (2017), and Spiegleworld's *Opium* (Las Vegas 2018). With Taylor Mac, Machine has collaborated on several projects, including *The Lily's Revenge* (2009), *Walk Across America for Mother Earth* (2012), and the Pulitzer Prize–nominated *A 24-Decade History of Popular Music* (2016–present). Conceptualist-as-artist meets DIY meets "glitter rhymes with litter," Machine was a corecipient the 2017 Bessie Award for Outstanding Visual Design and the winner of a 2017 Henry Hewes Design Award.

Viva DeConcini plays guitar like a flaming sword, screaming train, ringing bell, and a scratching chicken. She sings like Freddie Mercury if he had been a woman and a river of honey. Viva has played all over the world, from holes in the wall to Bonnaroo, Monterey Jazz Fest, and the Barbican, with her own band as well as artists ranging from Cyro Baptista to Taylor Mac. She has written and produced four full-length rock albums, four original music videos, a ten-episode podcast, and a poetry video for the Guggenheim's Works and Process. She has musically directed works at the Guggenheim Theater and the WP. Her work has charted on CMJ, been featured in *No Depression Magazine*, and she is one of the few females to be profiled in *Guitar Player Magazine*. She is currently working on an original web series queer feminist spaghetti Western operetta with sock puppets. www.vivadeconcini.com

Sean F. Edgecomb is associate professor of theater and performance in the PhD program at the Graduate Center and the coordinator of drama at the College of Staten Island, CUNY. He is the author *Charles Ludlam Lives: Charles Busch, Bradford Louryk, Taylor Mac and the Queer Legacy of the Ridiculous Theatrical Company* (University of Michigan Press, 2017). He is currently completing his second monograph, *A Queer Bestiary*, which critiques contemporary LGBTQIA+ performances that include animal symbolism and ritual anthropomorphism. Sean has published in a variety of edited collections and scholarly journals, most recently "Queer Rurality and the Closet Door Ajar on the Contemporary American Stage" in *Theatre Journal* (March 2021). In addition to his scholarly work and directing, Sean also paints and exhibits original queer folk art under the pseudonym "Peter Kunt" as an extension of his scholarship and commitment to creating queer, inclusive narratives drawn from mythical American histories. www.peterkunt.com/; @peterkunt_queerart

James Tigger! Ferguson is an actor and burlesque performance artist known as "The Godfather of Neo-Boylesque." He has performed in NYC since 1988 and around the world since 1993. A pioneer in the 1990s burlesque renaissance who won the first-ever "King of Boylesque/Mr. Exotic World" title at the Burlesque Hall of Fame in Las Vegas in 2006, Tigger! has headlined festivals all around Europe, Australia, North America, and South America. His act was banned in Rome. Tigger! has been delighted to perform in numerous original works with Taylor Mac since at least 2003, and also with Julie Atlas Muz, Penny Arcade, Target Margin Theater, the Talking Band, and other award-winning geniuses. @tiggerlesque

Lisa A. Freeman is professor of English at the University of Illinois at Chicago. She is the author of *Character's Theatre: Genre and Identity on the Eighteenth-Century English Stage* (University of Pennsylvania Press, 2002), and *Antitheatricality and the Body Public* (University of Pennsylvania Press, 2017), which was named the runner-up for the Association of Theatre in Higher Education Outstanding Book Award, a finalist for the Theatre Library Association George Freedley Award, and an honorable mention for the Joe A. Callaway Prize. Freeman is a founding member of the R/18 Collective: Reactivating Restoration and 18th-Century Drama for the 21st Century. She recently published in *Theatre Survey* on Elizabeth Inchbald's *Remarks for the British Theatre* and is currently working on two new book projects, an examination of race and successive adaptations on the eighteenth-century stage, and a study of contemporary playwrights of color and their engagements with the canonical stage.

Barbara Maier Gustern was a beloved New York–based voice teacher, singer, director, and writer. In addition to Taylor Mac, her students included Debbie Harry, Diamanda Galas, Tammy Faye Starlite, Machine Dazzle, and John Kelly. She graduated from Depauw and Columbia Universities. Her singing career included New York City Opera, Little Orchestra Society, off-Broadway, regional theater, and concerts. As a cabaret director and vocal coach, she worked with Austin Pendleton and Barbara Bleier, Tammy Faye Starlite, Penny Arcade, John Kelly, Sanda Weigl, and Carol Lipnik. Debbie Harry and Diamanda Galas were long-time vocal students. She taught in Poland and Mexico and was the vocal director for the Broadway productions of *Passing Strange*, *Metro*, and the revival of *Oklahoma!*. She recently worked on the concert production of *Most Happy Fella* at Bard Summer Stage.

Erika T. Lin is an associate professor in the PhD Program in Theatre and Performance at the Graduate Center, CUNY. She is the author of *Shakespeare and the Materiality of Performance*, which received the 2013 David Bevington Award for Best New Book in Early Drama Studies. With Gina Bloom and Tom Bishop, she edited the essay collection *Games and Theatre in Shakespeare's England* (2021). Her prize-winning articles have appeared in *Theatre Journal*, *New Theatre Quarterly*, and elsewhere. She is now writing a book on seasonal festivities and early modern commercial theater, a project recognized by various honors and grants, including an Andrew W. Mellon Long-Term Fellowship at the Folger Shakespeare Library. She recently served as the Book Review Editor of *Theatre Survey* and as a member of the Board of Trustees of the Shakespeare Association of America, and she continues to serve as the Board representative to the Bylaws Committee.

Sissi Liu is a RISD-certified jewelry designer who uses recycled and ethically sourced materials to create jewelry with healing powers. She is also a composer-lyricist and dramaturg whose work has been seen in venues such as Carnegie Hall, Joe's Pub, Lincoln Center, Time Square Alliance, and the Juilliard School. Her academic writing appears in *Theatre Topics*, *Performance Research*, *Studies in Music Theatre*, and several edited volumes, including *The Routledge Companion to the Contemporary Musical* and *iBroadway: Musical Theatre in the Digital Age*. She holds a PhD in theater and performance from CUNY Graduate Center and has been a visiting scholar/artist at Brown University. More at www.SissiLiu.net

Kim Marra is professor emeritus of theater arts and American studies at the University of Iowa. Her books include *Strange Duets: Impresarios and Actresses in the American Theatre, 1865–1914* (2006, winner of the Joe A. Callaway Prize) and the co-edited volumes *Passing Performances: Queer Readings of Leading Players in American Theater History* (1998) and its sequel *Staging Desire* (2002), as well as *The Gay and Lesbian Theatrical Legacy* (2005) and *Showing Off, Showing Up: Studies of Hype, Heightened Performance, and Cultural Power* (2017). She has published numerous articles on interspecies performance and directed the full-length documentary film *The Pull of Horses in Urban American Performance, 1860–1920* (2020). She currently serves as associate editor of the Animal Lives Series of the University of Chicago Press and as codirector of the Human-Animal Studies Summer Institute sponsored by the Animals and Society Institute and the University of Illinois at Urbana-Champaign.

Carrie Preston is the Arvind and Chandan Nandlal Kilachand Professor and director of Kilachand Honors College; a professor of English and women's, gender, and sexuality studies; and the founding codirector of the Initiative on Forced Displacement at Boston University. She is the author of *Modernism's Mythic Pose: Gender, Genre, and Solo Performance* (Oxford University Press, 2011) and *Learning to Kneel: Noh, Modernism, and Journeys in Teaching* (Columbia University Press, 2016). She is currently working on a new book, *Complicit Participation: The Liberal Audience for Antiracist Theater*, a critical examination of the political and pedagogical work of audience participation in antiracist theater.

Matt Ray is a Brooklyn-based pianist, composer, arranger, singer, songwriter, and music director. His arrangements have been called "wizardly" (*Time Out New York*) and "ingenious" (*New York Times*), and his piano playing referred to as "classic, well-oiled swing" (*New York Times*) and "to cry for" (*Ebony*). For his work on Taylor Mac's show *A 24-Decade History of Popular Music*, he and Mac shared the 2017 Kennedy Prize for Drama Inspired by American History. Notable live performances include Carnegie Hall with Kat Edmonson, the Hollywood Bowl with reggae legend Burning Spear, the Théâtre de Chaillot with Justin Vivian Bond, and touring the world as a US Department of State jazz ambassador. Other work includes arranging and music-directing Taylor Mac's Obie-Award-winning play *The Lily's Revenge*, and cowriting songs for and performing in Bridget Everett's one-hour Comedy Central special *Gynecological Wonder*. Ray has released three albums as a bandleader.

David Román is professor of English and American Studies at the University of Southern California. He is the author of several books, including *Acts of Intervention: Performance, Gay Culture, & AIDS*; *O Solo Homo: The New Queer Performance*, coedited with Holly Hughes; *Performance in America: Contemporary US Theatre and the Performing Arts*; and *Tarell Alvin McCraney: Theatre, Performance, and Collaboration*, coedited with Sharrell D. Luckett and Isaiah Wooden. Since 2018, he has been affiliated with the University of London's Royal School of Speech and Drama as a consultant on issues of equity and diversity. He's served as the scholar-in-residence at the Mark Taper Forum under the leadership of founding artistic director Gordon Davidson, and was the chair of the board of directors at Highways Performance Space under the leadership of founding artistic director Tim Miller. Currently, he serves on the board of directors of New York City's celebrated Labyrinth Theater.

Kevin Sessums is the editor-at-large of *Grazia USA*. He was also executive editor of Andy Warhol's *Interview* and a contributing editor at *Vanity Fair*. His work has appeared in myriad magazines over the last thirty-five years. Sessums also wrote the *New York Times* bestselling memoirs *I Left It on the Mountain* and *Mississippi Sissy*, the latter winning the Lambda Literary Award for Men's Memoir/Biography. He attended the Juilliard School's Drama Division.

Niegel Smith. A Bessie Award–winning director, Smith is the artistic director of the Flea Theater in lower Manhattan, and board member of A.R.T./New York. His directing credits include *The Fre (The Flea)*, *How To Catch Creation* (The Goodman), *Taylor Mac's Holiday Sauce* (Town Hall, world tour), *Father Comes Home from the Wars . . .* (The Goodman),

A 24-Decade History of Popular Music . . . (Pomegranate Arts, St. Ann's Warehouse, Melbourne Festival, et al.—a Kennedy Prize and Pulitzer Prize finalist), *Hir* (Magic Theatre, Mixed Blood, and Playwrights Horizons), *The Perils of Obedience* (Abrons Arts Center), *Neighbors* (the Public Theater), *Limbs: A Pageant* (HERE Arts Center), and *Rainy Days and Mondays* (FringeNYC). His participatory walks and performances have been produced by Abrons Arts Center, American Realness, the Brooklyn Museum, Dartmouth College, Elastic City, the New Museum, Prelude Festival, PS 122, the Van Alen Institute, and Visual AIDS. www.niegelsm ith.com

Paul Zimet is the founding artistic director of Talking Band. He wrote and directed *City of No Illusions, The Room Sings, The Golden Toad* (with Ellen Maddow), *Marcellus Shale, New Islands Archipelago, Imminence, Belize, The Parrot, Star Messengers, Bitterroot, Party Time, Black Milk Quartet,* and *New Cities.* He directed the premiere productions of Taylor Mac's *The Walk Across America for Mother Earth* and *The Lily's Revenge* (Part I). Recent performances include Mallory Catlett's *This Was the End* and Ellen Maddow's *Fusiform Gyrus.* He is recipient of an Obie Award for direction; three Obie Awards for work with the Open Theater and Winter Project directed by Joseph Chaikin; the Frederick Loewe Award in Musical Theater; and a Playwrights' Center National McKnight Fellowship. He is a playwright alumnus of New Dramatists and an associate professor emeritus in theater, Smith College.

Bibliography

Plays and Playwrights

Beckett, Samuel. *Waiting for Godot*. New York: Grove Press, 1954.
Beckett, Samuel. *Endgame*. New York: Grove Press, 1958.
Beckett, Samuel. *Happy Days*. New York: Grove Press, 1961.
Booth, Stephen. *Shakespeare's Sonnets*. New Haven: Yale University Press, 1977.
Busch, Charles. *The Tale of the Allergist's Wife and Other Plays*. New York: Grove Press, 2001.
Denton, Martin ed. *Plays and Playwrights 2007*. New York: New York Theatre Experience, 2007.
Evans, G. Blakemore, et al., eds. *The Riverside Shakespeare*. 2nd ed. Boston: Houghton Mifflin, 1997.
Greenblatt, Stephen, et al., eds. *The Norton Shakespeare*. New York: Norton, 1997.
Hinman, Charlton, ed. *The First Folio of Shakespeare*. New York: Norton, 1968.
Ibsen, Henrik. *A Doll's House*. Project Gutenberg (Ebook), 2001.
Ludlam, Charles. *The Complete Plays of Charles Ludlam*. New York: Harper Collins, 1989.
Mac, Taylor. *The Young Ladies of . . . .* New York: Black Wave Press, 2009.
Mac, Taylor. *The Lily's Revenge*. New York: Playscripts Inc., 2013.
Mac, Taylor. *Hir*. Evanston, IL: Northwestern University Press, 2015.
Mac, Taylor. *Gary: A Sequel to "Titus Andronicus."* Acting Edition. New York: Dramatists Play Service, 2020.
Miller, Tim. "My Queer Body." *Body Blows: Six Performances*. Madison: University of Wisconsin Press, 2002.
Tzara, Tristan. "How to Make a Dadaist Poem." https://www.writing.upenn.edu/~afilre is/88v/tzara.html

Books

Adorno, Theodor. *Prisms*. Cambridge: MIT Press, 1967.
Althusser, Louis. *Lenin and Other Essays*. Trans. Ben Brewster. New York: Monthly Review Press, 2001.

Baldrick, Chris. *In Frankenstein's Shadow: Myth, Monstrosity and Nineteenth-Century Writing*. Oxford: Oxford University Press, 1987.

Baudrillard, Jean. *Simulations*. Trans. Paul Foss, Paul Patton, and Paul Beitchman. New York: Semiotext(e), 1983.

Baudrillard, Jean. *Simulacra and Simulation*. Trans. Sheila Faria Glaser. Ann Arbor: University of Michigan Press, 1994.

Bechdel, Allison. *Fun Home: A Family Tragicomic*. Boston: Houghton Mifflin, 2006.

Binns, Henry Bryan. *Life of Walt Whitman*. London: Metheun, 1905.

Blalock, Stephanie M. *"GO TO PFAFF'S?": The History of a Restaurant and Lager Beer Saloon*. Bethlehem, PA: Lehigh University Press, 2014.

Brecht, Bertolt. *Brecht on Theatre: The Development of an Aesthetic*. Ed. and trans. John Willet. New York: Hill and Wang, 1977.

Brooks, Daphne. *Bodies in Dissent: Spectacular Performances of Race and Freedom, 1850–1910*. Durham, NC: Duke University Press, 2006.

Brown, William Wells. *Clotel, or the President's Daughter*. Ed. Robert S. Levine. Boston: Bedford/St. Martin's Press, 2000.

Butler, Judith. *Bodies That Matter: On the Discursive Limits of "Sex."* New York: Routledge, 1993.

Campbell, Alyson, and Stephen Farrier, eds. *Queer Dramaturgies: International Perspectives on Where Performance Leads Queer*. London: Palgrave, 2016.

Coviello, Peter. *Intimacy in America: Dreams of Affiliation in Antebellum Literature*. Minneapolis: University of Minnesota Press, 2005.

Cox, Karen L. *Dreaming of Dixie: How the South Was Created in American Popular Culture*. Chapel Hill: University of North Carolina Press, 2011.

Csordas, Thomas J. *Embodiment and Experience: The Existential Ground of Culture and Self*. Cambridge: Cambridge University Press, 1994.

Debord, Guy. *The Society of the Spectacle*. New York: Zone Books, 1994.

Delaney, Martin R. *Blake, or, the Huts of America*. Jerome McGann, ed. Cambridge: Harvard University Press, 2017.

Disch, Lisa, Mary Hawkesworth, and Brittney Cooper. *The Oxford Handbook of Feminist Theory*. Oxford: Oxford University Press, 2016.

Dolan, Jill. *Utopia in Performance: Finding Hope at the Theater*. Ann Arbor: University of Michigan Press, 2005.

Edgecomb, Sean F. *Charles Ludlam Lives! Charles Busch, Bradford Lourk, Taylor Mac, and the Queer Legacy of the Ridiculous Theatrical Company*. Ann Arbor: University of Michigan Press, 2017.

Emerson, Ken. *Doo-dah! Stephen Foster and the Rise of American Popular Culture*. New York: Simon & Schuster, 1997.

Erkkila, Betsy, and Jay Grossman, eds. *Breaking Bounds: Whitman and American Cultural Studies*. New York: Oxford University Press, 1996.

Esslin, Martin. *Theatre of the Absurd*. New York: Random House, 2004.

Folsom, Ed, ed. *Whitman East and West: New Contexts for Reading Walt Whitman*. Iowa City: University of Iowa Press, 2002.

Folsom, Ed. *Whitman Making Books/Books Making Whitman: A Catalogue and Commentary*. Iowa City: Obermann Center for Advanced Studies at the University of Iowa, 2005.

Foner, Philip S., ed. *The Life and Writings of Frederick Douglass*. Vol. 2. New York: New York International Publishers, 1950.

Freeman, Elizabeth. *Time Binds: Queer Temporalities, Queer Histories*. Durham, NC: Duke University Press, 2010.

Freeman, Elizabeth. *Beside You in Time: Sense Methods and Queer Sociabilities in the American 19th Century*. Durham, NC: Duke University Press, 2019.

Freeman, Lisa A. *Antitheatricality and the Body Public*. Philadelphia: University of Pennsylvania Press, 2017.

Greenberg, Marissa. *Metropolitan Tragedy: Genre, Justice, and the City in Early Modern England*. Toronto: University of Toronto Press, 2015.

Greenblatt Stephen, ed. *The Norton Shakespeare*. New York: Norton, 1997.

Halberstam, J. Judith. *In a Queer Time and Place: Transgender Bodies, Subcultural Lives*. New York: New York University Press, 2005.

Halberstam, J. Judith. *The Queer Art of Failure*. Durham, NC: Duke University Press, 2011.

Hartman, Saidiya V. *Scenes of Subjection: Terror, Slavery and Self-Making in Nineteenth-Century America*. New York: Oxford University Press, 1997.

Heathfield, Adrian, and Tehching Hsieg, eds. *Out of Now: The Lifeworks of Tehching Hsieh*. Cambridge, MA: MIT Press, 2009.

Johnson, Stephen, ed. *Burnt Cork: Traditions and Legacies of Blackface Minstrelsy*. Amherst, MA: University of Massachusetts Press, 2012.

Kalb, Jonathan. *Great Lengths: Seven Works of Marathon Theater*. Ann Arbor: University of Michigan Press, 2011.

Koestenbaum, Wayne. *The Queen's Throat: Opera, Homosexuality, and the Mystery of Desire*. New York: Poseidon, 1993.

Kramer, Larry. *The Tragedy of Today's Gays*. New York: Jeremy P. Tarcher/Penguin, 2005.

Lin, Erika T. *Shakespeare and the Materiality of Performance*. New York: Palgrave Macmillan, 2012.

Lott, Eric. *Love and Theft: Blackface Minstrelsy and the American Working Class*. New York: Oxford University Press, 2013.

Love, Heather. *Feeling Backward: Loss and the Politics of Queer History*. Cambridge: Harvard University Press, 2009.

Ludlam, Charles. *Ridiculous Theatre: Scourge of Human Folly*. Ed. Rick Roemer. New York: Theatre Communications Group, 1992.

Martin, Justin. *Rebel Souls: Walt Whitman and America's First Bohemians*. Philadelphia: Da Capo, 2014.

McRuer Robert. *Crip Theory: Cultural Signs of Queerness and Disability*. New York: New York University Press, 2006.

Muñoz, José Esteban. *Disidentifications: Queers of Color and the Performance of Politics*. Minneapolis: University of Minnesota Press, 1999.

Muñoz, José Esteban. *Cruising Utopia: The Then and There of Queer Futurity*. New York: New York University Press, 2009.

O'Connor, William Douglas. *The Good Gray Poet*. New York: Bunce and Huntington, 1866.

Petit de Julleville, Louis. *La comédie et les moeurs en France au moyen âge*. Paris: Adamant Media Corp., 2001.

Preston, Carrie. *Learning to Kneel: Noh, Modernism and Journeys in Teaching*. New York: Columbia University Press, 2016.

Rackin, Phyllis. *Stages of History: Shakespeare's English Chronicles*. Ithaca, NY: Cornell University Press, 1990.

Rancière, Jacques. *The Emancipated Spectator*. Trans. Gregory Elliott. London: Verso, 2009.

Roemer, Rick. *Charles Ludlam and the Ridiculous Theatrical Company: Critical Analysis of 29 Plays*. Jefferson, NC: McFarland and Co., 1998.

Román, David. *Performance in America: Contemporary US Culture and the Performing Arts*. Durham, NC: Duke University Press, 2005.

Ryan, Hugh. *When Brooklyn Was Queer*. New York: St. Martin's Press, 2019.

Savran, David. *A Queer Sort of Materialism: Recontextualizing American Theatre*. Ann Arbor: University of Michigan Press, 2003.

Schneider, Rebecca. *Performing Remains: Art and War in Times of Theatrical Reenactment*. London: Routledge, 2011.

Sedgwick, Eve Kosofsky. *Between Men: English Literature and Male Homosocial Desire*. New York: Columbia University Press, 1985.

Sedgwick, Eve Kosofsky. *Touching Feeling: Affect, Pedagogy, Performativity*. Durham, NC: Duke University Press, 2003.

Shiley, Charley, ed. *Calamus Lovers: Walt Whitman's Working-Class Camerados*. San Francisco: Gay Sunshine Press, 1987.

Smith, Emma, and Garrett A. Sullivan Jr. *The Cambridge Companion to English Renaissance Tragedy*. New York: Cambridge University Press, 2010.

Smith, Jack. *Wait for Me at the Bottom of the Pool: The Writings of Jack Smith*. J. Hoberman and Edward Leffingwell, eds. New York: Serpent's Tail, 1997.

Sontag, Susan. 2018. *Notes on Camp*. Penguin Modern. London: Penguin Classics.

Stewart, Susan. *On Longing: Narratives of the Miniature, the Gigantic, the Souvenir, the Collection*. Durham, NC: Duke University Press, 1992.

Traubel, Horace. *With Walt Whitman in Camden*. Vol. 6. Gertrude Traubel and William White, eds. Carbondale: University of Southern Illinois Press, 1982.

Turner, Steve. *Amazing Grace: The Story of America's Most Beloved Song*. New York: Ecco, 1992.

Turner, Victor. *From Ritual to Theatre: The Human Seriousness of Play*. New York: PAJ Publications, 1982.

Weiss, Penny A., ed. *Feminist Manifestos: A Global Documentary Reader*. New York: New York University Press, 2018.

Welsford, Enid. *The Fool: His Social and Literary History*. New York: Doubleday, 1961.

Whitman, Walt. *Leaves of Grass*. Boston: Thayer and Eldridge, 1860–61.

Zola, Emile. *Theatre/Theory/Theatre*. Ed. Daniel Gerould. New York: Applause, 2000.

Newspaper/Magazine Articles and Reviews

Berger, Arion. "Review of Meshell Ndegeocello's Album, *Cookie: The Anthropological Mix Tape*." *Rolling Stone*. May 22, 2002.

Bradley, Laura. "Colbert's Gift to Clinton: Naked-Man Butts Branded with 'I'm with Her.'" *Vanity Fair*. September 20, 2017.

Brantley, Ben. "Riffs on 9/11 and City Life and Lots of Liza Minellis." *New York Times*. July 18, 2003.

Butler, Isaac. "The Great American Living-Room Gets a Remodel." *American Theatre* (March 2000). https://www.americantheatre.org/2015/03/25/how-contemporary-pl aywrights-are-re-defining-the-living-room-play/

"Dress Like a Woman? What Does that Mean?" *New York Times*. February 3, 2017.

Elben, Tom. "Everyone Sings 'My Old Kentucky Home' at the Derby." *Lexington Herald*. April 27, 2018.

Evans, Suzy. "A Trip Around the Sun with Taylor Mac's '24-Decade History.'" *American Theatre Magazine*. October 14, 2016.

Feingold, Michael. "The Bold Soprano." *Village Voice*. February 27, 1983.

Gelt, Jessica. "Taylor Mac Brings 24 Decades of Delirium to Los Angeles." *Los Angeles Times*. June 20, 2017.

Hevesi, Dennis. "Ronald Tavel, Proudly Ridiculous Writer, Dies at 72." *New York Times*. March 27, 2009.

Hoban, Phoebe. "Sea Creatures Spare Nothing, Especially Not the Glitter, in 'Red Tide Blooming.'" *New York Times*. April 19, 2006.

Isherwood, Charles. "Protesters Armed with Wigs and Sequins." *New York Times*. January 20, 2011.

Isherwood, Charles. "Among the Huddles Masses." *New York Times*. January 29, 2013.

Isherwood, Charles. "Review: 'Hir' Sorts Through a Family in Transition." *New York Times*. November 8, 2015.

Jacobs, Leonard. "Papa Don't Preach: *The Young Ladies of . . .* Channels Big Daddy." *NY Press Review*. October 3–9, 2007.

Kaplan, Ilana. "Why Kathleen Hanna Spoke Up About 'Violent Alcoholic' Dad on New LP." *Rolling Stone*. July 6, 2016.

Kron, Lisa. "Taylor Mac's 'Hir': Just your Average Kitchen-Sink Genderqueer Family Drama." *American Theatre* (November 2014). https://www.americantheatre.org/20 14/11/26/taylor-macs-hir-just-your-average-kitchen-sink-genderqueer-family-dr ama/

Mac, Taylor. "Taylor Mac on 20 Songs that Made the Cut for *A 24-Decade History of Popular Music*." *Vulture*. September 19, 2016. https://www.vulture.com/2016/09/tayl or-mac-a-24-decade-history-of-popular-music.html

McNulty, Charles. "Tears of a Clown." *Village Voice*. June 15, 2004.

Phillips, Gretchen. "I Moshed at Mich." *Village Voice*. September 6, 1994.

Radosavljević, Duška. "Taylor Mac—*A 24-Decade History of Popular Music*: The First Act at the Barbican." *Exuent Magazine*. July 2, 2018.

Renkl, Margaret. "What It's Like to Wear a Mask in the South." *New York Times*. June 1, 2020.

Simon, John. "The Tale of the Allergist's Wife." *New York Times*. March 13, 2000.

Svich, Caridad. "Glamming It Up with Taylor Mac." *American Theatre* 25, no. 10 (2008): 36.

Tompkins, Calvin. "Profiles Ridiculous." *New Yorker*. November 15, 1976.

The *Voice* "Best of" Awards. "Best Be(a)sts New York 2007." *Village Voice*. May 21, 2007.

Weiss, Sasha. "Taylor Mac Wants Theater to Make You Uncomfortable." *New York Times Magazine*. April 2. 2019.

Winnant, Gabriel. "Rush Limbaugh's race to the bottom: Bend over, grab your ankles and submit to a mind-blowing rundown of the radio bully's obsessive butt talk!" *Salon*. May 21, 2009.

Journal Articles

Atkinson, Michael. "Flesh Journeys: Neo Primitives and the Contemporary Rediscovery of Radical Body Modification." *Deviant Behavior* 22, no. 2 (2001): 117–46.

Bisaha, David. "'I Want You to Feel Uncomfortable': Adapting Participation in *A 24-Decade History of Popular Music* at San Francisco's Curan Theatre." *Theatre History Studies* 38 (2019): 133–48.

Cvetkovich, Ann. "Sexual Trauma/Queer Memory: Incest, Lesbianism and Therapeutic Culture." *GLQ: A Journal of Lesbian and Gay Studies* 2 (1995): 351–56.

Edgecomb, Sean F. "The Ridiculous Performance of Taylor Mac." *Theatre Journal* 64, no. 4 (2012): 549–63.

Fitzgerald, Jason. "Review: *The Lily's Revenge*." *Theatre Journal* 62, no. 3 (October 2010): 457–58.

Folsom, Ed. "'A Yet More Terrible and Deeply Connected Problem': Walt Whitman, Race, Reconstruction, and American Democracy." *American Literary History* 30, no. 3 (Fall 2018): 531–58.

Gilmore, Paul. "'De Genewine Artekil': William Wells Brown, Blackface Minstrelsy and Abolitionism." *American Literature* 69, no. 4 (December 1997): 743–80.

Krasinski, Jennifer. "Everything You're Feeling Is Appropriate." *Theater* 47, no. 4 (2017): 8.

Pitts, Victoria. "Visibly Queer: Body Technologies and Sexual Politics." *Sociological Quarterly* 41, no. 3 (2000): 443–63.

Richardson, Niall. "Effeminophobia, Misogyny and Queer Friendship: The Cultural Themes of Channel 4's Playing It Straight." *Sexualities* 12, no. 4 (2009): 525–44.

Rivera, Takeo. "Do Asians Dream of Electric Shrieks? Techno-Orientalism and Eroto-historiographic Masochism in Eidos Montreal's *Deus Ex: Human Revolution*." *Amerasia Journal* 40, no. 2 (2014): 67–86.

Román, David. "Subjective Histories of Taylor Mac's 'Radical Faerie Realness Ritual' History." *Theatre Journal* 69, no. 3 (2017): 631–42.

Royster, Francesca T. "White-limed Walls: Whiteness and Gothic Extremism in Shakespeare's *Titus Andronicus*." *Shakespeare Quarterly* 51 (2000): 432–55.

Smolko, Joanna R. "Southern-Fried Foster: Representing Race and Place through Music in Looney Tunes Cartoons." *American Music* 30, no. 3 (Fall 2012): 344–72.

Switzky, Lawrence. "Marathon Theatre as Affective Labour: Productive Exhaustion in *The Godot Cycle* and *Life and Times*." *Canadian Theatre Review* 162 (Spring 2015): 26–30.

Westerling, Kalle. "Review of *A 24-Decade History of Popular Music*." *Theatre Journal* 69, no. 3 (September 2017): 408–9.

Dissertations and Theses

Jeffreys, Joe E. "An Outré Entrée into the Para-Ridiculous Histrionics of Ethyl Eichel-berger: A True Story." PhD dissertation. New York University, 1993.
Trinidad, Gaven D. "Queer Temporality and Aesthetics in Taylor Mac's *The Lily's Revenge.*" MA thesis. University of Massachusetts, Amherst, 2018.

Video and Radio

Don't Need You—The Herstory of riot grrrl. DVD. Directed by Kerri Koch. New York: Urban Cowgirl Productions, 2005.
Gary: A Sequel to Titus Andronicus, directed by George C. Wolfe, June 14, 2019 video-recording. (New York: Theatre on Film and Tape Archive, 2019), DVD, New York Public Library for the Performing Arts, Billy Rose Theatre Division, Theatre on Film and Tape Archive, NCOV 4269.
Mac, Taylor. Speech, Edwin Booth Award Ceremony, Martin E. Segal Theatre Center, City University of New York. April 28, 2017. https://www.youtube.com/watch?v=d IkOH8gVyqU
Mac, Taylor, Matt Ray, and Niegel Smith. "Sundance Theatre Lab: *A 24-Decade History of Popular Music.*" September 16, 2016. https://www.youtube.com/watch?time_conti nue=235&v=hldiCsWXWf8&feature=emb_logo
Shapiro, Ari. "Taylor Mac in Making a Better World in 24 Hours." *All Things Considered.* National Public Radio. December 28, 2016. https://www.npr.org/2016/12/28/50726 7783/taylor-mac-on-making-a-better-world-in-24-hours
Thunder: A Film About Ferron. Directed by Billie Jo Cavallaro, Bitch, and Ferron. Claw-son, MI: Short Story Records, 2013.

Index